SMALL FIRMS AND INDUSTRIAL DISTRICTS IN ITALY

Edited by
**Edward Goodman
and Julia Bamford**
with Peter Saynor

ROUTLEDGE
London and New York

First published in 1989
by Routledge
11 New Fetter Lane, London EC4P 4EE
29 West 35th Street, New York, NY 10001

© 1989 Acton Society Trust

Typeset by Mayhew Typesetting, Bristol

Printed and bound in Great Britain by
Mackays of Chatham PLC, Chatham, Kent

British Library Cataloguing in Publication Data

Small firms and industrial districts in Italy.
  1. Italy. Industrial development. Role of
  small firms
  I. Goodman, Edward F.W.
  338.0945

  ISBN 0-415-03563-5

Library of Congress Cataloging in Publication Data

Small firms and industrial districts in Italy/edited by
  Edward Goodman and Julia Bamford with Peter Saynor.
      p. cm.
  Includes index.
  ISBN 0-415-03563-5
  1. Small business — Italy. 2. Italy — Manufactures.
  3. Industrial districts — Italy. I. Goodman, Edward F.W.
  HD2346.I8S63 1989
  338.6'042'0945 — dc19

88-32174
CIP

Contents

20172

iii

Contents

List of figures

List of maps

List of tables

List of contributors

Dr Ash Amin is Senior Research Fellow at the Centre for Urban and Regional Development of the University of Newcastle.

Julia Bamford teaches in the Faculty of Economics at the University of Siena.

Dr Marco Bellandi is a research fellow in the Faculty of Economics at the University of Florence.

Giacomo Becattini is Professor of Economics at the University of Florence.

Sebastiano Brusco is Professor of Economics at the University of Modena.

Edward Goodman is Chairman of the Acton Society.

Dr Mario Pezzini is a research associate at Nomisma, an industrial economics research institute.

Guido Rey is Professor of Economics at the University of Rome and President of ISTAT (the Italian statistical institute).

Dr Margherita Russo teaches economics at the University of Pescara.

Dr Fabio Sforzi teaches at the University of Florence and is a research associate at IRPET.

Dr Carlo Trigilia teaches in the Political Science Department of the University of Florence.

Preface

In 1983 the Acton Society set up a continuing study addressed to the question, 'Whatever happened to Freedom?' This was not intended as a device for discussing the fate in modern times of the great constitutional freedoms but, rather, of the forms and expressions of freedom curtailed under the impact of modern industrial civilization and of how the wide general vision had shrunk into slogans coined to encapsulate narrowly defined rights. It referred to the time when it could be said that freedom, itself, was the ideology of the age. What mattered very much was freedom in daily life, especially in work: the freedom associated with small organizations, the expression of skills and the network of productive relationships formed in local communities. All this had disappeared under the impact of mass production. The values of material progress, so necessary to the overcoming of poverty, suddenly seemed incompatible with those of freedom. Increasingly large and centralized organizations, scientific methods of management and ever more minute divisions of labour ruled the day.

But how inevitable could the continuation of these trends be seen to be? Was there not already a beginning of a human reaction to these tendencies? Already the computer and numerically controlled tools pointed to material tendencies which could be harnessed towards the achieving of greater individual freedom. Eventually for the purposes of setting up an agenda for medium- to long-term study, the Acton Society invented the idea of a two-tier economy.

The first tier is the tier of the impersonal, the large and the centralized. Typically, it is the tier dominated by big business, bureaucracy and the powerful unions. The second is the tier of the small, skilled and self-responsible. It depends for its efficiency and success upon the spontaneous and dedicated co-operation of its workers.

In thinking about the second tier we began with ideas we had already discussed at our seminar on the techniques of small

Preface

organizations held in Siena in 1977. This had a section under the title of 'Firms of Tomorrow', many subjects for which were suggested by Professor Marcello de Cecco. Therefore it was to him that I referred in 1985 for help in preparing a bibliography of the new technologies which seemed to promise a horizontal division of labour in place of a vertical one. This brought my attention to the American literature on the subject, notably the work of Charles Sabel and Michael Piore, to which we have all been indebted. At the same time I became aware of the rich Italian literature on this and allied subjects which led me to the trading estates and factories on my doorstep in Tuscany and beyond. Here, it seemed, was a model for the second-tier economy.

At this point, Krishan Kumar outlined the scope of a book he thought I ought to produce, and the project was started in England, with Graham Field organizing a series of meetings. In Italy Julia Bamford agreed to help me, and she gathered together and edited the most suitable articles which had appeared in Italian journals. With the advice of Giacomo Becattini and Sebastiano Brusco, we then commissioned new material, and we were particularly fortunate to obtain an authoritative contribution from Guido Rey.

A debt of gratitude is owed to Marcello and Julia de Cecco for hospitality at their house in Fiesole, where we held a number of seminars. It was there that a group of colleagues gave shape to the project – among them Giacomo Becattini, Sebastiano Brusco, Fabio and Anna Sforzi, Mario Pezzini and Marco Bellandi. I would also like to thank Adriana Zini for providing me with essential data on Emilia, some of which I have incorporated as Appendix 5 (p. 121). As on previous occasions I have benefited from the advice of Franco Romani and Giovanni Grottanelli. I am also grateful to Mary Martin for help in preparing the Introduction.

In England another group took part in discussing the work, and I am especially grateful to Krishan Kumar, a fellow trustee of the Acton Society, for his contribution. Others who gave support and advice at different stages included John Samuels, Richard Scase, Susan Mendus and Simon Carter. Ash Amin was of great help, working as he was from both Newcastle and Naples. Peter Saynor was a very active member of the English group and was indefatigable in the final editing.

A big vote of thanks is due to several typists and checkers on successive drafts: Margaret Horton and Karen Ludlow in Italy, and Gaenor Amory, Jennifer Jones and Nicola Reid in England.

Edward Goodman
Montefioralle
July 1988

Note on the Acton Society

This book was sponsored by the Acton Society. The Acton Society Trust is an independent, non-profit-making organization, set up in 1948 as a charitable trust. It takes its name from the nineteenth-century historian Lord Acton, who held that the justification of liberty lay in the realization of human values. The Society has carried out or sponsored many research projects in economic and social fields.

A catalogue of the resulting publications is available from the Acton Society, 9 Poland Street, London W1V 3DG (01 437 8954).

Introduction: the political economy of the small firm in Italy

Edward Goodman

The fastest growing economy in Europe in the first half of the 1980s was the Italian. Figures from the OECD indicated that by 1986 Italy's GDP at $673 billion was higher than that of the UK. Later estimates from the Italian Institute of Statistics put the Italian figure below the British. But the difference is slight, and it is not a matter of doubt that an 'economic miracle' took place. In a surprisingly short space of time a relatively backward economy was transformed and Italy emerged as a major industrial power. As in Britain, the resultant prosperity was more evident in one half of the country than the other – in Italy's case, the north. The role of the small firm in the Italian success story has been crucial; in the area of central and north-east Italy, known as the *Terza Italia*[1] where the small manufacturing firms are concentrated, the increase in the rate of production has far outstripped that of the rest of the country.

To those accustomed to thinking of Italy as the home of a happy-go-lucky, at times irresponsible life-style, with shabby workshops and an electoral system incapable of producing stable government, the figures on industrial production may appear surprising. But appearances are deceptive. True, the workshops are shabby, and the electoral system throws up many more parties and coalitions that are candidates for government than does the British system; true, too, these are engaged in constant debate that reflects the ever-changing climate of opinion and fashions of intellectual dilettantism as well as the continuous emergence of new critical issues. Yet the system has shown itself to be capable of a kind of long-term economic stability, and the changes in direction of public policy since the war have been less erratic than those brought about by the first-past-the-post method of registering electoral success in Britain.

It has to be remembered that Italy has been a unified nation-state for less than 130 years and that it was much later than most other European countries in developing an industrial economy. The boundaries

1

of the medieval city states remain amongst the hills and plains, crossed as they are by the efficient communication-network of the modern autostrada; but within these boundaries are still autonomous, purpose-bent groups, assertive, and immensely confident of themselves and of the smaller communities to which they belong. Evidence of these different cultures remains in the distinctive architecture and other art forms for which each of the cities or regions has become renowned.

At a less exalted level, each has still its characteristic commercial achievements in the crafts and urban skills that derive from the practical traditions going back into the remote past and continuing in modern forms, some within the confines of the industrial districts that have become one of the principal features of present-day Italy's industrial economy. Right at the heart of these are, as ever before, the really vital entrepreneurial groups of ten workers or fewer.

It is the visual image of Italy's industrial performance which has given confidence to the OECD's assessment of her achievements and to the prediction that better is to come. This is a picture of fickle markets, constant innovation and the fusion of art with high technology resulting in beautiful new forms and highly saleable and adaptable designs of swift appeal to the world of fashion. Beneath these are cleverly conceived prototypes that are quickly converted for mass markets and then broken down into small batches of customerized production and a plethora of low-cost, eye-catching items, useful, but intentionally not lasting. This is a market which understands itself well: a 'Janus-type market', a fragmented market, able to respond almost instantly to fashion and changed demands, alert to quick openings, with flexible programmes and short production runs, what Giacomo Becattini calls the 'amoeba-like ability of the Italian small firm to respond to changing demands'.[2]

How does this image of brittle success and disposable production square with the more ordinary picture of the run-of-the-mill Italian small business? The fact has to be admitted that small firms are not inherently smart, nor are they run by a set of temperamental genius-designers, but by steady inventive entrepreneurs with a feeling for aesthetic values and a flair for knowing where to buy and where to sell, and often with the tenacity to perfect their own skills and to adapt them to the tasks in hand rather than to be forced into paying high prices for new tools and technology. If an image is required, it is of the converted makeshift workshops abutting on to narrow streets with hardly room for a van to turn, cheek by jowl with residential accommodation; or the new, small, cramped trading estate built on to the dirt roads, and the family-based group of six or seven talkative workers grouped round one of the older craftsmen, whilst the quick-thinking entrepreneur listens at a desk of his own, making notes and determined to get on.

Beneath the surface of both these images – the highly polished one and rougher one – are the most important achievements of the Italian economy to which thousands of small firms contribute in quality markets, where well-tested traditions of individual workmanship as well as good looks and unique design are hallmarks, and the very label 'Made in Italy' attracts custom.

A question of style

In all these achievements style is an important ingredient, uniquely and conspicuously Italian; a style that is rooted in the self-confidence of the individual workman and of the entrepreneur himself. Brought up in the security of family and community relationships and in a set of cultural assumptions resting upon instinctively shared values, no job is too menial for him and all jobs are worth doing well.

How is it that these very likeable personal qualities have been incorporated into an impersonal commercial economy and what are the mechanisms through which the values contained in these images have been transmitted to world markets? And how is it that the Italian Lilliputian firms have stood up to a world of giants?

It is tempting at this point to give reasons for the declining influence of the economies of scale based on extensive production lines, and to introduce the concept of the model of flexible production together with that of the division of labour according to firm specialization. The large manufacturing firm, according to this argument, is out of date and its machinery is as obsolete as the steam engine. The numerically controlled tool and the computer have transferred the ability to meet demand promptly, cheaply and efficiently from the large to the small firm. Customerized production in small batches is here to stay and the market likes it. There are several disadvantages in continuing to argue in this way. For example, one could counter-argue that the recent success of the small firm will be short-lived and that the large multi-product undertaking will make a comeback, that its financial power will enable it to organize the setting-up of a variety of interdependent units of production, sharing the same economies of scale and fitting into an overall pattern of organization. Or it can be suggested that the innovative skills and adaptability of the small firm will be more than offset by the greater resources of the giant firm when it comes to exploiting the next wave of high technology. There is a third view, not incompatible with the first, which sees the success of the small firm in modern Italy as stemming from the explosive power of the values of the craft firm and of the self-employed worker based, as they are, on family and community. According to this view, the ability to introduce new technology stems also from the same set of values: and this makes it necessary to discuss at least part of the Italian industrial success in terms of what one may simply call the political economy of the small firm.

In such a discussion, by way of leitmotif, it is helpful occasionally to make comparisons with England's experiences at similar stages of development. The most conspicuous differences between the two countries lie historically in their attitudes to trade and money-making and the importance they attach to design and ordinary good appearance. This second is noticeable in everyday things, such as the wrapping up of a parcel or the design of a five-bar gate. Good design and a quality of thought-out artistry have always formed the essential basis of authentic Italian workmanship. Men of every trade seem to possess a good eye and a sense of acceptable appearance. In considering what design and ornament are appropriate, the craftsman has to take into consideration what his customer can afford just as much as what exactly he wants the appearance to be. Whenever there is a gap between the two, he is trained to evolve new techniques to abridge it. This is the basis of much of his capacity to adapt and innovate. Sebastiano Brusco says, for example, 'the tools used by traditional artisans are in general simple and multi-purpose. The skill of the artisan lies here: in being able to cope in complex situations working with few tools, often with unsuitable material.'[3]

The idea of money-making is not disreputable nor trade a dirty word, and they have never been looked down upon socially as they have been in England. In Italy it has always been thought legitimate for the dealer and tradesman 'to make a turn' and for the man with entrepreneurial spirit to be one of the most admired in the local community; indeed, success as an entrepreneur has always been regarded as at least a rung on the ladder to social recognition. For the same reason, the earning of money as a means of securing positional goods has never been discouraged. Display and ornament associated with wealth have been from the earliest times implicit in the ambition of almost every talented person who has had the opportunity to succeed. In the Middle Ages, as the merchant classes grew rich, some cities became something like plantations of towers attached to the largest houses as signs of prestige. Armour and weapons of war were finely ornamented, and of course the dresses of both men and women were beautifully designed and richly embroidered. The courts of the city-states and the merchants themselves were the patrons of the crafts and of good design.

4

All this of course was reflected in the nobleman's palaces and the town houses of merchants. Much of the furniture and tapestry were made *in situ*; so also the paintings – for example, in the Ducal Palace at Urbino, where a Raphael portrait of a lady is still on the easel where he painted it. At the time of the Renaissance, painters and architects had no separate status; they were superior dignified decorators or designers, and it was in these roles and belonging to teams of equally talented colleagues that they designed the courtyards and decorated in fresco the walls of cloisters and the interiors of churches, palaces, and large houses alike. It was to this tradition that the artist and the skilled tradesmen belonged. Their contemporary conventions and social attitudes go back to these roots.

In order to obtain their original stock of wealth, the merchants had to display something similar to what centuries later was identified as the entrepreneurial spirit. At first they were little more than dealers, buying and selling commodities that were quickly resold in the market places. However, in time their biggest profits came from international trade, and soon after they became lenders of money; the merchant bankers of today are derived from them.

When life in the cities became orderly and trading on a wide scale became possible, the growth of the entrepreneurial spirit provided one of the first pieces of evidence of the Italian admiration of commercial skills and of the ability to make use of an idea, show initiative and maintain control of undertakings. But historically Italians do not have a taste for large-scale administration, nor do Italian men of spirit like being organized, or being obliged to obey superiors without question.

Because of the entrepreneur's reluctance to administer large organizations, the businesses organized by him tend to remain small. Expansion for him means the possibility of allowing things to develop beyond his control. Though he takes risks, his key role is to be in control of things and to keep intact his own independence and powers of initiative. He is the ideas man searching out new niches in the markets of today. He is accustomed to ducking authority and getting by on his own. The local market is important to him both as a means of selling his goods and of learning what the public wants and what designs are coming into fashion. The ultimate of his ambition is not growth, but recognition.

There are other visual images of modern industrial Italy besides those that derive from the small firm's successes in the *Terza Italia* and the prestigious consumer goods and design centres of the north-eastern industrial triangle; and some of these other images are not only unattractive but lead one to wonder, if they do indeed represent a reality, how Italy has managed to appear in the industrial league table at all. Its bureaucracy has a reputation for being, with the exception of the Russian, the most cumbersome in Europe. With feet of stone and head of ancient iron, and with a file of forms in quin-triplicate, it is a monster from Byzantium that has long held Italy in its claws: a cumbersome spirit of delay and obstruction, it sometimes seems to drag upon every transaction. The postal service is surely the most unreliable in Europe, so secure in its bad ways that it seems incapable of making any improvement.

Yet another image of Italy is the poverty of many areas in the south; it is only in the centre and north that prosperity reigns. Finally, there is the very recent expansion of the large private companies, with an era of mergers and takeovers already begun. But none of this is part of the present volume.

The *artigiani* and the family firm

The merchant and the entrepreneur are the two figures who, larger than life, stand in the background of Italian small-firm development. In the foreground is the master craftsman, the *artigiano*. Pre-eminently a man of skill and sensitivity, he is also independent, and in order to stay so he has to economize on tools and almost every-thing else he needs. It is this which gives him the impetus constantly to sharpen his repertoire of skills with new techniques and to improvise. A passion for detail and a flair for design run in his blood. He is not well educated and his class, the artisan class, is not far up the social hierarchy, but he is inventive and he believes in himself and in his craft. He likes solving problems in his work, but he does not like the solutions that the big firm offers. It is for him to use the machine and not for the machine to rule him. It is love of work that explains the pleasure he takes in life, and this provides a strong contrast to the British utilitarian idea that all work is painful and has to be endured to gain the needs of existence. The Italian craftsman delights in pleasing his customers and unashamedly wants to see their appreciation of what he does for them. He likes display and to have social confirmation of his mastery of craft skills and his ability to run a small firm successfully – but no more than a small firm, just the number of people whom he can know intimately and whose work he can criticize and control. Above all, he has an eye for relevance; his life is one which cannot afford mistakes. It is a combination of these qualities which has kept the *artigiano* firm in business for so many centuries and made it a model of nearly all Italian small businesses from the earliest times down to the high-technology small firm of the *Terza Italia*.

The role of the family

Underpinning the entire *artigiano* economy is the family. The firm is rooted both in the family and in the *artigiano*'s exceptional personal skills. This creates a more or less permanent tension. The family is a conservative force depending for its effectiveness on its solidarity. Members of the entrepreneur's own family work in the business, as well as the in-laws (*cognati*). Many of them may live in residential quarters attached to the workshop. In times of economic recession it is usually found that employment in *artigiano* firms increases as young members of the family can now find a place of some sort working in the family business. Starting-up capital is usually found in the family before the entrepreneur goes to the local bank. In contrast to the conservatism which such a structure creates, is the colourful individualism and single-mindedness of the entrepreneur himself and of his most-talented craftsmen. It is remarkable that with contradictions such as this at their core such firms survive year after year and generation after generation. That they do is due to the fact that the family itself is the breeding ground of strong character and has its own rules of give and take, which assert that, to be productive, all differences must be exercised within commonly accepted limits. It follows also that there must be limits to the size of the firm.

To the observer what seems even more surprising is that into this conservati٠e structure of a family conducting its affairs in a manner resembling a small debating society have been successfully introduced the tools and equipment of sophisticated modern technology. The enthusiastic reception of new technology by traditional industries is one of the most promising features of the *Terza Italia*.

Characteristics of the small firm

Since very early times there have been two main categories of *artigiano* firm. The first was very small, centred around the personality of the master craftsman himself, doing purely craftwork. The second was somewhat larger and, under the leadership of a more entrepreneurial type of craftsman, produced goods for wider sale in the retail market; for example the small shoe firms of northern Italy or the makers of ceramics around Deruta. The larger firms might make use of sub-contracting or putting out to home-workers. In recent times, especially since the trade unions tended to make life difficult for managers and skilled workers in large firms, new types of *artigiano* firm have grown up in industries using high technology. Two are of chief importance and have been selected, together with the traditional *artigiano* firm, by Brusco as the archetypes of the genre. One is the dependent subcontractor and the other the small specialist firm, usually employing flexible production methods. Both types flourish in the industrial districts of the *Terza Italia* and are described in subsequent parts of this book.

There are many factors to be taken into account in order to understand what it really is that makes the Italian small firm a stimulating place to work, and how, in the modern world, it has come to produce goods that attract a world-wide reputation. The Italian craftsman's capacity to adapt and innovate has already been noted (to quote Brusco again, it is 'an integral part of his own make-up'), and one of the secrets of Italian success has been the ability to revive traditional industries by the careful application of new technology. Equally significant is the urge to compete and the entre-preneur's intense awareness of his competitors. These are fundamen-tal characteristics of the protagonists in this remarkable economy.

The size of the typical *artigiano* firm varies from about five to ten persons. Limitation of size has been, and in many circumstances still is, an important consideration for the small firm, since it gives exemption from certain legislative requirements and local authority controls and regulations. It is also, by virtue of the small numbers employed, easy for the firm to avoid trade union pressures and many of the more vexatious items of the rule book. Perhaps most impor-tant of all, size is very much a function of the style of the firm and relationships which characterize it. These relationships include those between the owner or the entrepreneur and those whom he employs. Ideas flow freely in the workshop, and those participating often include the customer who may be waiting for his work to be finished. There may be buyers anxious to see what the next year's fashions are likely to be or to ask for modifications to suit their own requirements. Their comments will often provoke a general discus-sion. The entrepreneur will rarely comment, except to make notes of the suggestions he likes or to smile at justified criticisms. At the end of the week or month these will be incorporated into new models which will be put on display whilst the old ones will be sold off cheaply. This example shows that smallness of both firm and factory is indeed one critical factor, not only because of the close relation-ships that it fosters between the workers but also for two other reasons: it makes possible an unacknowledged system whereby each worker tends to monitor and encourage the other according to a tradition of workmanship and design to which they all belong; and it stimulates the discussion of new ideas in a wider circle. In these ways it leads to flexibility and innovations, small and large. These advantages can be seen equally well in one of the small ceramic workshops described by Margherita Russo or in one of Italy's most sophisticated fashion houses. They are not just the standards of a particular craft; they are part of the intrinsic qualities of the Italian tradition of workmanship that govern the small-firm economy.

What matters eventually, however, is not so much the exact numbers of employees working in a given firm as the fact of whether or not a project or plan can be understood, shared and worked upon as an act of collaboration by a group of the size chosen by the entrepreneur. How does an idea travel between its members, how easy do they find it to identify problems they encounter and to devise innovations – perhaps no more than little improvements and original ways of doing things better? How, too, does the firm react to the society around it? It is their interest in each other's work and the means they adopt for fulfilling their role in the common project that renders unnecessary detailed surveillance and other associated costs. (In the United States, according to Samuel Bowles, these costs in large firms are usually as great as the annual net profits.[4]) The Italian small firm is thus more of a cultural entity than the English equivalent. It has familial, social and artistic aspects as well as economic, offering its workers a wide range of satisfactions besides that of earning a living. Its standards are those of excellence.

There are no sleeping partners or equity shareholders in the *artigiano* firm. Thus right at the beginning the idea of a takeover is made unlikely and small Italian firms cannot be regarded as fodder for the larger growing firm to feed on and eventually completely devour, which was the prevalent view in Britain in the 1960s and early 1970s.[5] Thus too, neither growth nor profit maximization for capital value purposes can be regarded as the raison d'être of the *artigiano* firm.

The Italian small firm has one other advantage: because of the absence of class barriers, it has few of the communication problems that can beset the larger hierarchical firms. Indeed, it is this lack of hierarchy and the very informality of the boss–worker relationship, often accompanied by a certain untidiness of procedure, that stimulates the flow of invention from the small workshops.

This, then in outline is the *artigiano* firm which dominates the traditional industries such as fabrics and clothing, shoe-making and leather goods, ceramics, carpentry, and furniture. There is much common ground, of course, between the traditional *artigiano* firm and the new high-technology firm which began to emerge in the late 1960s; for example, in the contemporary engineering industries the ancient idea of bespoke production for individual customers has been transformed under the impact of modern technology into the concept of 'customerized production'. Bespoke production is the habit of the traditional craft firm serving either a particular customer or the local market. Such a firm is always on the lookout for small differences in design that may constitute novelty and frequently uses its customers' ideas as its own inspiration. When the design is judged to be successful, the entrepreneur first tries out no more than a dozen or so copies of it on his local market. In his workshop, he aims to be one or two steps ahead of fashion and to avoid producing long runs of anything which would have to be destroyed were new designs to be adopted. In the high-technology *artigiano* firms using the most up-to-date equipment, short runs are nearly always favoured. The difference is, of course, that they have the advantage of computers which forecast demand and of numerically controlled tools which give expression to it quickly in economically regulated batches.

Where there has been a changeover in production methods from those based on craft traditions to those of high technology, the character of the working lives of many of the workers has also changed. Automation has taken away the skills from the hands of some of them and in doing so has created a new type of worker whose skills are mental and conceptual and whose main value to the firm is often his judgement rather than his manual dexterity.

In 1985 it was estimated that small firms employing fewer than ten workers made up 80 per cent of all Italian manufacturing firms, and they comfortably outperformed the larger firms in the same industrial sector; moreover, their wages at that time were significantly higher. Guido Rey in Chapter 2 gives plenty of evidence to put this achievement into perspective, suggesting that there is no need to make a fetish of small numbers of employees. There is no magic number. The point is that the ethos of the *artigiani* firm is not simply valuable in its own context but also as a wider influence on Italian industry.

The community and a concept of freedom

The *artigiano* firm, as well as being rooted in family, is grounded in community. This familiar statement has, of course, cultural and political implications, besides economic and organizational.

The word 'community' gives rise to a wide range of interpretations. For the moment, suppose five sets are taken:

(1) An aggregate of individuals but not a collective, who live in the same territory, who also know each other by name, speak the same language, have a common history and, in some minimal sense, share the same interests.

(2) Values, beliefs, loyalities or interests held in common; this gives rise to the idea of people sharing these things and having aspirations and projects in common, so that they identify with each other and work together to achieve common goals.

(3) More abstract and metaphysical meanings which include (2) but go beyond it: the community is an organic entity and has a value independent of those who compose it. This meaning is derived from times when communities were autonomous and self-contained and geographically cut off from each other; they each had an idiosyncratic sense of justice which they administered.

(4) Union of separate peoples or states, as in European Community.

(5) A concrete legal entity with interests to protect and functions to carry out. The Italian word *comune* can be used in several general senses, but its specific meaning is the administrative organization of the district, that is the local authority.

All five usages of 'community', although quite separate, give a particular intellectual flavour when taken together. However, (1) and (2), when combined with the values encapsulated in the claim for the *artigiani* to be rooted in community, yield valuable insights into the nature of personal liberty that underpins the Italian small-firm political economy. This commences with the idea of freedom as related by, for example, Simone Weil: 'Freedom is not to be defined in terms of a relationship between desire and its satisfaction', but by a relationship between, on the one hand, thought, judgement, and imagination and, on the other, the action and sequence of means needed to achieve the images so constructed. 'The absolutely free man would be he whose every action proceeded from a preliminary judgment concerning the end which he set himself and the sequence of means suitable for attaining this end.'[6]

In order to achieve the co-ordination between the workers needed to carry out a given project, each worker would have to employ methodical thought and to have the same mental blueprint in his head and this blueprint would need to give clear ideas of all the specialized procedures needed for its exact execution.

The *artigiano* version of freedom in activity also starts with the need of a shared image of the end to be achieved, but in place of Weil's methodological co-ordination through mental and manual discipline, it relies for its realization upon the knowledge each worker has acquired of the other workers through his life in the community and upon the skills and spontaneous forms of co-operation which the community, through tradition and practice, has shaped for all to use. The family and the community also provide necessary resources, which on occasion may be capital or institutional support. This view of liberty emphasizes the individual's desire to be free and to attain his freedom through the realization of consciously formulated mental blueprints; but at that point it leaves Weil's Cartesian description of methodical thought and its specialized procedures, and substitutes one that is less static. This version of freedom involves an on-going interaction, a negotiation as it were, between the craftsman and the tools he uses, and it is sustained by an actively participating community in which the individual lives and works. (In Chapter 6 Sforzi takes up a similar point in his identification of industrial districts.)

What is really being described is the working-out in real situations of 'freedom as integrity'. It is the freedom of the whole man, and what makes the man whole is his establishing his identification with the plans and projects of others (though his ability to identify with his own plans and projects is of course crucial). The important metaphors are those of wholeness, community, integrity: freedom in activity is not solely J.S. Mill's freedom as autonomy, but freedom as integrity. This emphasizes both the need of the individual to be true to himself – to fulfil his own plans and projects – and the need to be true to a common project, to perceive and recognize the aspirations and needs of those with whom he is working. Also, it gives a new slant on the concept of 'alienation', since alienation constitutes an attack on the integrity of the individual, fragmenting his own life and at the same time his relationships in the rest of the community.[7]

This description of freedom in the small-firm economy relies on two conditions. The first is a decentralized economy and the second is a small-sized working group, which Weil's description fits: 'collectives should never be sufficiently vast to pass outside the range of the human mind'.[8]

These reflections provide the basis of the distinction between a first and second tier of the modern technological economy, which, as already noted, underlies the current studies by the Acton Society.

The *comune* and political subcultures

The family and communal characteristics which make for small entrepreneurial firms coincide with another set of notable features of contemporary Italian life: the strength of the traditions and tendencies directed towards decentralization. These tendencies are not solely political; they also arise spontaneously from the vitality and self-interest of local communities and the common life and beliefs of those living in them. The geography of the country is also a factor, and features of the terrain which in the past have isolated the regions and cities from each other still help to preserve some ancient differences.

The origins of the tradition of decentralization are to be found in Italy's peculiar history. After the break-up of the Roman Empire it eventually emerged as a country made up of city-states, with hinterlands of rural communities, that were almost self-contained. Not surprisingly they each developed distinctive characteristics, heightened in some cases by different ethnic mixes. At the end of the first millennium some cities in central and northern Italy were electing consuls and by the twelfth century the prototype of what was to be the *comune* was well established. The cities of Tuscany were among the first to be self-governing. By the end of the fifteenth century the great city-states had absorbed many smaller towns and had themselves been converted into duchies or principalities, later to be ruled by foreign powers or by the Vatican in the extensive Papal States. But certain functions and, in some cases, rights were retained by the *comuni*, even if their role was confined to the more pedestrian administrative work.

In these respects it is important to separate two entities: first, the local authority, the *comune*, with its mainly administrative functions, and second, the community itself, which has a past and present identity, and consists of individuals, who can at least recognize each other, and who, more often than not share values, attitudes, and priorities. The common life tends to be closer than that lived in a territory of similar size in England, and in comparatively recent times this has spurred on the *comune* to attempt to take political initiatives in furtherance of the collective interest or the interests of particular groups of citizens, such as the unemployed.

As the *comune* developed, the ideas it represented tended to be radical and republican. For example, during the period when these states fell under Vatican or foreign rule, the *comune* functioned as the egalitarian organ of local administration directly under the occupying powers. Both the Vatican and the Habsburgs are known to have encouraged a sense of responsibility in those they ruled, and hence *comuni* in territories in the north and centre occupied by either of these powers would have gained experience in local government earlier than those elsewhere. However dependent upon the occupying powers' connivance such a form of local participatory government had to be, it gave the local citizens political maturity and a confidence in their decision-making abilities.

It was thought that the unification of Italy would abridge the role of the *comune* but this is not what happened. In time the *comune* became a very important feature of social and industrial life, filling

Small firms and industrial districts in Italy

some of the gaps left in default of central government action. Local interest groups also began to thrive and helped to create a movement towards decentralization. As Carlo Trigilia shows in Chapter 7, new political forces developed within the boundaries of the old allegiances and adapted the old social habits to modern economic and industrial conditions.

It is within this context of political and economic decentralism that a new philosophy of localism emerged in the nineteenth century, to be revived with renewed vigour in the 1970s. Following the unification of Italy the two most intellectually vigorous and socially dedicated political cultures in the *Terza Italia* were effectively exiled from political life: the Catholics because of Leo X's vendetta against them for their part in the expropriation of the Papal States, and the Socialists because in the public mind they had come to be associated with anarchists and other revolutionary forces. As a result, Catholics with abilities well-suited to public life were left without roles to play, and instead of contributing to the new politics of united Italy, they joined the Socialists in giving their talents to the public life of the region in other ways. For example, together they helped develop new co-operative movements throughout the territory; others turned to forming a strong local banking system to absorb the savings of local people and to channel them into *artigiano* firms and the new forms of enterprise beginning to grow up in the neighbourhood. New forms of political organization were created, some of them deriving from municipal socialism, some from what became the Catholic Action movement, which helped to form associations in order to further particular communal activities. These various structures provided niches for men of ability to occupy. In this way the community mobilized local wealth for the development of businesses, and out of all this eventually grew up the mid-twentieth-century movements which are the principal subject of this study. Another local activity of much significance for the future was adult education, especially technical and professional education. The movement was particularly strong in Emilia-Romagna, Tuscany, Friuli and parts of the north-west. No less important than these practical activities was the discussion of intellectual and ideological issues. This increased in intensity after the turn of the century when the issues themselves became more timely. The expression which gave the whole movement significance was the somewhat rhetorical one 'in defence of local society'. This not only voiced a virtuous form of local patriotism and crystallized local feelings of caution towards the new centralized government of united Italy, but also expressed the misgivings of many politically conscious Italians, the Socialists especially, about economic developments which they saw as

14

manifestations of social disintegration: the mass-based markets and industrialization coming from Anglo-Saxon societies. There was also considerable agreement with the critique of the capital-investment process made by Marx and Engels. A perception of 'exploitation' was certainly shared by both parties and has survived into recent times. In looking for a method of investment that did not rely upon equity capital sharing the profits, these thinkers drew upon the experience of the *artigiani* who managed to build up their enterprises without having to raise capital in this way.

Was there not a Christian or Socialist alternative to the hard-faced mechanized society that seemed fast approaching and about to pour the culture of northern and central Italy into its mould? This question persisted, and many who asked it saw in co-operatives and small-scale enterprises a sound moral alternative to capitalism. It may even be that the development of an industrial society in Italy was delayed two generations by these misgivings. The keynote sounded in both Socialist and Catholic cultures was the virtue of conserving local society and the values that they believed it embodied. It was in a world of this intellectual and moral quality that the new spirit of localism found expression.

Later, after the interregnum of Fascism and the Second World War, two political movements (or subcultures, as Trigilia describes them) came to dominate the regions of central and north-east Italy: the Italian Communist Party (PCI) and the Christian Democrats (DC), the former more powerful in the centre (the red areas), the latter in the north-east (the white areas). Different as they were, they both inherited the spirit of localism and began to develop economic policies which in various ways, and often in co-operation with local interest groups, helped to stimulate industry in their areas. This ensured that the communes devoted their available resources to supporting the infrastructure of local industry and also that the trade unions co-operated. As Trigilia's chapter explains, these two political parties 'favoured a localist regulation of the small firm economy through their influence on industrial relations and the activity of local governments. On these bases a social compromise was reached which brought about high levels of economic flexibility.'

This compromise brought about the paradox of Prato – the small-firm area perhaps best known outside Italy – where a Communist local authority presided over an industrial district which exemplifies in extremely efficient form all the characteristics of a capitalist system described by the classical economists: some thousands of small textile firms (many of them employing fewer than ten people) competing with each other, producing high-quality goods, achieving remarkable success in export markets and bringing great prosperity to the district.

Reserves of labour: leaving the land

Between 1945 and 1960 Italy seemed set to be well on the way to becoming a successful industrial nation following the models of American capitalism and the British mixed economy. The war was over and the post-war recession in Italy had left behind no marks of permanent damage. Industries that had been nationalized for wartime production were being dismantled to make room for efficient peacetime enterprises; others returned to their previous owners to meet the demands of new markets. Heavy industry was being methodically built up in what has since become known as the northern industrial triangle – based on Turin, Milan, and Genoa. Into this triangle would soon be drawn an army of migrant workers from the south. Light industry, mostly engineering, was beginning to be attracted into adjoining areas and the infrastructures of many cities in the north and centre of the country were being improved. As employment and investment increased, the need for subsidiary and secondary industries arose, and these were developing in districts where there had been industrial establishments before: engineering for example, in and around Bologna and Modena; textiles in Prato; refrigerators, furniture, and other consumer durables in the region of Venice and the northern part of Tuscany. The labour situation at that time seemed likely to remain particularly favourable. As the mechanization of agriculture got under way, so it was argued, there would be released in the north and centre of the country large reserves of skilled and experienced labour.

It is worth having a look at a sample of the small farmers and agricultural workers that made up this reserve. They were hardworking and knowledgeable people versed in the many skills needed for success on the hillside farms: grapes and olives to cultivate and harvest; corn between the rows of vines to grow; sheep and oxen to care for as well as the dozen or so subsidiary occupations that helped to make a living in winter. The men were also able to repair equipment and knew enough about the petrol engine to keep their vehicle on the road. The women, besides making the family's clothes, and probably the linen too, collected and prepared the orris roots to take to the perfume factories, made the honey and vinegar and preserved the fruit and still had time to box and tan the animal hides for leather for sale or their own use. The family was not only skilled in all these land-based occupations, but it had also, over the centuries, acquired hard-headed business experience. The agricultural system which they worked and which survived in parts of central and northern Italy until after the Second World War was the *mezzadria*. The land was worked by extended families, and the head of the family would be experienced at organizing the varied operations, in negotiating with the *fattore* (the land agent or estate manager) and in selling the produce in the local market. Here in fact was a flexible division of labour practised in the countryside. The houses stood together in groups by the side of their ample barns in a way that suggests a small industrial complex. Moreover, as Becattini has pointed out in relation to Tuscany, many of the agricultural units were related to each other and bound together by having a common landowner in a system that had characteristics later to be found in the industrial productive process.

This labour force of multi-purposed skills would be redeployed as machines came to take on many of the burdens of its heavy work. It was only a matter of time before Lamborghini and Fiat tractors would become commonplace. Most of the workers when they left the land, it was believed, would adapt their repertoire of skills to enable them to meet the newly articulated needs of the northern triangle or go into the traditional industrial areas as they developed new ranges of consumer goods. There were other options: some abandoned manual work and became stall-holders or dealers in one of the markets of nearby cities. In any event, they took with them a basic entrepreneurial ability.

At the same time as the *contadini* in the north were leaving their farms, workers from the south were coming to the north-eastern industrial triangle in search of work in the factories. Permanent employment in the prosperous factories did not easily come to them, and when it did, they discovered that the work itself bore little relation to that to which they were accustomed. They felt themselves regarded as unskilled and resented strangers who were putting pressure on the already scarce stock of housing resources. They wanted to be accepted and to have some kind of social standing which at that time no union or political party offered them. They needed to make a convincing gesture to show that they were willing to take on the values of the northern industrial proletariat, and to do this they adopted a militancy and a trade-union loyalty not known in the north before. They followed four aims. The first was to become accepted by the northern workers as good union members, and in the course of a few years they led many of the strikes. Second, they agitated for better working conditions and better housing. The third aim was to remove what was for them the wounding distinction between skilled and general work; at least the money value of the distinction could be progressively whittled away; time after time they successfully proposed to union leaders the same wage increase for all grades of workers irrespective of skill differentials. Their fourth aim was to ensure that their wages were high enough for them to make

17

generous allowances to their families still in the south, and the way to do this was to make themselves a militant force to be feared. They were the first to occupy the factories where they worked, on a 24-hours-a-day basis. Another feature of their radicalism in the late 1960s was their desire to be involved in new forms of political action, alongside the students. This they believed would create a new political force that would take in much besides the conventional list of Marxist grievances. Eventually, political and economic objectives combined to create demands in an atmosphere which intimidated management and alarmed skilled workers, whose wage differentials were already threatened. As a result, the power of the general workers' unions dramatically increased. One of the fruits of their success was the 1970 *Statuto dei Lavoratori*, the first of a series of legislative measures which provided almost cast-iron security of employment and also gave the unions the right to organize elections in the factories and to establish factory councils. It seemed as though the unions would take full control when factory councils were given additional powers in 1972 and 1973. A policy of radical action continued to be pursued by the unions, though by the beginning of the late 1980s their strength was diminishing.

In a comparatively short time this unrest and its aftermath came to play an increasingly decisive part in a nation-wide debate on decentralization. It challenged many of the ideas of the left and centre-left concerning the nature of collectivism and the desirable qualities of working life. Localism once again became a strong force. Discussion centred on the objectives of local policies and how the ways of perceiving them differed from those of central government. The doctrine of popular participation also became the subject of debate. This was a new concept, and as it developed it became part of the political vocabulary of the left as well as of others, finding a place alongside the traditional ideas of decentralization. Finally, decentralization crossed into the economic and industrial vocabulary and gave yet another boost to the small firm rooted in the fertile ground of local community.

The small firms had in fact benefited from the *Statuto dei Lavoratori*. During the debate leading up to the legislation, the associations of small business had exerted the maximum political influence to persuade the political parties of the need for concessions in their favour, which the statutes duly embodied. Small firms, defined first as having fifteen members or fewer (later increased to twenty) were exempted from the principal provisions of the *Statuto dei Lavoratori*, especially those concerned with trade-union representation in factories. In addition, they were given fiscal concessions, such as exemption from VAT up to a generous limit, and they were also exempted from social security payments. A third privilege which they shared with the *contadini* was to be assessed for local taxes at a lower rate. The central government also enabled local authorities to build trading estates where small factories could be built or let at advantageous terms to small firms wishing to have better working space or to come out of their back garden, garage, or kitchen-workshop. Another legislative measure authorized local authorities to denote certain areas within their boundaries as 'depressed zones' and to provide subsidies or other forms of special treatment to those starting new businesses there.

The role of the small firm in the local economy became an important issue which was heightened by the wave of unemployment in the wake of the oil crisis of 1973. This was supplemented by a renewal of interest in the need for a more active and concerned local government. The pressures that were exerted by interest groups and local institutions resembled the scene at the beginning of the century when localism first became an issue. This time, however, the pressures had very much greater practical content: there was a consensus on the need for local economic development and the capital expenditure to accomplish it. The *comuni* became aware of the need to find employment for those who had lost their jobs as a result of the oil crisis. The *artigiano* firms themselves formed pressure groups which were well received by the leading political party in the *comuni*, whether the DC or PCI. They were concerned to fill, in practical ways, the gaps they believed central government had left in their political attitudes to local economic issues. Thus, as Trigilia points out, in a great many different and distinctive ways, Communist and Catholic local parties (PCI and DC) 'fostered a localist regulation of the small firm economy through their influence on industrial relations and the activity of local government'.

At the same time, the general unions themselves recognized that they were losing their bargaining power, because of technical developments which enabled management to abandon the assembly line and to use instead new, flexible methods of production, and because of rising unemployment.

Even before this, the owners and managements of many large firms, especially in the northern triangle, had begun to extend the practice of subcontracting important pieces of work; and this process was taken further by encouraging their skilled men, sometimes the entire workforce of a crucial department, to turn themselves into independent specialist firms under separate management. In order to be exempt from further union pressure and from the provisions of union-instigated legislation, these new firms had to be seen to be independent of any outside ownership. They were then able to enter into contractual relationships with their previous employer, who often helped them by making loans as starting capital. Some remained in the area and can be recognized as dependent subcontractors. Others moved further afield. The alternative for some large firms was liquidation, so the arrangement had some guarantee of permanence; and so it has proved. However, the small firms had to face the danger of being dependent on a single, large client who would find it easy to exploit them, and therefore they had to develop relationships with other customers. Eventually, the number and variety of their customers became a measure not only of their independence but also of their commercial solidity and viability. This was the origin of that particular characteristic of the high-technology *artigiano* firm, namely that it was not only highly specialized but also flexible. Each contract it made was for a different product demanding from the workers skills in different sequences of work.

The industrial district

Four tendencies have been discussed above: localism, participation; resistance to the organized pressures of the unskilled workers; and the formulation of a new type of skilled industrial enterprise. Together these factors generated the force to create a distinctive type of manufacturing complex which has been identified as a contemporary form of the 'industrial district'. It may be too early to judge the success of the Italian industrial district in meeting the needs of modern society or how permanent a social and economic structure it will prove to be. But even with this reservation and the added one that the area of the *Terza Italia* where it has been created is but a small part of Italy and a tiny part of the industrial world, it is yet clear that the high-technology industrial district is an innovation of great importance in the realm of ideas which carries with it few of the moral objections to capitalism and few of the political objections to communism.

Since a large part of this book is involved with industrial districts, the notes that follow are designed to introduce the English reader to the modern Italian concept of what has previously been described mainly in terms of British nineteenth-century experience. It will be seen that there are broadly two types of industrial district, one conventional and, in economic terms, classical, and the other with certain collectivist features. Roughly speaking, the former tended to evolve naturally; the latter was more positively encouraged and more systematically supported by local interest groups.

The term 'industrial district' is a concept made familiar by the English economist Alfred Marshall. The division of labour which characterizes the area is not by individual workers in a single factory but by different highly specialized firms which both compete with each other and complement one another. The ultimate refinements are the flexible use of resources, including manpower, and a specialized vertical production process. The more specialized the process the fewer the firms in the pyramid. This is illustrated by Brusco's maxim that in an industrial district only one type of specialist firm corresponds to each stage of production. The definition of the industrial district is at present a subject of debate, especially in Italy, among economists and industrial sociologists. Initially, it can be said that an industrial district is an 'exclusive and restricted locality which has both industrial and residential characteristics'. The classic type described by Marshall had a number of features that still have validity today. Two of Marshall's comments are worth quoting for the flavour they give: ' "The Mysteries of Industry" that children learn unconsciously and others breathe in through the air'; 'Workers by associating with one another teach one another'. A third is worth summarizing: opportunities for innovation are enhanced when small firms operate within industrial districts and can draw on the pooled resources and the generational accumulation of skills that are stored there. Innovations are born in this industrial atmosphere and the harder the challenge, the more likely it is that simpler and more efficient ways of responding to it will be found.

The industrial district is essentially a territorial system of small and medium-sized firms producing a group of commodities whose products are processes which can be split into different phases. This definition was given by Becattini.[9] Other authors refer to it as a system of firms rather than as an exact geographical concentration. It is interesting that in this connection they do not think it impossible for two or three industrial districts to thrive in the same geographical area, or in overlapping or contiguous areas. Where a given area of specialization in interrelated forms of production lacks some of the features of an industrial district, it is convenient to call it a 'product specialist area', a label which points to the continuation of craft traditions, as in some parts of Tuscany or in the south of Italy.

Fabio Sforzi follows a meticulous path, seeing the industrial district as a well-defined part of a particular kind of geographical system. For him it is 'an organised complex of local interdependence within which the interrelations between family systems and firm systems takes place'. Its primary purpose is as a local labour market, where 'the majority of the local population can find work or change jobs without having to change their place of residence'. He infers that there is a strong relationship, almost by definition, between social class and industrial district. He quotes Marshall as saying that an industrial district has to be organized as 'a totality of integral parts' and also that its population has to have social characteristics, just as the manufacturing firms it includes have to have 'productive characteristics' and to be specialized in different phases of production. For him, an industrial district is a predominantly working-class area where most wives go out to work, and he tends to reject candidate-areas for inclusion on the grounds that they have too many white-collar workers. His point about the class basis of the industrial districts opens up many topics of discussion, and, of course, begs the question of white-collar workers in areas such as machine-tool making, where an educational qualification and white collar or similar symbol of class may be very nearly inevitable.

From these remarks it ought not to be inferred that in modern Italy class distinction is an important factor. In fact, it should be stressed once again that the Italian small firm has few of the communication problems that beset larger hierarchic firms in many parts of the world. What is significant about an industrial district, and often other kinds of industrial areas too, is that its inhabitants tend to be homogeneous. Living and working together is a precondition of specialization.

Becattini claims that the basic unit of economic analysis should be the industrial district or industrial area and not a particular firm or industry. He likes the expressions 'systems of firms' and 'network of firms', which make the system of industrial districts themselves seem a more flexible and adaptable idea. Moreover, the concentration of skills and the rapid circulation of ideas within these areas, and the constant experimenting with new practical forms of them, leads to innovation, which is especially important in businesses committed to high technology. What holds together the firms in an industrial district, according to Becattini, is 'a complex and tangled web of economies and diseconomies, of joint and associated costs, of historical and cultural vestiges, which envelop both inter-firm and interpersonal relationships'. Russo's fascinating study of the ceramic tile makers, introducing innovations made by their neighbours the machine-tool makers, is an example ready to hand to illustrate Becattini's point.

Central to the understanding of the industrial districts is the notion of internal and external economies of scale. An internal economy of scale is, of course, an economy organized and achieved within a firm for the benefit of all its parts: a typing pool, an accounts department, a drawing office and sometimes, a research department, perform the functions of internal economies. Other examples will be obvious. An external economy arises where it is cheaper for an external firm or agency, and sometimes an institution, to carry out specialized work for all the firms in an industry, rather than for each of the constituent firms to do it in-house. In general terms, therefore, it can be said that in an industrial district, economies of scale are internal to the district but external to the firms that make it up.

The unique feature of an industrial district is that by one of two methods it carries out the external economies for all the firms in the district. These two methods correspond to the type of industrial district they serve. In the first, the classical type of district with its strong historical traditions and other features very much resembling Bellandi's account of the Marshallian system, there is no collective provision of external services. (This type prevails in Tuscany, for example.) Instead, the external economies of scale here are provided through specialist firms and through one or two large firms that existed in the district before the small firms came and which now act as training centres for workers and transmitters of old skills and traditions.

By contrast, in the red areas (dominated by the PCI) a collectivist model of the industrial district is the more usual form, and the method of providing common services is through centralized agencies. This system can be quickly comprehended in Chapter 3, by Ash Amin. It is as though an entire industrial district specializing in one type of production had become a kind of corporation housing a number of independently owned, interlocking small firms.

Competition in industrial districts, especially in the engineering sectors, is exceptionally severe, because each firm is very specialized, and the smaller and more specialized, the more deter-mined are its members to win the contract. Having won a contract, a firm may subcontract parts of it to other even more specialized firms, all of which collaborate with each other to complete it with maximum efficiency. Moreover, many of these specialist subcontrac-tors may again subcontract to yet other specialized firms. This holds especially true of the Emilian industrial districts. Any individual firm may enter into any number of contracts during the course of a year: between twenty and thirty is normal. The firms sell their products either to the local market or, more usually, to each other. The more specialized the product, the more likely it is that the sale will be to another specialist firm. Eventually, of course, the completed product reaches the national or international market.

These remarks point to the significance of the dualism of competi-tion and collaboration in the modern industrial district. The firms may work together to find new techniques or devise new tools, but competition remains fierce. They may pass to another firm, orders they cannot fulfil; and the relationship may become contractual, which justifies the reference to some small specialist firms as subcontractors.

In his idealized model Amin describes even closer collaboration by a 'cluster' of small firms making up integrated production units and then selling their finished goods to 'strategic entrepreneurs composed of other small firms from provincial cities'. These latter firms come from different family units and share the bargain of the strategic entrepreneur on a contractual basis. All contracts are short term and can be adjusted to actual market conditions. This leads Amin on to the subject of flexibility of contracts, which he sees as the logical and symmetric counterpart of flexible production.

Flexible production is the second most conspicuous feature of the industrial district which has attracted public attention. It can be regarded as the Italian industrial district's unique contribution to lowering the cost of modern technology. In mass production specially designed plant and machinery is used to achieve the economies of scale, but the plant is costly and needs a very long series of production to justify it. The use, instead, of flexible methods of production – in the deployment of labour and the use of tools – makes possible short series of production in batches. It also gives scope for customized production. Modern technology, in particular the computer and numerically controlled tools, makes small-scale production possible and leads to variations in output which would not have been possible in systems of production based on the conventional economies of scale and conventional production plans. Such flexibilities are particularly appropriate for markets concentrating on quality-based products the demand for which fluctuates, sometimes dramatically, in terms of both quality and design. The adaptability of the labour force, a salient characteristic of the *Terza Italia*, is of course crucial to flexible production methods.

The financial backing for small firms in Italy shows a sharp contrast to the contemporary British banking system, dominated as it is by a few centralized national banks. A significant part of the Italian system is formed by local banks, often called savings banks or artisans' banks. They have counterparts in Germany, variously called co-operative, savings, or *Handwerk* banks, and bear some resemblance to nineteenth-century British provincial banks before the amalgamations took place. These Italian banks derive their funds from local sources and lend to local firms. Their directors and managers have a close working relationship with the firms in their area and a personal knowledge of anyone setting up in business and needing to borrow money to do so. In some cases the bank may be involved in the decision-making of the business and may even lend staff. Some banks subsidize centres for providing specialist services to small firms. But equally important is the fact that the decisions of the bank will be based on an understanding of the economy of the district rather than on rules laid down by a distant head office. Another institution, called *Intermediatore con l'Estero*, provides help to small firms in import–export business. It is a private-enterprise common-service agency performing the function of intermediary between producer and buyer. Sometimes, in the case of long-term contracts, the *Intermediatore* is in a position to vary the contract (e.g. to initiate changes in price) when it seems realistic to do so.

The difference that the existence of an industrial district makes to the success of the small firm is illustrated in two other chapters: the one on Ravenna by Mario Pezzini and the one on Naples by Ash Amin. In Ravenna the small manufacturing firms hardly get off the ground, or if they do there are few others with whom they can develop markets and trade-offs, and there are no reserves of trained and experienced labour. In Naples there certainly are small manufacturing businesses, but few of them flourish. Amin describes some really excellent firms of shoemakers, but they enjoy neither the growth nor the profits of the firms in the industrial districts of the north.

Summing up

Brusco's chapter introduces comments on two justly celebrated pieces of economic literature which give a perspective on our present study of the small firm economy in Italy. One is Adam Smith's maxim that the division of labour is limited by the extent of the market, and the other is George Stigler's article in the *Journal of Political Economy* in June 1951 which refers at length to the book by G.C. Allen, *The Industrial Development of Birmingham and the Black Country 1860–1927*.[10] This latter opens up the vista of that part of Birmingham centred around St Mary's Church, where two industrial districts coincided: that where jewellery was manufactured and where the specialist parts of guns were assembled and the gun finished. Stigler's comment is as appropriate today as it was in 1951 when his article was first published. 'The division of labour is not a quaint practice of eighteenth-century pin factories: it is a fundamental principle of economic organisation.'

This is not, however, the primary reason for bringing up again Stigler's discussion of the specialism carried out in the Birmingham small arms industrial district in 1860. The intention was rather to be able to add, 'So we have all been here before!' The population of this particular small firm economy was as skilled, as knowledgeable and as productive as that of any Italian district now; yet in the 1920s it disappeared. The mass-production motor industry took its place, drawing on its reservoir of skilled workers. There are of course important differences of tradition and culture, especially the important role of family and community. Nevertheless, on first rereading the passage from G.C. Allen's book quoted by Stigler, a chill goes down the spine of any of us who are concerned about the future of the Italian small firm: history may repeat itself.

With their familial relationships, their generational build up of skills, their asymptotic dependence upon both competition and co-operation, their obvious sense of community and camaraderie, the industrial manufacturing districts of Italy are important cultural entities. What we have been describing, and the chapters in this volume refer to, is not only a small-firm economy. It is a polity as well, and if British economic history were to be repeated, this might soon be in jeopardy from monopolies and conglomerates.

Yes, we have been here before. Consider the small-arms industry in 1860, when Birmingham was still the leading production centre of the world:

> Of the 5,800 people engaged in this manufacture within the
> borough's boundaries in 1861 the majority worked within a small
> district round St Mary's Church. . . . The reason for the high
> degree of localisation is not difficult to discover. The manufacture
> of guns, as of jewellery, was carried on by a large number of
> makers who specialised on particular processes, and this method
> of organisation involved the frequent transport of parts from one
> workshop to another. The master gun-maker – the entrepreneur –
> seldom possessed a factory or workshop. Usually he owned
> merely a warehouse in the gun quarter, and his function was to
> acquire semi-finished parts and to give these out to specialised
> craftsmen, who undertook the assembly and finishing of the gun.
> He purchased materials from the barrel-makers, lock-makers,
> sight-stampers, trigger-makers, ramrod-forgers, gun-furniture
> makers, and, if he were engaged in the military branch, from
> bayonet-forgers. All of these were independent manufacturers
> executing the orders of several master gun-makers. Once the parts
> had been purchased from the 'material makers', as they were
> called, the next task was to hand them out to the 'setters up',
> each of whom performed a specific operation in connection with
> the assembly and finishing of the gun. To name only a few, there
> were those who prepared the front sight and lump end of the
> barrels; the jiggers, who attended to the breech end; the stockers,
> who let in the barrel and lock and shaped the stock; the barrel-

strippers, who prepared the gun for rifling and proofing; the hardeners, polishers, borers and riflers, engravers, browners, and finally the lock-freers, who adjusted the working parts.[11]

History may not repeat itself, and there is much in the Italian tradition of small firms that will delay whatever ineluctable economic forces there may be. Let's try to be clear about what some of its advantages are: intimate-sized working units based on family and community relationships between men and women who traditionally support each other; the relentless pursuit of skill both as a means of maximizing economic gain and of the individual's response to the challenges set out by his work; no need for surveillance, no free riders, and the rich opportunities for improvization and the discussion of technical problems that so often result in innovation. All these provide economic advantages to the firm as well as satisfaction to the workers.

One needs to refer again to Brusco's work and to Stigler's article to put this optimism to the test and discover the real threats to the small-firm economy. In 1951 Stigler pointed to one threat and in 1986 Brusco took it up: vertical integration. Specialist small firms develop a new high-technology product which becomes indispensable to a large manufacturer, the raw material, as it were, of the essential output of the large firm. It is assumed that sooner or later the small firms will be taken over by the big manufacturer, giving it vertical economies and adding to its size and security.

However, Brusco is confident that this is a situation with which a well-organized industrial district can deal successfully. Specialization takes the place of vertical integration, 'thus enabling the industrial district to have at its disposal high level skills'.

Brusco's main fear seems to be whether the system of disintegrated firms will be able to survive the introduction of new electronic technologies. Will the small manufacturer be able to develop new products in competition with giant firms which can devote massive resources to research and development? His solution is a much more systematic provision of central services in industrial districts, with both public and private support. Some degree of collectivism is of course implied.

Brusco relates two views of technical progress: one from Schumpeter, the *élan vital* which sees progress created by intuitive leaps occurring in daily experience in the workshop, the other a more institutional approach, associated with the name of Rosenberg, whose advance is by small successive steps. There can be little doubt that those who believe in the small firm economy will find the creative theory of technical progress more attractive. Nevertheless, progress of this nature would be well served by the underpinning that a solid institution could give. Leaps forward are safer in the light than in the dark, and research and scientific expertise can provide the light. So it may be that these are not two contradictory models, and that there is a role for specially designed centres for common services in the patient and systematic follow-up of innovative ideas. It needs to be said that a danger for the future of industrial districts is that those responsible will imitate more closely the blueprint efficiency of the large firm and reinforce the collectivist trends, already strong in the institutions of the high-technology districts. The superiority of the small *artigiano* firm has been founded on the belief in the efficacy of the 'bottom-up' form of organization, and on the ability of these firms to handle the tools of high technology. Why diminish these strengths? A debate on this issue might illuminate the problem of how better these industrial districts may be supported.

At the immediately practical level it seems obvious to suggest that if the causes for sounding the alarm are the predatory noises, still some way off, coming from the centres of international capital, the most effective safeguard is to make sure that the money supply line to the constituent firms is at least as effective as it would be if international capital were actually to take them over. Statistics show that wages in some of the districts of the *Terza Italia* are falling below the level of a year or two ago, and this may indicate a levelling off of the upward curve of prosperity.

Is it realistic to expect the present structure of the industrial district to remain intact in the face of the financial pressures and inducements that are likely to come? These are issues the EEC might address itself to. For one of the threats to the political economy of the small firms comes from developments in the EEC itself. Among the changes under the single market in 1992 will be the removal of the current restrictions in Italy which prevents a foreign company owning more than 49 per cent of an Italian business. Possibly more alarming is the prospect of foreign banks freely entering the Italian market, since, as we have seen, the Italian local banks give vital support to the small firms. The Italian central bank has already let it be known that the arrival of European competition will necessitate bigger banks.

The question above all that the chapters of this book invite to be asked is this: are these small independent craft firms simply efficient agents of economic purpose at this particular time in Italy's industrial history or do they also embody important human values which might well cease to find expression if the firms were to suffer the fate of their counterparts in the industrial districts of England in the time of Alfred Marshall? This is a question addressed to the political theorist and the educated public as well as to the economist and the industrial sociologist. Possibly enough has been said to show that the Italian small-firm economy offers at least one approach to the liberal dream of free and creative work as an essential part of liberty.

As the work on this book progressed, it became more and more evident that the distinction implied in the title of the Acton Society's continuing study of the two-tier economy has a reality and perhaps a universal significance. The first tier is defined as the sphere of the large-scale organization, of mass production and the unskilled worker, of the vertical division of labour and hierarchical relationships, and inevitably, of impersonal and bureaucratic systems of control. The second tier is the tier of skill, imagination, and adaptability, where production is for the market-place where people's needs differ; the sphere of worker satisfaction and personal service, involving a type of work that has to be done on a human scale and where relationships operate *al livello umano*. It is clear that the first and second tiers have separate characteristics, not only in economic terms but in social, cultural, and political terms as well; and it may be that they should be governed by quite separate rules. It may also be true that these considerations apply as strongly to Britain as to Italy. The belief that the interests of economic and political liberalism are identical, that economic progress by whatever means achieved is political progress, and the belief that there is only one way to a desired economic or political end – these false theories are refuted in this book, which points to an industrial future that will preserve and extend the human as well as the economic values enshrined in these small firms and the complex of relationships that bind them together.

Notes

1. The term *Terza Italia*, the third Italy, distinguishes the area of north-central and north-east Italy from the south of the country and from the area of heavy industry in the north-west. It consists of the regions of Tuscany, Emilia-Romagna, Umbria, Marche, Veneto, Friuli-Venezia-Giulia and Trentino-Alto Adige. Arnaldo Bagnasco is credited with inventing the term.

2. Professor Becattini is a distinguished economist and an authority on the subject of this book. See, for example, his *Mercato e forze locali: il distretto industriale*, Bologna: Il Mulino: 1987 and 'Dal settore industriale al distretto industriale', in *Rivista di Economia e Politica Industriale*, no. 1, 1987.

3. Professor Brusco is the leading authority on the Emilian economy. See, for example, 'The Emilian model: production, decentralisation and

social integration', *Cambridge Journal of Economics* 6, 1982; 'Small firms and industrial districts', in D. Keeble and E. Wever (eds.) *New Firms and Regional Development*, London: Croom Helm, 1986.

4. At an Acton Society seminar in Florence, 1987.

5. See *Bolton Committee of Inquiry on Small Firms*, Cmnd 4811, HMSO, 1971.

6. S. Weil, *Oppression and Liberty*, London: Routledge & Kegan Paul, 1958.

7. I owe much of the insight in this section to discussions with Dr Susan Mendus of York University. See her 'Liberty and autonomy', *Proceedings of the Aristotelian Society*, 1986.

8. Weil, op. cit.

9. In an address to an Acton Society seminar at Eynsham Hall, Oxford, October, 1987.

10. G.J. Stigler, 'The division of labour is limited by the extent of the market', *Journal of Political Economy* 59 (31), June 1951.

11. G.C. Allen, *The Industrial Development of Birmingham and the Black Country 1860–1927*, quoted in Stigler.

Chapter 1

The role of small firms in the development of Italian manufacturing industry

Marco Bellandi

(Translated by Stephen Coffey)

Italy
6110
1223
6310

31 – 68

Introduction

The purpose of the present chapter is to present a simple quantitative analysis of the role played by small and medium-sized firms in the industrial development of Italy in the 1960s and 1970s.

The boom in Italian industry in the 1950s saw the formation of many small and medium-sized industrial firms, thus adding to the small number of large firms which had grown up in an earlier period (Isotta and Rispoli 1979). The 1960s seemed to indicate that the natural continuation of this growth would be along the inevitable road towards modernization, characterized by a general increase in the size of both firms and production plants and by a progressive shift towards those industrial sectors and techniques considered to be more characteristic of modern economies; for example, mechanical engineering, chemicals, iron and steel, and mass production in general. The 1970s, however, which might have been expected to confirm this process of modernization, held a number of surprises in store. Growth continued, but it was characterized by a further proliferation of small firms and also by the fact that many large firms found themselves in serious difficulties. In addition, those industries considered to be older and more traditional (e.g. textiles, clothing, footwear, leather and leather goods, the manufacture of furniture and other wooden objects, glass and ceramic goods) showed considerable liveliness, especially in regions where the growth of smaller-sized firms had been greater, and continued to make a decisive contribution to, amongst other things, Italian exports. This change of direction in industrial development rekindled debate and controversy in Italy as regards the role played by small firms. Later on we shall try to give a brief outline of this debate.

Since the principal aim of this chapter is to offer a simple but incisive illustration of the real importance of this change, we shall make use primarily of the information contained in the Trade and

Industry Censuses of 1961, 1971, and 1981 provided by ISTAT, the Italian national institute of statistics. These data concern *employees* in the manufacturing industries and are organized according to type of economic activity, geographical region, and size of *plants*.

It should be noted that the information we shall be considering relates to the workforce in plants and not in firms. Strictly speaking, therefore, if we take into consideration the phenomenon of multi-plant firms, results deriving from the percentage distribution of plants according to size of workforce should not automatically be indicative of the size structure or change in size structure of the firms themselves. However, as there is high correspondence between the number of single-site firms and the number of plants in all the aggregate subdivisions we have used, the phenomenon of multi-plant firms may be considered as being limited to medium and large plants. Thus, an examination of the figures relating to individual plants should not result in any excessive overestimation of the impor-tance of small and very small firms.

Another statistical problem concerns the reliability of the census data. It has been pointed out that the 1981 census was more accurate and extensive than its predecessors, and that this led to the appearance of populations of very small industrial firms which had previously existed but not been registered. We shall attempt to take into account this problem of comparability, the importance of which, however, should not be overestimated (Appendix 1, p. 53). It should also be remembered that the ISTAT censuses are the most complete survey available in Italy dealing with the facts we are considering.

Another point to note is that the information on the employment sector, geographical region, and size of plants, has been reorganized in various ways in order to facilitate the work of analysis and comparison. The detailed size classification of the censuses has been reduced, ignoring minor incomparabilities, to four groups: (1) *very small* plants, in which the workforce has a maximum of nine employees; (2) *small*, from ten to forty-nine employees; (3) *medium*, from fifty to 499 employees; (4) *large*, more than 499 employees. As far as geographical division is concerned, reference is made both to individual regions and to the following three regional aggregates: (1) the industrial triangle of the north-west (TRI), comprising Lombardy, Piedmont, Liguria, and Val d'Aosta, which includes the oldest industrial parts of Italy; (2) the north-central and north-east area (NEC), comprising Tuscany, Umbria, Emilia Romagna, Marche, Veneto, Trentino-Alto Adige, and Friuli-Venezia-Giulia, the area of the *Terza Italia*; and (3) the centre, including Latium, the south and the islands of Sicily and Sardinia (SCI). Employment sectors have been aggregated according to two main criteria, one statistical and one economic. The statistical criterion is the result of the need to find aggregates which are more or less comparable between the different censuses. The economic criterion arises from the need to work with aggregates which are as homogeneous as possible. In an attempt to satisfy these criteria, manufacturing industry is divided into three large aggregates: (1) metal goods and engineering; (2) traditional industries; (3) other industries, among which are iron and steel, chemicals, and the production of vehicles and transport equipment, henceforth referred to as 'heavy and other' industries. Within the traditional industries there are also sub-aggregates.

Employees in Italian manufacturing industry between 1961 and 1981

The starting point of the analysis is 1961. In that year in Italian manufacturing industry as a whole, the most important size category of plant, from the point of view of employment figures, is that of medium-sized plants (32 per cent), and the least important is that of small plants (19 per cent); very small plants are second in importance and large plants third.

Between 1961 and 1981 the workforce in Italian manufacturing industries grew considerably (36 per cent); between 1961 and 1971 the increase was about 800,000 employees (18 per cent), and between 1971 and 1981 the increase was just as great in absolute terms, though consequently smaller as a percentage of the workforce – the figures relating to this second decade have been partly inflated by the greater accuracy of the 1981 census in respect to its predecessors (Appendix 1). After the boom of the 1950s, when there was an increase of more than one million employees, the following twenty years thus saw an appreciable strengthening of manufacturing industries.

Between 1961 and 1981 the proportion of employees in small plants increased progressively until it overtook the proportion in large plants and came close to that of both very small plants and medium-sized plants. The latter three categories showed percentage decreases, which were the result of different trends in the two decades. In 1971 the very small plants proved to have remained more or less stationary from an employment point of view and therefore to have lost quota with respect to 1961, but in the following decade they made up most of this loss. The large and medium size categories both increased proportionately between 1961 and 1971, but in the course of the following decade declined to proportionate levels below those of 1961; it must be emphasized, however, that

Small firms and industrial districts in Italy

Figure 1.1 Manufacturing industries (=100%): % of employees by size of plant (in employees). Regional aggregates, 1961, 1971, 1981

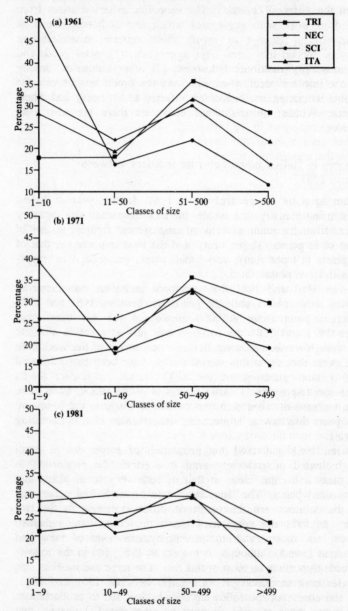

Note: See introduction to this chapter for the meaning of the aggregates.
Source: Elaboration on ISTAT, 1961, 1971, 1981.

this decline was more pronounced in the case of large plants, which in fact underwent a reduction in manpower in absolute terms between the years 1971 and 1981 (Fig. 1.1).

1961–71: a decade of modernization

As far as sectoral distribution is concerned, it is to be noted that the position of clear supremacy at a national level held in 1961 by the traditional industries (more than 40 per cent) had by 1971 undergone considerable change, this as a result of the very low increase in the number of employees in the traditional sectors (less than 3 per cent). The shift seen towards the larger size of plant between 1961 and 1971 in the manufacturing industries as a whole may be explained on the one hand by the decrease in proportional importance of the traditional sectors (in which smaller plants typically prevail), and on the other hand by the general shift towards plants of larger sizes. The latter factor is to some extent relevant to the traditional sectors, where small and medium-sized plants become more important at the expense of large and above all very small plants, but is to be seen most clearly in metal goods and engineering (where the large plants become more important at the expense of the other three categories) and in the industries which we have termed 'heavy and other' (where small and large plants undergo proportional increases). It should, however, be pointed out that the sectoral aggregate with the highest employment growth, that is metal goods and engineering (37 per cent), tends towards the larger size of plant to a considerably lesser extent, even after expansion in the 1960s, than the heavy and other industries (employment growth of 22 per cent).

When the data for the manufacturing industries is viewed according to a geographical split between the three regional aggregates, considerable differences between these areas show up in the 1961 figures. The manufacturing industries in the NEC regional aggregate do not indicate the marked predominance of any one size of plant, although there is a tendency towards the very small and medium-sized plants. In the TRI area the medium and large plants predominate when grouped together, while in the SCI it is the very small plants alone which are predominant (we say that a size category predominates when its proportion of the workforce is 40 per cent or more, and that two contiguous size categories predominate when, although not individually predominant, their combined proportion is 60 per cent or more).

The 18 per cent increase in the workforce in the Italian manufacturing industries between 1961 and 1971 finds different expression in the three areas we are dealing with. In the TRI there is an increase of 10 per cent (+239,000 employees), which represents a decrease in importance of the area with respect to the national total from 51 per cent to 48 per cent. In the NEC employment growth is 29 per cent (+406,000 employees), with a proportional increase from 31 per cent to 34 per cent of the national total. Employment growth in the SCI is 20 per cent (+161,000 employees), a proportional increase of half of 1 per cent, remaining at approximately 18 per cent of the national total.

Between 1961 and 1971 the TRI experiences an increase in the proportional importance of large plants (reaching 30 per cent in 1971). This is due to a number of factors: the considerable decrease in the importance of traditional activities (−116,000 employees); the significant increase in metal goods and engineering (though in percentage terms below the increase recorded in the other aggregate areas) within which sector there is an increase in the importance of large plants; the increase of heavy and other industries (above the national average), where large plants account for as much as 46 per cent of the workforce.

In the NEC area during the same period, the very small plants decrease in importance in terms of employment, but the large plants fail to increase in importance. This may be explained by the very marked increase in metal goods and engineering, where very small plants lose ground in favour of larger plants; and also by the increase in importance of the medium-sized and especially of the small plants, at the expense of the very small and large plants, in the traditional industries and in the heavy and other industries, which also experience good employment growth during this period.

In the SCI during the period 1961–71, the very small plants lose considerable ground (from 51 per cent of the total in 1961 to 39 per cent in 1971) in favour of the medium-sized and large plants in particular. There is a decrease in the importance of the traditional sectors, which in absolute terms remain static with regard to employment figures, while the proportional importance of large plants in the heavy and other industries reaches a noteworthy 31 per cent in 1971.

In the light of this small amount of data, the picture of change during the 1960s seems clear, and seems, moreover, to confirm the interpretative schema which was undoubtedly popular during that period and which anticipated development towards progressively larger firms and production plants and towards more modern industries where the larger sizes of firms would prevail. Moreover, the decrease in importance of the industrial triangle (TRI) in manufacturing industry as a whole, and above all in the traditional sectors, seems to conform, more or less, to a complementary interpretation, that of the 'inter-regional cycle of production' according

Figure 1.2 Metal goods and engineering industries (=100%): % of employees by size of plant (in employees). Regional aggregates, 1961, 1971, 1981

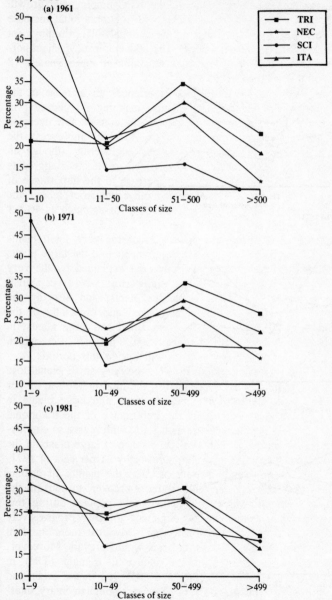

Note: See introduction to this chapter for the meaning of the aggregates.
Source: Elaboration on ISTAT, 1961, 1971, 1981.

Figure 1.3 Traditional industries (= 100%): % of employees by size of plant (in employees). Regional aggregates, 1961, 1971, 1981

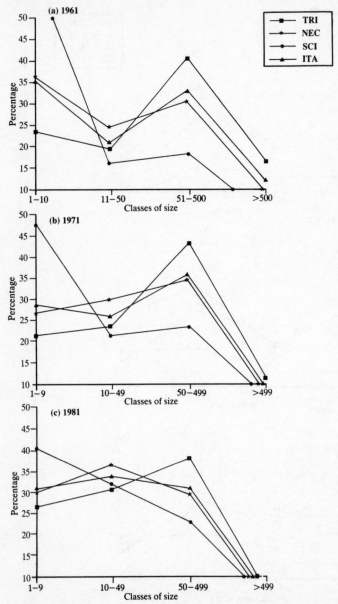

Note: See introduction to this chapter for the meaning of the aggregates.
Source: Elaboration on ISTAT, 1961, 1971, 1981.

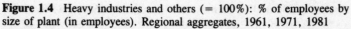

Figure 1.4 Heavy industries and others (= 100%): % of employees by size of plant (in employees). Regional aggregates, 1961, 1971, 1981

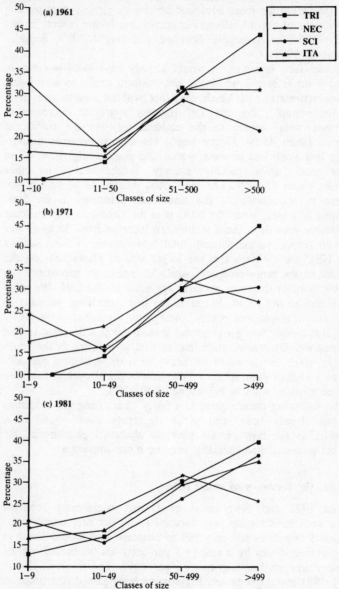

Note: See introduction to this chapter for the meaning of the aggregates.
Source: Elaboration on ISTAT, 1961, 1971, 1981.

to which there is a shift of the older production industries from the centre to the periphery, and growth of more modern activities in the centre (including the more advanced service industries), thus leading to a decrease of the manufacturing importance of the centre, in this case the TRI (see Arcangeli, Borzaga, and Goglio 1980; Becattini and Bianchi 1982).

In actual fact, however, it would already have been possible in 1971 to point to details which did not conform totally to such interpretative schemata, and which were not without significance. It is true, for example, that the TRI regional aggregate decreases in importance with respect to the national total in the traditional industries (from 45 to 37 per cent), but it also becomes proportionally less important in metal goods and engineering (from 60 to 54 per cent), whilst gaining, slightly, in the heavy and other industries (from 53 to 54 per cent). And what is to be said of the decrease in importance of the traditional industries in the less-developed SCI area, when the NEC is at the same time experiencing considerable growth in these sectors (an increase from 36 to 44 per cent with respect to the national total)? Moreover, in these sectors in the NEC the shift towards the larger size of plants halts on the threshold of the large category, which decreases in importance, as indeed it does in the same sectoral aggregate in the TRI. We must also emphasize the slight, but none the less surprising, increase in the number of employees in very small plants registered in the NEC, whilst in the other two geographical areas there is a decrease in this size category. Of course, state intervention in industry in the south of Italy, which concentrated on heavy industry activities, partially explains a certain interruption of the inter-regional cycles. But how does one explain what is happening in the NEC?

In the following decade there is a fairly clear change in dynamics – it has already been seen at an aggregate level – and it is interesting to see how certain previous abnormal phenomena, far from being assimilated, actually become more important.

1971–81: the recovery of small firms

Between 1971 and 1981 metal goods and engineering achieves another very considerable leap forward (+36 per cent employees). Traditional industries not only fail to decrease, but indeed increase in employment terms by a rate (+5 per cent) not far behind that of the heavy and other industries (+6 per cent). The result of this is that by 1981 metal goods and engineering have gained first place in terms of the number of employees, while the heavy and other industries have not yet managed to overtake the traditional industries, although this might have seemed probable given the trends of the previous decade. It is to be noted that the increased number of employees in the very small firms is distributed among all three aggregate sectors (see also Appendix 1). These trends, together with an increase in the proportion of both small and very small plants in all three sectors at the expense of the medium and large categories, are consistent with the analogous trend in proportional structure of the manufacturing industry as a whole. In the resulting size structure of the manufacturing industries, the small plants have become comparable in importance to the very small and medium-sized plants, while the large plants have remained quite clearly behind (Fig. 1.1c).

This structure finds its clearest expression in the traditional sectors, where the three smaller size categories are all above 30 per cent and large plants are reduced to 5 per cent. In metal goods and engineering, very small plants are clearly more important than in the manufacturing industry as a whole, where they are pushed downwards by the heavy and other industries in which medium-sized and large plants still predominate. Sixty per cent of the employees in large plants are now concentrated in this sector.

With regard to the dynamics of geographical division, we observe a considerable reduction in the importance of manufacturing employment in the TRI (from 48 to 42 per cent), with the corresponding increase divided between the NEC (a little more than 3 per cent) and the SCI (a little less than 3 per cent). The NEC, with 37 per cent of the manufacturing workforce, has now almost reached the proportion of the TRI, while the SCI, which has not yet made a decisive leap forward, remains clearly behind (20.5 per cent). It should be remembered than in 1981 the resident population of the SCI was 44 per cent of the national total.

In the TRI there are changes in the size structure of manufacturing industry which are analogous to the changes at a national level: an increase in the importance of small and very small plants and a decrease in that of the medium-sized and large plants. Naturally, there is a greater tendency towards the larger size of plant when compared with the national average. The larger categories, however, lose their predominance; indeed, the proportion of small plants reaches that of the large plants (about 23 per cent) – in 1971 the respective proportions had been 19 and 30 per cent – and it approaches that of the medium-sized plants (32 per cent). In terms of employment it is notable that small plants in metal goods and engineering take an even higher proportion in the TRI (25 per cent) than in the national aggregate. In the traditional sector, large plants slump to 5 per cent. Noteworthy, too, is the fact that while the number of employees in metal goods and engineering increases by 20 per cent during the decade, in the other two aggregate sectors the workforce diminishes, thus allowing metal goods and engineering to claim 40 per cent of the workforce in the TRI in 1981 (Figs. 1.1c, 1.2c, 1.3c, 1.4c).

In the NEC, in conformity with the national trend, there is an increase in importance of small and very small plants and a reduction in importance of the other two categories. Combining categories in two different pairs – small and very small, and small and medium-sized – we find that both combinations produce a figure close to 60 per cent. The small plants, with 30 per cent (25 per cent at national level), have reached first position, while larger plants fall to 12 per cent. In employment we must note the predominance gained by the two above-mentioned pairs of size categories in the traditional industries, both reaching in the NEC the very high proportion of 66 per cent. In the heavy and other industries we find that the pair medium-sized and large fail to predominate; this is the result of the minimal importance of large plants with respect to the national average (26 per cent as opposed to 35 per cent), a fact which is not compensated for by the relatively high percentage of medium-sized plants (32 per cent as opposed to 30 per cent).

In the SCI, the dynamics of firm size are atypical with respect to the other two areas and the national situation. The importance of very small plants diminishes, though at 34 per cent it is still significantly higher than the national average (26 per cent), and the large plants increase in importance. The latter category, in contrast to the situation in the other two areas, experiences an increase in the number of employees, and a considerable increase at that (+85,000). The proportional importance of this category within the SCI even exceeds its importance at a national level (21 per cent as opposed to 19 per cent); in 1961 the respective proportions had been 11 and 21 per cent. A single category or pair of categories still does not predominate since simultaneously the small plants have gained in importance and the medium-sized plants decreased in importance. The resultant size structure, when compared with the national average, shows an accentuation of the smallest and largest size categories. A similar picture of change is seen in the three sectoral aggregates, except for the decrease in importance of large plants in the traditional industries. It should also be noted that there is a further increase in the importance of the heavy and other industries in the SCI (in contrast to the other two geographical areas); that the importance of metal goods and engineering in the SCI exceeds that of the same employment sector in the NEC (33 per cent as compared with 31 per cent); and that the importance of the traditional industries in the SCI is now below the national average (30 per cent as compared with 33 per cent).

Interpretative paradigms: top-down growth or multi-regional development?

We observe, therefore, a process of convergence between the large territorial aggregates, which, however – and this is the difference which has become a central issue – does not tend towards that which had been the size structure of the TRI, but rather towards a fairly uniform structure wherein the small plant gains in importance. The decrease in manufacturing importance of the TRI and the tendency towards metal goods and engineering would seem still to be congruent with the existence of inter-regional production cycles. But the latter sectoral aggregate has grown even more (in employment terms) in the other two areas; also, those industries considered to be older and more traditional remain concentrated in the NEC, and lose importance in the SCI, which area tends more and more to be characterized by the heavy and other industries. A major inter-pretative problem arises which has sparked off a very heated debate in Italy over the last ten years. Within this debate there are a number of distinct standpoints. Two main interpretative paradigms may be distinguished and two main positions within each of these paradigms (see Becattini 1987).

The first interpretation suggests that the relationship between small firms and economic development in Italy may be reduced to a single pattern of development which emanates from the economically central regions and/or centres of capitalism, and then manifests itself in accordance with the specific socio-territorial conditions it encounters. This schema is of course consistent with the model of the inter-regional cycle and that of the tendency towards larger firms and production plants. Furthermore, the developments witnessed in the 1970s, despite being contrary to the expectations of these two models, have nevertheless been accommodated within the centralist paradigm, as is witnessed by studies on industrial reorganization, the decentralization of production, the segmentation of the labour market, and peripheral and marginal economies. In these studies two positions emerge, though not always clearly distinguishable. The first is characterized by its economic approach, concentrating on the ability of large firms to adapt themselves in due time to the changes and upheavals which assailed the home and international markets in the 1970s. Multi-plant investment, collaboration agreements, flexible automation, and financial reorganization are forms of adaptation

which are compatible with a decrease in the size of the production
plant while still remaining within the overall strategies of large firms.
At the same time, moonlighting, access to non-unionized labour
markets, and tax evasion would easily explain the temporary success
of smaller firms. The second position has more of a political
approach, according to which the external decentralisation of production in the 1970s was a central component in the owners' strategy
against the increased power of the trade unions within large firms.
Such decentralization has manifested itself in the creation of a myriad
of small firms which are formally autonomous but which in reality
are economically dependent on the large firms, and which effectively
bring about the splitting up of the working class together with the
reduction in power of the trade unions and of the political left
(Varaldo 1979; Goglio 1982).

The second interpretation is that of the 'autonomy' of growth of the
small firm. On the one hand, we find here the concept 'small is
beautiful' adapted to the exigencies of independence of the young
post-'68 generations. On the other hand, there are studies which
stress the importance of the endogenous forces sustaining some local
and regional developments of systems of small firms. 'Multi-regional
development', 'industrial districts', 'system areas', and 'flexible
specialization' are terms which are representative of the latter position
and which take their part in the debate in the 1980s on the relationship between small firms and economic development in Italy. It is
maintained that the small can in its own way be big, when it is organized through the appropriate systems of relationships (labour division
among firms, external economies, etc.), and that the creation and
reproduction of these systems is often facilitated by the existence of
deep-rooted substrata of local and regional production traditions (Fua
and Zacchia 1983; Piore and Sabel 1984; Brusco 1986).

We do not intend to enter into the merits of these positions. The
data we have presented certainly does not allow us to reach any
definitive conclusions in favour of one position or the other. It is
possible, however, to make a few relevant comments.

The first is that the debate on the relationship between small firms
and economic development is not merely a result of the writing of
academic papers in response to other papers, but rather responds to
socio-economic events of great significance. The second consideration
is that these events and the debate that has accompanied them have
delivered a heavy blow to organization determinism, which would
like to see the inevitable success of certain industrial models and the
inevitable failure or marginal importance of others, as a result of the
existence of certain economic conditions. A third consideration lies in
the recognition that the variety of industrial change observed in terms

of both territory and employment sector not only makes room for different interpretations, but is probably also compatible with the co-existence of different *types* of development.

We shall now return to the statistical data and examine individual geographical regions and employment sectors, and thereby try to identify signs which are more clearly interpretable as the expression of different types of development.

Regional differences and different types of development

We shall concentrate our analysis on the traditional and metal goods and engineering sectors in the regions of the NEC, where the importance of small plants is most evident, and compare these with the historically central regions, that is those of the TRI, where there was also significant growth in the workforce in small plants in the 1970s. We must attempt to discern signs of, on the one hand, the 'decentralization of production', and on the other, 'endogenous development of the small firm at a regional level'. Three observations seem to be of importance in relation to this. We shall deal with two of these in the present section, and the third in the following.

First, it should be noted that the type of changes in size structure which occurred during the twenty-year period 1961–81 is largely the same for the various regions and sectors we are now considering, and reflect what has already been observed for the larger territorial and sectoral aggregates; that is, a constant decrease in the importance of a size structure characterized by the prominence of the smallest and largest category. In the first decade this resulted from a continuous increase in the importance of small plants, a decrease in the importance of very small plants, an increase in the importance of the large and especially of medium-sized plants; and in the second decade, a recovery by the very small plants and a decrease in the importance of the medium-sized and above all large plants.

These changes, and in particular the increase in importance of the small plants, would seem, therefore, to respond to important systematic factors. Of the explanations previously mentioned, this would give support to those of a non-regional type.

There exist, however, points of difference which are far from negligible and which are the subject of our second set of observations. We should remember that the TRI and the NEC differ as regional aggregates, the former having a size structure which tends towards medium-sized and large plants and a growth rate which was low in the period 1961–71 and very low in the period 1971–81; and the latter, the NEC, having a size structure which tends towards the smaller-sized plants, and very high growth rates in both decades. It is important to emphasize now, however, that within these two geographical entities there exist important regional differences.

Within the TRI (excluding the very small region of Val d'Aosta), Liguria, which in 1961 had the highest percentage of employees in the large category (36.5 per cent) and the highest percentage in the heavy and other industries (47 per cent), experiences continuously decreasing employment figures in the manufacturing industries as a whole, in the traditional sectors, and also in the heavy and other industries themselves, a certain increase being achieved only in metal goods and engineering. Piedmont, which in 1961 had a high concentration of employees in the medium-sized and large categories (68.5 per cent), records an employment growth rate higher than that of Lombardy in the first decade (14 per cent as opposed to 10.5 per cent), thanks especially to the high growth achieved in the heavy and other industries, and a further concentration of size structure towards the medium-sized and especially the large plants. In the following decade, however, there is a decline in employment in Piedmont; while there is an increase, though only slight, in Lombardy, which traditionally offers, compared to the two other regions, a size structure less dominated by the large plants and a sectoral structure less dominated by the heavy and other industries. This could be interpreted as a sign of the importance of regional and sectoral traditions in the development of small firms even in areas of relatively old industrialization.

The regions of the NEC can be characterized by the convergence of *some* of the following traits; employment in small and very small manufacturing plants proportionally above the national average; growth rates in the manufacturing industries above the national average; proportional importance of traditional industries above that of the national average; and positive employment growth rates in the traditional sectors. On the basis of these characteristics, it is easy to draw important distinctions between the regions of the NEC.

To begin with, Trentino-Alto Adige and Friuli-Venezia-Giulia differ from the other five regions by virtue of the absence of one or two of these characteristics. In particular, both regions show low growth rates in the traditional industries taken as a whole, and a certain tendency (especially in Friuli) towards larger sizes of plants. Of the other five regions, Marche and Umbria show a decisive leap forward towards industrialization in the twenty-year period I am considering, with very high employment growth rates in the manufacturing industries. The other three regions had already experienced massive industrialization before 1961; however, Veneto and Emilia-Romagna continue to record high employment growth rates in the manufacturing industries as a whole; in Tuscany these same growth rates are only marginally above the national average. Tuscany preserves the most

marked tendency towards the smaller sizes of plants and towards traditional industries. Tuscany also differs from all other regions of the
NEC by virtue of growth rates in metal goods and engineering which
are below the national average; these growth rates reinforce Tuscany's
last place, in terms of employment figures, of metal goods and engineering in relation to the manufacturing industries as a whole (20 per
cent as against the national average of 35 per cent and Emilia-
Romagna's 41 per cent).

The very high employment growth rates in the manufacturing industries in Umbria (+36 per cent in the first decade and +41 per cent
in the second) and in Marche (+52 per cent and +53 per cent) could
be interpreted as being an indication of the processes of relocalization
and decentralization from other regions. However, in order to explain
such very high growth rates, it also seems plausible to assign an
important role to pre-existing traditions of production, perhaps in
handicraft and commercial activities. The presence of both types of
development, internal and external, may also explain the high growth
rates in Veneto and Emilia-Romagna. The presence of a single type of
development might, on the other hand, explain the less outstanding
results in Tuscany, where external influence and control have probably
played a weaker role, and in Trentino-Alto Adige and Friuli-Venezia-
Giulia, where, in contrast, self-sustaining, endogenous development
might seem less strong. These are, of course, very hypothetical suggestions, to which we will now add a small number of further
considerations.

Regional differences and different types of development: an examination of certain classes of activity

We thus arrive at our third set of observations. Here we shall
consider the data for the various regions of the NEC in the following
sectors (classes or aggregates of classes): 'textiles', 'leather and
leather goods', 'footwear and clothing', 'timber and wooden
furniture', 'manufacture of non-metallic mineral products' – which
together comprise the traditional industries – and 'metal goods and
engineering'. Let us consider in particular those regional sectors
which stand out either for having recorded particularly high employment growth rates in relation to the national average for that sector,
or for showing in 1981 a high regional specialization in those
sectors. The majority of these cases show the now familiar pattern
of development: more or less high growth rate during the twenty-
year period, with a trend towards the top end of the size structure
in the period 1961–71, and vice versa in the period 1971–81. The
regional sectors concerned are textiles in Veneto, Emilia-Romagna,

and Umbria; leather and leather goods in Veneto and Marche; footwear and clothing in Tuscany; timber and wooden furniture in Veneto, Friuli-Venezia-Giulia, and Umbria; and metal goods and engineering in Veneto, Emilia-Romagna, and Umbria.

The sectors in which Tuscany is prominent, apart from footwear and clothing, show some significant variations with respect to the above-mentioned pattern: textiles, leather and leather goods, and timber and wooden furniture, although experiencing considerable growth, show no signs of shifting towards the larger size of plant, not even in the 1960s. In addition, the footwear and clothing of Veneto, Umbria, and Marche make the same sector in Tuscany also seem an exception, although the latter fits into the normal pattern. In the other three regions, in fact, the normal pattern appears in a significantly accentuated form in the first decade; for example, between 1961 and 1971 the importance of the very small plants in Veneto decreased from 42 to 18 per cent, in Umbria from 83 to 32 per cent, and in Marche from 58 to 26 per cent (in Tuscany only from 36 to 22 per cent), and growth rates in the three regions were very high indeed, ranging from +55 to +87 per cent (the national average was +15 per cent and in Tuscany the rate was +44.5 per cent).

Different patterns of development are to be found in the manufacture of non-metallic mineral products and metal goods and engineering. This might partly reflect the high level of heterogeneity within these two sectors. However, it is still worth mentioning some of these patterns. The manufacture of non-metallic mineral products in Emilia-Romagna records a very high growth rate, constantly centred around medium-sized plants, the proportional importance of which category is 56 per cent in 1961 and 58.5 per cent in 1981. In metal goods and engineering Friuli-Venezia-Giulia, Trentino-Alto Adige, and Marche are to be noted. In Marche there is a very high growth rate, with a continuous shift towards the upper end of the size structure, though by 1981 the sector has not reached the levels of the national average. In Trentino-Alto Adige there is a notable shift towards the upper end of the size structure in the first decade and a very slight shift towards the lower end in the second decade. In Friuli-Venezia-Giulia, a very high rate of growth is reached in 1971 in this sector (with 40 per cent of the employees in large plants), but in the second decade there is a relatively slow growth rate together with a sudden decrease in the importance of the large plants, which, however, can still boast 30 per cent of the workforce in that sector as against a national average of 17 per cent.

The normal pattern of growth could, in fact, reflect two different types of development; one external and one internal. The change of size structure from the first decade to the second could be the result of the presence of factors which have been highlighted by such explanations as the inter-regional cycle and the decentralization of production. However, in those regional sectors we have considered above which do conform to the normal pattern, growth normally takes off from situations in which there are a significant number of employees in the small and very small plants. Naturally, large regional and extra-regional firms could have been the guiding force behind the swing in the 1970s; however, the developments of the preceding decade did not allow the very small firms to disappear, and strengthened the small firms. We might, therefore, conceive of a probable and significant relationship between the growth recorded in the 1970s and pre-existing substrata of smaller-sized firms. Following from this, it would also be easy to interpret the other patterns in ways which seem to conform to the previous hypotheses regarding the types of development which might have occurred in the various regions of the NEC.

Size of firm and economic viability in the Italian manufacturing industries of the 1970s

One of the limits of analyses based on data concerning employment figures is that such data can give a distorted picture of the underlying economic situation. For example, the decrease in importance in a certain period, in employment terms, of large firms in favour of small firms, might reflect not the greater buoyancy of the latter so much as an accentuation of the processes of capitalistic intensification in the former. It is difficult to assess this question either in general or in its particular relevance to the argument we have been discussing in the previous pages. There are various problems, of both statistics and economic interpretation.

We shall here limit ourselves to observing that two important series of surveys, those of the ISTAT concerning gross product and those of the Mediocredito concerning manufacturing firms in Italy, seem clearly to confirm the existence in the 1970s of greater overall buoyancy in the small-to-medium sector than in the medium-to-large sector.

Let us first consider the data of the ISTAT survey as presented in the important in-depth analysis on the 'Reorganization and Development of Industrial Firms' to be found in the 1987 annual report of the Governor of the Bank of Italy. Here, a distinction is made between small-to-medium firms, with between twenty and ninety-nine employees, and large firms, with 200 employees or more. From this data we learn that at a national level in the 1970s the small-to-medium firms almost always fared better than the large firms as regards indices of growth of value added, investment, and employment (diminishing in large firms). The share of annual gross profit on value added was constantly higher in the small-to-medium firms. Absenteeism was much lower in the smaller firms, while the income per employee was higher. It is to be noted that while the figures on absenteeism could be used to stress the importance of conditions promoting the decentralization of production, the figures concerning labour income per employee do not confirm such conditions.

The data of the Mediocredito come from a survey on a sample of firms with more than ten employees (we shall here consider only the surveys of 1973, 1977–8, and 1981). Our processing of the data for the national aggregate confirms the higher profitability of the small firms (between eleven and fifty employees) compared with medium-sized firms (between fifty-one and 500 employees), and of the latter compared to large firms (over 500 employees); profitability is indicated here by considering the difference between gross product and labour costs in relation to the value of invested capital. This is true both for 1973 and for 1977–8, for the manufacturing industries as a whole and for class aggregates partly comparable to those we have considered in the previous pages – that is, textiles, clothing, footwear, leather and leather goods, timber and wooden furniture, metal goods and engineering (the only exception is the timber and wooden furniture sector in which we find the highest index of profitability in the large firms, followed by the small firms, and the lowest index in the medium-sized firms).

Two other interesting points emerge from the same analysis of the data. The first concerns the capital intensity of the firms and in particular the average investment per employee in machinery and other equipment. This ratio predictably increases with the employment size of the manufacturing firms. However, it is to be noted that between 1973 and 1977–8 there is a reduction in the proportion of the increase. Moreover, with reference to the class aggregates already discussed, we observe that the differentials are very much reduced, or indeed reversed in the case of the traditional industries, and are below the manufacturing average in 1977–8 in metal goods and engineering.

The second point concerns exports. As is predictable, the ratio between the number of exporting firms and the total number of firms generally increases with the employment size of the firms. The same is true for the relationship between the value of exports and the total sales value. However, in the second type of relationship the increase is generally less marked and, in certain class aggregates, nullified (textiles in 1977–8, clothing, footwear and leather in both 1973 and 1977–8), or inverted (textiles in 1973). This indicates that within the set of small firms as a whole, there are subsets, especially in the traditional sectors, which present a very high profile as regards exporting capability, and therefore a high level of international competitiveness.

The 1980s

Before concluding, we must ask what has happened in the first half of the 1980s and what is happening today. According to the ISTAT survey on gross product there has continued to be, until 1984 at least, a decrease in the workforce in large firms, and an increase in small-to-medium firms. It is probable, although we have no relevant data with regard to this matter, that large firms are continuing to show a tendency towards multi-plant diversification; it may therefore be concluded that the shift towards the smaller sizes of plants is continuing. The increase in the total number of employees in the manufacturing industries observable in the 1970s has probably ceased.

Another very important change since the 1970s has already been noted in the ISTAT survey, in the observations of the Bank of Italy, and in the 1984 Mediocredito survey. Large firms, whether private or state-owned, are achieving considerable progress in productivity and economic and financial strength. Financial reorganization, in particular, has played a very incisive role, coinciding with a new take-off of the Italian stock market and rapid internationalization. All this has brought back into the public imagination the image of important private entrepreneurs and public managers. In other words, the large firm in Italy has come out of its corner. The end of this decade, therefore, will probably see a rekindling of the debates on the marginal status of small firms, which, however, at least until 1984, do not show overall signs of a weakening of that economic buoyancy which characterized them in the 1970s.

Bibliography

Arcangeli, F., Borzaga, C., and Goglio, S. (1980) 'Patterns of peripheral development in Italian regions, 1964–1977', *Papers and Proceedings of the Regional Science Association* 44.

Banca d'Italia (1987) *Relazione annuále agli azionisti. Esercizio 1985*, Rome.

Becattini, G. (1987) 'Il distretto industriale marshalliano: cronaca di un ritrovamento', in G. Becattini (ed.) *Mercato e forze locali: il distretto industriale*, Bologna: Il Mulino.

Becattini, G. and Bianchi, G. (1982) 'Sulla multiregionalità dello sviluppo economico italiano', *Note Economiche* 5–6.

Bruni, L. (1986) 'Dinamica strutturale dell'industria italiana nel trentennio 1951–1981', *L'Industria* 2.

Brusco, S. (1986) 'Small firms and industrial districts: the experience of Italy', in D. Keeble and E. Wever (eds) *New Firms and Regional Developments*, London: Croom Helm.

Fuà, G. and Zacchia, C. (eds) (1983) *Industrializzazione senza fratture*, Bologna: Il Mulino.

Goglio, S. (ed.) (1982) *Italia: centri e periferie*, Milan: F. Angeli editore.

Isotta, F. and Rispoli, M. (1979) 'La dimensione d'impresa e di stabilimento nell'evoluzione dell'industria manifatturiera italiana', in G. Franco (ed.) *Sviluppo e crisi dell'economia italiana*, Milan: Etas libri.

ISTAT (1961) *IV Cens. Gen. dell'industria e del commercio*, Rome.

—— (1971) *V Cens. Gen. dell'industria e del commercio*, Rome.

—— (1981) *VI Cens. Gen. dell'industria e del commercio, dei servizi e dell'artigianato*, Rome.

—— (1985) *Popolazione residente e presente dei comuni. Censimenti dal 1861 al 1981*, Rome.

Mediocredito Centrale (1977) *Indagine sulle imprese manifatturiere, 1973*, Rome.

—— (1981) *Indagine sulle imprese manifatturiere, 1977*, Rome.

—— (1986) *Indagine sulle imprese manifatturiere, 1984*, Rome.

Piore, M. and Sabel, C. (1984) *The Second Industrial Divide*, New York: Basic Books.

Varaldo, R. (ed.) (1979) *Ristrutturazioni industriali e rapporti fra imprese*, Milan: F. Angeli editore.

Appendix 1

The purpose of this appendix is to make three observations regarding the statistical significance of the data used.

1. L. Bruni (1986), taking as his starting-point the observation that the Italian census of 1981 differs from its predecessors by virtue of its being more accurate and extensive, has attempted to appraise the order of magnitude of the improvement of the last census in terms of the number of employees in industry (manufacturing or otherwise), and therefore of the relative underestimation of the pre-1981 censuses.

To this end Bruni hypothesized a distinction between real increases in employment and statistical increases:

> we consider it improbable that between 1971 and 1981 there was an increase in the number of employees in plants of less than 10 employees in activities of employment [four-digit industries] in which the average workforce per plant was already very low in 1971, and in which total employment increased considerably between 1971 and 1981.

This hypothesis is justified by the fact that the improvement in census coverage concerned those plants which are more difficult to observe in a survey, in general very small production units. An additional hypothesis is that there are in fact no differences in the extent of coverage of the three censuses previous to that of 1981. The results of applying these hypotheses are shown in Table A1.1.

Bruni also gives estimates of the extent to which the pre-1981 censuses, when compared with the 1981 census itself, underestimated employment figures as regards the first twelve activities. These figures demonstrate that over half the underestimation may be attributed to non-manufacturing activities. This clearly reduces considerably the importance of the aggregate distortion in the manufacturing industries, given that the latter have a very important

Table A1.1 Assumed evaluation errors of pre-1981 censuses in Italian industry

	1951	1961	1971	1981
Workforce in 000s				
Data obtained	4,112	5,584	6,469	7,415
Corrected data	4,485	5,957	6,842	7,415
Presumable error	−373	−373	−373	−
% variation	51/61	61/71	71/81	51/81
Data obtained	+36	+16	+14	+80
Corrected data	+33	+15	+8	+65

Source: L. Bruni, 'Dinamica strutturale dell'industria italiana nel trentennio 1951–1981',
Industria 2 (1986): 316.

position in Italian industry as regards employment (more than 80 per cent in 1981). About 20 per cent of the increase in the number of manufacturing employees recorded between 1971 and 1981 would be attributable to statistical effect. Among the manufacturing activities which show considerable underestimation, there are some activities in the clothing and footwear class (Appendix 2), that is tailored outerwear, millinery, and so on, and footwear, which, with an underestimation (or, re-estimation) of 55,000 employees, would account for almost all the increase observed in that aggregate sector between 1971 and 1981. Also important, in relative terms, is the underestimation calculated for leather goods, 10,000 employees, which would account for a third of the increase in employment in the leather and leather goods class between 1971 and 1981.

Although we have to recognize the probability of a higher incidence of statistical affect within the traditional sectors (Appendix 2), characterized by a myriad of very small plants, at the same time it should not be forgotten that the above-presented results are based on a hypothesis whose validity is not indisputable, involving, (a) the exclusion of phenomena of underestimation in sectors which, although of not very low average size of plant, include quite a large number of very small plants, and (b) the exclusion of the possibility of real employment growth in sectors where the plants are of very small average size. This second possibility is not so outlandish when we consider the well-known phenomenon of the increase in new handicraft initiatives during the 1970s.

Moreover, more specific doubts exist regarding the figures for tailored outerwear and millinery, and so on, and footwear. In the first case there is a considerable decrease between 1971 and 1981 in the number of employees in very small plants, and in the second case the increase in employees in very small plants could also be explained by hypothesizing real growth in the specialist production of parts and accessories for footwear. In our discussion we have deliberately avoided giving any fundamental importance to employment trends observed in very small plants, especially to the two above-mentioned classes. It should also be noted in this regard that the figures given for the footwear and clothing class are also affected by the absence in 1981 of the repairing of footwear activity (Appendix 2), almost entirely composed of the very small firms of cobblers. The latter comprised 28,000 employees in 1971 and around 17,000 in 1981. In 1981 this sector appears in the metal goods and engineering aggregate, where, however, given the size of the aggregate, they have a minimal distorting effect.

2. The size classifications in the 1971 and 1981 censuses allow us to make the aggregate size groups which we have referred to during our discussion, that is 1–9 employees, 10–49, 50–499, above 499 employees. The size classification of the 1961 census does not conform completely to such grouping. Here the size groups are 1–10, 11–50, 51–500, and over 500. We have supposed that the consequent incomparability would not have any considerable effect, although we recognize that this factor adds a statistical effect, although minimal, to the decrease in importance of the very small plants and to the increase in importance of the large plants, as generally observed between 1961 and 1971.

3. The concentration in medium-sized and large plants of the phenomenon of multi-plant firms is illustrated in detail in Isotta and Rispoli (1979). The ratio between single plant firms and the total number of plants is in general very high, as is shown in Table A1.2.

Table A1.2 The ratio of mono-plant firms to the total number of plants and the average size of workforce per plant in Italian manufacturing industry; regional aggregates, 1961, 1971, 1981

	1961		1971		1981	
	Mono-plants %	Average size	Mono-plants %	Average size	Mono-plants %	Average size
TRI	93	12.4	90	12.9	90	10.4
NEC	94	6.7	93	8.3	91	7.5
SCI	94	3.7	94	4.5	93	5.6
Italy	94	7.4	93	8.4	91	7.9

Source: Elaboration of ISTAT data, *Cens. Gen. dell'industria e del commercio*, Rome, 1961, 1971, 1981.
Note: For explanation of aggregates see Appendix 2.

Appendix 2

Table A2.1 Resident population in Italian regions, 1961, 1971, 1981

	1961 %	1971 %	1981 %	Increase/decrease 1961–71 %	1971–81 %
Piedmont	7.73	8.19	7.92	13.23	1.06
Valle d'Aosta	0.20	0.20	0.20	7.92	2.75
Lombardy	14.63	15.78	15.72	15.34	4.09
Liguria	3.43	3.42	3.20	6.86	−2.48
TRI	25.99	27.59	27.04	13.54	2.36
Trentino-Alto Adige	1.55	1.56	1.54	7.12	3.68
Friuli-Venezia-Giulia	2.38	2.24	2.18	0.83	1.65
Veneto	7.60	7.62	7.68	7.17	5.38
Emilia-Romagna	7.24	7.11	7.00	4.91	2.89
Tuscany	6.49	6.42	6.33	5.69	3.11
Umbria	1.57	1.43	1.43	−2.39	4.12
Marche	2.66	2.51	2.50	0.97	3.82
NEC	29.50	28.88	28.66	4.71	3.68
Latium	7.82	8.66	8.84	18.44	6.68
Abruzzi	2.38	2.16	2.15	−3.23	4.37
Molise	0.71	0.59	0.58	−10.61	2.50
Campania	9.41	9.34	9.66	6.24	7.99
Apulia	6.76	6.62	6.85	4.74	8.07
Basilicata	1.27	1.11	1.08	−6.37	1.16
Calabria	4.04	3.67	3.64	−2.79	3.67
Sicily	9.33	8.65	8.68	−0.85	4.83
Sardinia	2.80	2.72	2.82	3.88	8.14
SCI	44.51	43.53	44.30	4.57	6.33
Italy	100.00	100.00	100.00	6.94	4.47
Italy (000s)	50,624	54,137	56,557		

Source: Elaboration from ISTAT, 1983. *Popolazione residente e presente dei Comuni. Censimenti del 1861 al 1981. Roma, 1983.*
Note: The Italian regions are here arranged in three groups:
  TRI – The industrial triangle of the north-west, based on Milan, Turin and Genoa.
  NEC – The north-central and north-east, which forms the *Terza Italia.*
  SCI – Latium, the south and the islands.

Appendix 3

Table A3.1 Number of employees by size of plant in selected manufacturing sectors in Italian regions, 1961, 1971, 1981

(a) Manufacturing

Pl.size	1961					1971					1981				
	1–10	11–50	51–500	>500	Total	1–9	10–49	50–499	>499	Total	1–9	10–49	50–499	>499	Total
Piedmont	115,429	104,217	224,114	251,707	695,467	108,391	116,762	236,281	329,378	790,812	151,635	143,947	231,059	252,975	779,616
Val.Ao	2,092	549	1,039	7,150	10,830	1,833	1,074	816	6,810	10,533	2,502	1,044	1,709	5,692	11,147
Lombardy	256,452	288,997	561,743	338,007	1,445,199	252,264	340,042	628,444	376,209	1,596,959	349,630	434,133	574,393	229,960	1,648,116
Trent.AA	22,142	9,707	12,375	8,935	53,159	18,438	14,485	20,686	11,290	64,889	23,580	17,203	26,392	9,512	76,687
Veneto	98,371	78,475	127,508	73,600	377,954	105,745	126,173	184,054	81,852	497,824	159,489	200,151	210,881	70,950	641,471
Friu.VG	27,623	18,875	33,985	26,863	107,346	25,438	26,072	41,294	42,236	135,040	32,524	33,220	48,528	31,765	146,037
Liguria	36,945	22,910	42,563	58,636	161,054	35,576	23,628	44,253	50,139	153,596	37,463	25,095	33,594	51,661	147,813
Emil.Rom	122,222	78,900	118,391	35,705	355,218	127,566	115,449	167,486	51,491	461,992	170,139	161,854	190,935	60,556	583,484
Tuscany	115,828	89,043	94,351	57,055	356,277	129,671	126,425	112,520	63,614	432,230	169,410	167,662	108,559	65,266	510,897
Umbria	17,512	6,850	11,829	13,651	49,842	17,467	13,769	18,704	18,300	68,240	24,083	25,096	28,614	18,313	96,106
Marche	39,257	21,526	21,059	5,882	87,724	41,385	42,309	40,423	9,252	133,369	62,708	73,053	57,934	10,812	204,507
TRI	410,918	416,673	829,459	655,500	2,312,550	398,064	481,506	909,794	762,536	2,551,900	541,230	604,219	840,755	600,488	2,586,692
NEC	442,955	303,376	419,498	221,691	1,387,520	465,710	464,682	585,167	278,025	1,793,584	641,933	678,239	671,843	267,174	2,259,189
SCI	404,351	127,347	174,700	89,095	795,493	375,501	167,434	231,815	181,612	956,362	426,264	261,198	296,422	266,832	1,250,716
ITA	1,258,224	847,396	1,423,657	966,286	4,495,563	1,239,275	1,113,622	1,726,776	1,222,173	5,301,846	1,609,427	1,543,656	1,809,020	1,134,494	6,096,597

(b) Metallic engineering

Pl.size	1961					1971					1981				
	1-10	11-50	51-500	>500	Total	1-9	10-49	50-499	>499	Total	1-9	10-49	50-499	>499	Total
Piedmont	42,410	36,320	56,415	52,739	187,884	46,387	37,430	68,239	82,877	234,933	74,158	61,903	87,544	61,671	285,276
Val.Ao	600	73	0	0	673	721	301	308	0	1,330	1,079	402	192	0	1,673
Lombardy	87,797	97,028	170,710	92,503	448,038	102,186	121,936	208,666	132,249	565,037	163,730	178,130	216,604	114,308	672,772
Trent.AA	5,884	1,998	2,790	0	10,672	6,045	4,105	5,905	2,558	18,613	9,514	5,540	9,055	2,549	26,658
Veneto	28,083	18,933	28,055	13,326	88,397	37,188	30,208	43,354	21,852	132,602	64,123	56,907	66,628	18,250	205,908
Friu.VG	8,564	5,432	5,708	3,887	23,591	9,980	7,472	9,106	17,619	44,377	15,165	11,566	14,143	17,687	58,581
Liguria	11,697	7,233	12,588	15,985	47,503	14,242	8,801	12,513	13,729	49,285	17,876	11,160	11,518	23,360	63,914
Emil.Rom	40,198	23,931	31,223	11,012	106,364	51,758	38,755	47,621	20,054	158,188	78,841	66,060	68,914	27,259	241,074
Tuscany	26,934	13,202	13,113	8,172	61,421	32,664	18,222	15,598	12,177	78,661	44,700	28,703	21,458	10,820	105,681
Umbria	4,741	1,122	2,607	642	9,112	5,830	2,397	4,170	1,099	13,496	8,635	5,939	8,057	633	23,264
Marche	8,925	3,142	3,094	0	15,161	12,095	6,499	6,540	507	25,641	18,593	12,443	11,624	1,693	44,553
TRI	142,504	140,654	239,713	161,227	684,098	163,536	168,468	289,726	229,855	850,585	256,843	251,595	315,858	199,339	1,023,635
NEC	123,329	67,760	86,590	37,039	314,718	155,560	107,658	132,294	76,066	471,578	239,591	187,158	200,079	78,891	705,719
SCI	88,595	21,029	23,022	11,284	143,930	118,935	35,057	47,156	46,161	247,309	178,971	67,782	87,168	74,159	408,080
ITA	354,428	229,443	349,325	209,550	1,142,746	438,031	311,163	469,176	351,062	1,569,472	675,405	506,535	603,105	352,389	2,137,434

(c) Heavy industry

Pl.size	1961					1971					1981				
	1–10	11–50	51–500	>500	Total	1–9	10–49	50–499	>499	Total	1–9	10–49	50–499	>499	Total
Piedmont	19,089	28,541	69,353	140,488	257,471	23,207	38,301	82,135	213,825	357,468	35,728	38,743	74,866	178,343	327,680
Val.Ao	341	252	563	7,150	8,306	306	328	508	6,810	7,952	477	335	879	5,892	7,583
Lombardy	45,520	75,673	161,467	171,549	454,209	50,443	94,975	203,565	196,836	545,819	70,082	107,929	188,609	156,336	522,956
Trent.AA	3,311	2,822	5,305	8,337	19,775	3,531	4,284	7,754	8,722	24,291	4,059	4,293	11,147	6,963	26,462
Veneto	16,161	20,005	34,286	32,691	103,143	19,288	29,399	46,711	31,953	127,351	26,148	37,138	50,948	34,182	148,416
Friu.VG	4,699	4,850	11,947	16,621	38,117	4,429	6,031	11,873	16,690	39,023	5,065	6,673	12,998	10,874	35,610
Liguria	7,733	8,945	20,806	38,203	75,687	7,937	9,324	21,772	34,977	74,010	9,164	8,958	15,418	28,301	61,841
Emil.Rom	22,702	22,930	40,812	20,514	106,958	26,312	31,272	49,720	19,728	127,032	31,172	37,468	52,805	22,684	144,129
Tuscany	17,624	14,324	22,797	32,210	86,955	20,560	21,467	27,821	36,045	105,893	24,868	26,979	28,683	45,604	126,134
Umbria	3,412	1,851	3,998	11,120	20,381	3,243	3,454	5,373	15,242	27,312	4,474	5,158	7,237	15,754	32,623
Marche	7,133	4,637	7,139	5,882	24,791	7,836	7,207	10,723	5,532	31,298	10,556	10,256	13,135	7,210	41,157
TRI	72,683	113,411	252,189	357,390	795,673	81,893	142,928	307,960	452,448	965,249	115,451	155,965	279,772	368,872	920,060
NEC	75,042	71,419	126,284	127,375	400,120	85,199	103,114	159,975	133,912	482,200	106,342	127,965	176,953	143,271	554,531
SCI	94,660	49,605	86,343	64,582	295,190	84,964	56,038	100,454	110,048	351,504	96,431	74,342	123,581	171,838	466,192
ITA	242,385	234,435	464,816	549,347	1,490,983	252,056	302,080	568,409	696,408	1,818,953	318,224	358,272	580,306	683,981	1,940,783

Source: Elaboration on ISTAT, 1961, 1971, 1981 censuses.
Note: See Appendix 2 for the meaning of the aggregates.

Table A3.2 Number of employees by size of plant in selected manufacturing sectors in Italian regions, 1961, 1971, 1981

(a) Traditional

Pl.size	1961 1-10	11-50	51-500	>500	Total	1971 1-9	10-49	50-499	>499	Total	1981 1-9	10-49	50-499	>499	Total
Piedmont	53,930	39,356	98,346	58,480	250,112	38,797	41,031	85,907	32,676	198,411	41,749	43,301	68,649	12,961	166,660
Val.Ao	1,151	224	476	0	1,851	806	445	0	0	1,251	946	307	638	0	1,891
Lombardy	123,135	116,296	229,566	73,955	542,952	99,635	123,131	216,213	47,124	486,103	115,818	148,074	169,180	19,316	452,388
Trent.AA	12,947	4,887	4,280	598	22,712	8,862	6,096	7,027	0	21,985	10,007	7,370	6,190	0	23,567
Veneto	54,127	39,537	65,167	27,583	186,414	49,269	66,566	93,989	28,047	237,871	69,218	106,106	93,305	18,518	287,147
Friu.VG	14,360	8,593	16,330	6,355	45,638	11,029	12,569	20,315	7,727	51,640	12,274	14,981	21,387	3,204	51,846
Liguria	17,515	6,732	9,169	4,448	37,864	13,397	5,503	9,968	1,433	30,301	10,423	4,977	6,658	0	22,058
Emil.Rom	59,322	32,039	46,356	4,179	141,896	49,496	45,422	70,145	11,709	176,772	60,126	58,326	69,216	10,613	198,281
Tuscany	71,270	61,517	58,441	16,673	207,901	76,447	86,736	69,101	15,392	247,676	99,842	111,980	58,418	8,842	279,082
Umbria	9,359	3,877	5,224	1,889	20,349	8,394	7,918	9,161	1,959	27,432	10,974	13,999	13,320	1,926	40,219
Marche	23,199	13,747	10,826	0	47,772	21,454	28,603	23,160	3,213	76,430	33,559	50,354	32,975	1,909	118,797
TRI	195,731	162,608	337,557	136,883	832,779	152,635	170,110	312,088	81,233	716,066	168,936	196,659	245,125	32,277	642,997
NEC	244,584	164,197	206,624	57,277	672,682	224,951	253,910	292,898	68,047	839,806	296,000	363,116	294,811	45,012	998,939
SCI	221,096	56,713	65,335	13,229	356,373	171,602	76,339	84,205	25,403	357,549	150,862	119,074	85,673	20,835	376,444
ITA	661,411	383,518	609,516	207,389	1,861,834	549,188	500,359	689,191	174,683	1,913,421	615,798	678,849	625,609	98,124	2,018,380

(b) Non-metallic mineral products

Pl.size	1961					1971					1981				
	1-10	11-50	51-500	>500	Total	1-9	10-49	50-499	>499	Total	1-9	10-49	50-499	>499	Total
Piedmont	3,742	9,260	13,115	3,278	29,395	3,942	8,070	9,913	2,245	24,170	3,905	6,480	8,010	1,656	20,051
Val.Ao	113	61	0	0	174	79	110	0	0	189	118	149	0	0	267
Lombardy	7,908	17,353	27,497	4,313	57,071	8,447	14,505	23,188	4,741	50,881	8,655	14,404	17,701	5,033	45,793
Trent.AA	636	1,156	1,321	0	3,113	624	1,404	986	0	3,014	865	1,419	1,043	0	3,327
Veneto	4,973	11,840	19,159	1,547	37,519	6,563	16,336	13,342	804	37,045	8,341	16,684	12,567	1,717	39,309
Friu.VG	1,013	1,951	3,219	0	6,183	1,314	1,995	2,188	1,940	7,437	1,460	1,929	2,890	830	7,109
Liguria	1,655	2,067	5,420	1,092	10,234	1,435	1,634	4,188	1,433	8,690	1,479	1,573	4,072	0	7,124
Emil.Rom	3,907	8,229	18,770	2,619	33,525	4,442	11,486	31,249	6,664	53,841	4,759	12,541	36,339	8,664	62,303
Tuscany	8,312	13,268	20,581	3,943	46,104	9,030	13,691	15,762	3,054	41,537	8,367	14,163	12,790	2,542	37,862
Umbria	1,015	1,882	2,920	0	5,817	1,377	2,671	2,545	0	6,593	1,899	3,270	3,583	0	8,752
Marche	1,372	3,206	3,750	0	8,328	1,680	4,321	2,403	0	8,404	1,832	4,172	1,980	0	7,984
TRI	13,418	28,741	46,032	8,623	96,874	13,903	24,319	37,289	8,419	83,930	14,157	22,606	29,783	6,689	73,235
NEC	21,228	41,532	69,720	8,109	140,589	25,030	51,904	68,475	12,462	157,871	27,523	54,178	71,192	13,753	166,646
SCI	18,650	21,051	34,735	6,832	81,268	19,165	26,454	33,096	9,971	88,686	23,048	32,797	34,595	7,528	97,968
ITA	53,296	91,324	150,487	23,624	318,731	58,098	102,677	138,860	30,852	330,487	64,788	109,581	135,570	27,970	337,849

(c) Textiles

Pl.size	1961					1971					1981				
	1-10	11-50	51-500	>500	Total	1-9	10-49	50-499	>499	Total	1-9	10-49	50-499	>499	Total
Piedmont	7,183	13,829	63,212	47,593	131,817	6,968	16,950	46,623	21,871	94,412	9,927	17,881	38,148	6,642	72,598
Val.Ao	46	21	425	0	492	20	33	0	0	53	27	34	297	0	358
Lombardy	18,351	44,070	136,191	64,274	262,886	15,301	45,816	111,511	31,016	203,644	23,604	48,586	89,724	10,976	172,890
Trent.AA	452	410	1,100	598	2,560	276	504	2,736	0	3,516	264	533	2,136	0	2,933
Veneto	5,869	5,512	20,084	20,324	51,789	5,108	10,913	27,275	13,817	57,113	8,497	15,303	21,963	8,254	54,017
Friu.VG	1,246	889	5,429	5,456	13,020	667	945	6,102	4,742	12,456	606	926	4,518	929	6,979
Liguria	957	1,067	1,775	2,512	6,311	796	831	2,613	0	4,240	596	692	1,233	0	2,521
Emil.Rom	9,036	5,722	8,172	1,560	24,490	10,040	9,321	13,021	2,388	34,770	17,501	12,849	9,252	0	39,602
Tuscany	18,856	17,592	17,074	8,820	62,342	23,935	24,087	18,641	4,767	71,430	36,410	31,857	13,517	1,736	83,520
Umbria	1,029	409	1,335	1,889	4,662	1,581	1,370	2,513	1,322	6,786	2,712	2,806	2,327	1,062	8,907
Marche	2,193	1,194	978	0	4,365	2,431	2,228	1,916	0	6,575	2,937	3,218	1,753	0	7,908
TRI	26,537	58,987	201,603	114,379	401,506	23,085	63,630	162,747	52,987	302,349	34,154	67,193	129,402	17,618	248,367
NEC	38,681	31,728	54,172	38,647	163,228	44,038	49,368	72,204	27,036	192,646	68,927	67,492	55,466	11,981	203,866
SCI	13,316	5,485	9,975	5,055	33,831	15,311	8,006	15,667	7,051	46,035	10,736	10,202	13,904	6,395	41,237
ITA	78,534	96,200	265,750	158,081	598,565	82,434	121,004	250,618	86,974	541,030	113,817	144,887	198,772	35,994	493,470

Source: Elaboration on ISTAT, 1961, 1971, 1981.
Note: See Appendix 2 for the meaning of the aggregates.

Table A3.3 Number of employees by size of plant in selected manufacturing sectors in Italian regions, 1961, 1971, 1981

(a) Leather goods, etc.

Pl.size	1961 1-10	11-50	51-500	>500	Total	1971 1-9	10-49	50-499	>499	Total	1981 1-9	10-49	50-499	>499	Total
Piedmont	1,133	1,581	2,634	2,416	7,764	764	1,363	2,114	572	4,813	991	1,146	1,989	0	4,126
Val.Ao	1	19	0	0	20	0	0	0	0	0	13	0	0	0	13
Lombardy	4,212	5,414	5,508	0	15,134	4,002	4,568	5,698	0	14,268	5,392	5,741	4,436	0	15,569
Trent.AA	86	104	0	0	190	84	97	54	0	235	109	135	141	0	385
Veneto	994	2,540	2,873	0	6,407	1,169	4,321	4,440	0	9,930	3,377	6,362	5,544	0	15,283
Friu.VG	91	163	339	0	593	73	180	0	526	779	217	165	443	693	1,518
Liguria	243	166	53	844	1,306	201	113	557	0	871	330	150	252	0	732
Emil.Rom	1,139	1,252	882	0	3,273	1,309	1,568	887	0	3,764	2,511	2,964	924	0	6,399
Tuscany	3,204	3,793	1,597	0	8,594	5,328	5,757	1,537	0	12,622	9,285	10,480	2,136	0	21,901
Umbria	79	35	452	0	566	77	98	181	0	356	144	243	86	0	473
Marche	191	380	463	0	1,034	186	638	875	0	1,699	1,507	1,501	1,785	0	4,793
TRI	5,589	7,180	8,195	3,260	24,224	4,967	6,044	8,369	572	19,952	6,726	7,037	6,677	0	20,440
NEC	5,784	8,267	6,606	0	20,657	8,226	12,659	7,974	526	29,385	17,150	21,850	11,059	693	50,752
SCI	2,737	1,311	968	0	5,016	3,270	2,616	1,588	0	7,474	6,011	5,844	3,079	0	14,934
ITA	14,110	16,758	15,769	3,260	49,897	16,463	21,319	17,931	1,098	56,811	29,887	34,731	20,815	693	86,126

(b) Footwear and clothing

Pl.size	1961					1971					1981				
	1-10	11-50	51-500	>500	Total	1-9	10-49	50-499	>499	Total	1-9	10-49	50-499	>499	Total
Piedmont	23,068	7,084	12,667	5,193	48,012	13,090	8,390	18,308	7,988	47,776	10,483	10,501	16,479	4,663	42,126
Val.Ao	433	12	0	0	445	190	161	0	0	351	85	48	341	0	474
Lombardy	48,528	27,163	39,726	4,776	120,193	32,440	34,003	56,252	9,490	132,185	34,130	49,004	40,455	3,307	126,896
Trent.AA	4,821	230	208	0	5,259	2,430	839	2,280	0	5,549	1,224	809	1,655	0	3,688
Veneto	21,774	9,515	14,270	4,508	50,067	13,647	18,604	33,430	11,808	77,489	18,363	41,929	36,699	8,026	105,017
Friu.VG	6,439	1,398	2,074	899	10,810	3,623	2,249	2,239	0	8,111	2,189	1,826	1,664	0	5,679
Liguria	7,916	1,423	1,436	0	10,775	5,640	1,634	1,298	0	8,572	3,257	1,327	614	0	5,198
Emil.Rom	24,731	8,232	12,828	0	45,791	17,948	12,560	17,133	736	48,377	18,413	19,131	14,492	683	52,719
Tuscany	20,067	17,461	14,763	3,910	56,201	18,201	27,759	27,696	7,571	81,227	24,291	39,646	25,670	4,564	94,171
Umbria	4,130	527	330	0	4,987	2,590	1,942	2,925	637	8,094	2,968	5,292	6,204	864	15,328
Marche	12,495	4,925	3,951	0	21,371	10,475	12,911	13,368	3,213	39,967	18,474	28,934	21,152	1,909	70,519
TRI	79,945	35,682	53,829	9,969	179,425	51,360	44,188	75,558	17,478	188,884	47,955	60,880	57,889	7,970	174,694
NEC	94,457	42,288	48,424	9,317	194,486	68,914	76,864	99,071	23,965	268,814	85,922	137,617	107,536	16,046	347,121
SCI	113,657	13,260	11,220	1,342	139,479	76,398	21,300	24,722	8,381	130,801	48,488	45,207	25,977	6,912	126,584
ITA	288,059	91,230	113,473	20,628	513,390	196,672	142,352	199,651	49,824	588,499	122,365	243,704	191,402	30,928	648,399

(c) Furniture, etc.

Pl.size	1961					1971					1981				
	1-10	11-50	51-500	>500	Total	1-9	10-49	50-499	>499	Total	1-9	10-49	50-499	>499	Total
Piedmont	18,804	7,602	6,718	0	33,124	14,033	6,258	6,949	0	27,240	16,443	7,293	4,023	0	27,759
Val.Ao	558	111	51	0	720	517	141	0	0	658	703	76	0	0	779
Lombardy	44,136	22,296	20,644	592	87,668	39,445	24,239	19,564	1,877	85,125	44,037	30,339	16,864	0	91,240
Trent.AA	6,952	2,987	1,651	0	11,590	5,448	3,252	971	0	9,671	7,545	4,474	1,215	0	13,234
Veneto	20,517	10,130	8,781	1,204	40,632	22,782	16,392	15,502	1,618	56,294	30,640	25,828	16,532	521	73,521
Friu.VG	5,571	4,192	5,269	0	15,032	5,352	7,200	9,786	519	22,857	7,802	10,135	11,872	752	30,561
Liguria	6,744	2,009	485	0	9,238	5,325	1,291	1,312	0	7,928	4,761	1,235	487	0	6,483
Emil.Rom	20,509	8,604	5,704	0	34,817	15,757	10,487	7,855	1,921	36,020	16,942	10,841	8,209	1,266	37,258
Tuscany	20,831	9,403	4,426	0	34,660	19,953	15,442	5,465	0	40,860	21,489	15,834	4,305	0	41,628
Umbria	3,106	1,024	187	0	4,317	2,769	1,837	997	0	5,603	3,251	2,398	1,120	0	6,759
Marche	6,948	4,042	1,684	0	12,674	6,682	8,505	4,598	0	19,785	8,809	12,479	6,305	0	27,593
TRI	70,242	32,018	27,898	592	130,750	59,320	31,929	27,825	1,877	120,951	65,944	38,943	21,374	0	126,261
NEC	84,434	40,382	27,702	1,204	153,722	78,743	63,115	45,174	4,058	191,090	96,478	81,979	49,558	2,539	230,554
SCI	72,736	15,606	8,437	0	96,779	57,458	17,963	9,132	0	84,553	62,579	25,024	8,118	0	95,721
ITA	227,412	88,006	64,037	1,796	381,251	195,521	113,007	82,131	5,935	396,594	225,001	145,946	79,050	2,539	452,536

Source: Elaboration on ISTAT 1961, 1971, 1981.

Note: See Appendix 2 for the meaning of the aggregates.

Table A3.4 Ratios of the economic structure of Italian manufacturing firms in selected sectors by size of firm, 1973, 1977, 1984

	1973				1977				1984			
	11–50	51–500	>500	Total	11–50	51–500	>500	Total	11–50	51–500	>500	Total
(a) Total manufacturing												
Assets/employee	11.209	10.307	16.457	13.431	27.023	24.966	35.583	29.792	73.188	75.915	102.780	84.965
Equipm./employ.	3.178	3.544	8.893	6.088	7.999	8.885	15.713	11.604	20.764	25.847	42.959	30.803
Gross pr./employ.	4.765	5.069	5.914	5.434	11.873	12.714	14.891	13.484	30.692	36.270	38.177	35.612
Prod./gross pr.	2.900	2.779	2.558	2.678	3.168	3.072	3.006	3.056	3.604	3.295	3.595	3.475
Profits/assets	0.204	0.183	0.092	0.132	0.176	0.164	0.122	0.145	0.151	0.157	0.105	0.133
Exp. firms/firms	0.338	0.625	0.845	0.444	0.424	0.711	0.871	0.524	0.452	0.739	0.927	0.523
Export/sales	0.126	0.191	0.227	0.200	0.165	0.251	0.269	0.245	0.172	0.249	0.297	0.252
(b) Textiles												
Assets/employee	10.914	9.010	10.051	9.830	23.522	23.108	22.731	23.099	79.559	74.909	59.344	73.586
Equipm./employ.	3.032	3.334	4.908	3.845	7.598	8.666	8.892	8.505	25.083	25.474	23.779	25.079
Gross pr./employ.	4.848	4.214	4.470	4.407	11.864	11.379	10.153	11.177	33.317	33.856	32.640	33.534
Prod./gross pr.	2.328	2.446	2.177	2.328	2.584	2.697	2.605	2.652	3.551	3.228	2.474	3.193
Profits/assets	0.237	0.175	0.114	0.163	0.228	0.166	0.094	0.161	0.174	0.168	0.185	0.172
Exp. firms/firms	0.377	0.637	0.800	0.484	0.437	0.689	0.800	0.532	0.432	0.717	0.923	0.512
Export/sales	0.272	0.253	0.176	0.230	0.289	0.335	0.268	0.310	0.253	0.289	0.283	0.277

(c) Footwear, clothing, leather

	1973				1977				1984			
	11–50	51–500	>500	Total	11–50	51–500	>500	Total	11–50	51–500	>500	Total
Assets/employee	5.837	4.687	6.568	5.306	15.334	11.703	12.244	12.638	41.563	39.089	46.546	40.920
Equipm./employ.	1.110	1.001	1.501	1.120	2.837	2.382	2.777	2.558	6.827	7.171	9.940	7.373
Gross pr./employ.	3.116	3.118	3.692	3.226	8.701	8.487	8.961	8.622	23.320	26.102	30.875	25.622
Prod./gross pr.	2.662	2.577	2.544	2.589	3.010	2.758	2.518	2.771	3.510	3.146	3.036	3.255
Profits/assets	0.201	0.190	0.125	0.177	0.205	0.193	.155	0.190	0.197	0.200	0.200	0.199
Exp. firms/firms	0.493	0.661	0.833	0.557	0.585	0.775	1.000	0.659	0.537	0.734	0.892	0.588
Export/sales	0.308	0.352	0.178	0.305	0.371	0.422	0.307	0.389	0.318	0.368	0.393	0.353

(d) Furniture, timber

	1973				1977				1984			
	11–50	51–500	>500	Total	11–50	51–500	>500	Total	11–50	51–500	>500	Total
Assets/employee	9.873	9.359	8.711	9.538	25.834	25.364	21.727	25.319	73.063	72.699	61.753	72.611
Equipm./employ.	2.216	2.541	2.138	2.389	5.891	7.228	6.603	6.642	15.536	18.521	13.699	16.733
Gross pr./employ.	3.932	4.152	4.874	4.096	9.707	10.315	11.143	10.121	24.946	30.415	27.597	27.299
Prod./gross pr.	2.552	2.675	2.983	2.644	2.770	2.927	2.853	2.860	3.280	3.354	3.029	3.308
Profits/assets	0.171	0.154	0.179	0.162	0.130	0.099	0.099	0.112	0.099	0.116	0.094	0.106
Exp. firms/firms	0.199	0.483	1.000	0.275	0.375	0.698	0.889	0.456	0.382	0.753	1.000	0.499
Export sales	0.053	0.121	0.145	0.097	0.145	0.236	0.340	0.209	0.156	0.172	0.337	0.168

	1973				1977				1984			
	11–50	51–500	>500	Total	11–50	51–500	>500	Total	11–50	51–500	>500	Total
(e) Metallic general engineering												
Assets/employee	10.134	10.101	16.432	13.354	24.725	24.280	30.583	27.471	66.943	70.191	96.734	80.194
Equipm./employ.	2.920	3.178	8.728	5.992	7.511	8.274	12.193	10.108	18.536	22.269	36.781	27.323
Gross pr./employ.	4.960	5.318	5.884	5.561	12.407	13.419	14.042	13.581	31.608	36.615	37.233	35.803
Prod./gross pr.	2.448	2.597	2.317	2.428	2.695	2.835	2.591	2.691	2.966	2.908	3.187	3.055
Profits/assets	0.225	0.187	0.087	0.128	0.188	0.169	0.111	0.139	0.158	0.161	0.977	0.129
Exp. firms/firms	0.365	0.686	0.921	0.495	0.444	0.749	0.930	0.556	0.492	0.789	0.977	0.570
Export/sales	0.123	0.224	0.278	0.240	0.156	0.284	0.364	0.306	0.172	0.297	0.431	0.338

Source: Elaboration on Mediocredito Centrale, *Indagine sulle imprese manifatturiere*, Rome, 1977, 1981, and 1986.

Note: Assets/employees: fixed and real current assets (millions of lire) per employee.

Equipment/employee: machinery and equipment (millions of lire) per employee.

Gross product/employee: profits before salaries depreciation and tax (millions of lire) per employee.

Profits/assets: profits before depreciation and tax (millions of lire)/fixed and real current assets (millions of lire).

Exporting firms/firms: number of firms which export some of their production/total number of firms.

Export/sales: exports (millions of lire)/total sales, millions of lire).

Chapter 2

Small firms: profile and analysis, 1981–85

Guido Rey

(Translated by Stephen Coffey)

69 – 110

Italy
6110
6300

Introduction

Examination of the industrial census data of 1981 showed that there had been an increase in the importance of small and medium-sized firms within Italian manufacturing industry. This increase may be interpreted in different ways according to the theoretical standpoint from which one starts. According to the traditional models of oligopoly and dualism, the increase in importance of smaller firms is a transitory phenomenon linked to a particular phase of economic development (crisis of the larger-sized firms, ease of entry to markets, innovatory role of the small and medium-sized firms). Once this phase has been passed through, markets will expand and it will once more be possible to take advantage of economies of scale. Larger firms will then prevail once more, relegating the smaller firms to a merely dependent and supportive role. An alternative theory sees the progress made by the small and medium-sized firms as the result of radical changes in the production environment, and thus a more permanent feature in the larger industrial context.

The first studies on the decentralization of production appeared in Italy in the mid-1970s. These were based on the results of ad hoc surveys carried out in a limited number of geographical regions and economic sectors. In these surveys, a significant number of large firms stated that they 'decentralized' parts of their production process, sometimes entire phases, to smaller units. The studies which examined the decentralization of production interpreted this behaviour as a means of overcoming the obstacles created by too rigid a use of the workforce in large firms. In a situation such as this, the small firm which receives production orders from the larger firm might on the one hand find itself in a position of total dependence on the latter; it would be sure of retaining its position in the market thanks above all to the exploitation of a minimally skilled workforce with poor conditions of employment. There again,

69

the smaller firm might have a greater or lesser degree of autonomy with respect to the larger firm, and therefore have a very different role to play. This might range from participation in the planning phase to exclusive specialization in a particular stage of the production process, together with the possibility of eventually being released from its commitment to the larger firm and perhaps placing what had now become its own product on the intermediate goods market.

The idea that the smaller firms would employ a skilled workforce, take a central role in innovatory processes, and become more or less independent of the larger firms, has found a place within what is known as the 'model of flexible specialization'. This states that within a productive system characterized by the decentralization of various stages of the production process, the small and medium-sized firms will tend towards specialization in a limited number of phases of production but for many different types of goods. According to the model of flexible specialization, radical changes in the production environment are the cause of this new structure of the industrial system. Technological innovation is no longer to be found principally in large firms, and its effects are to be felt throughout the productive system. It helps to make machinery more efficient and more flexible, and allows the progressive substitution of machinery for human labour in more repetitive work areas. Above all, it enables firms to react more quickly and more efficiently to changes in product demand. The advantages which larger firms have derived from their being able to take advantage of economies of scale will progressively decrease, and indeed will be outweighed by the disadvantages inherent in the growing demands of the workforce in large firms. These demands relate above all to wages and the organization of labour, and are linked to the increase in job dissatisfaction caused in its turn by highly repetitive tasks of a very restricted nature.

In short, according to the model of flexible specialization, the growth of small and medium-sized firms is due above all to the progressive decrease in importance of economies of scale, and to the reduction in the minimum efficient size of firm. The latter phenomenon is caused by changes in the production process brought about in their turn by technological innovation.

It is important to point out, however, that within the categories of small and medium-sized firms a highly diversified situation is to be found, with innovative firms operating alongside technologically backward firms. It must also be said that in their process of reorganization, large firms may take advantage of new technology to reunite the various phases of the production process within medium and large plants. These two factors may place limitations on a productive system such as that hypothesized by the model of flexible specialization, and may signal the beginning of a new phase of domination by the large firm.

A recent series of studies in the field of industrial economics has taken as its starting-point the complex and highly diversified nature of the categories of small and medium-sized firms. These studies have attempted to go beyond the traditional opposition between 'small' and 'large', arguing that the concept of size is an inadequate tool for the analysis of the structure of the productive system, and that the central issue to be examined is that of the new forms of organization and behaviour to be found within firms, and the relation of these to the use of the new technologies which are now available to all.

The current debate on the role of small and medium-sized firms in the industrial system asks a number of questions, which may be summarized as follows:

(1) The modifications to the size structure of industry in favour of smaller firms have been accompanied by a more general, deeper process of restructuring. Has this process of restructuring been towards the greater efficiency, profitability, and competitiveness of the individual economic sector?

(2) Has there been a progressive widening of the gaps between different sectors, or on the contrary, has industry become more homogeneous?

(3) Is the size of firm still enough to explain the differences in variables observable within each sector of economic activity?

In order to present an overall picture of the structural development of industry which will allow us to give an initial, though necessarily partial, answer to these questions, we have availed ourselves of the following sources of information: the industrial censuses of 1971 and 1981; the annual survey on gross product in firms of twenty employees or more, and the survey on a sample of small firms (ten to nineteen employees) carried out by ISTAT in 1983 and 1985 (the figures for 1985 are to be treated as provisional); the ISTAT survey on technological innovation; and the survey of the *Mediocredito Centrale* into the characteristics of the accumulation process and the financial state of firms.

With regard to the definition of small and medium-sized firms, in this study we have used the size of the workforce as the defining criterion, and 100 employees as the cut-off point. We are well aware that there is no single definition of small and medium-sized firms, whether from an economic or a legal point of view, and, above all, that it is not totally satisfactory to have the size of the workforce as the sole defining parameter. Moreover, we are not interested in merely comparing the performance of one group of firms designated as 'small' or 'small-to-medium' with another designated as 'large' (though we shall at times also do this); rather, we are interested in examining the differences which exist within these size categories.

Our analysis takes the following form. First, we give a brief description of the main structural changes which have occurred within the manufacturing industries in recent years (sections 1 and 2). We then identify those variables which may be considered as being indicators of the state of economic viability of firms, and the dynamics of these variables has then been analysed in relation both to the size of firm and to other variables. The first two variables we have considered concern the innovative capacity of firms, the one regarding production techniques and the other the firm's internal information system (sections 3 and 4). We then examine the dynamics of gross profits, considered here as an index of profitability and, at the same time, the dynamics of labour productivity, seen as an indicator of how efficiently the most important factor of production is used (section 5). In order to interpret the dynamics of the latter two variables, it has been necessary to carry out a detailed analysis of wages, of employment structure, and of hours worked. In section 6 we examine the degree of interdependence between firms within the productive system and the modifications this has undergone in recent years, in order to see whether this variable has also had a role to play in determining the degree of profitability and efficiency of firms. Finally, we have considered the degree of penetration into international markets, as measured by the ratio value of exports to total turnover (section 7).

1. Comparison of census data

Between the years 1971 and 1981 there was a substantial increase in the number of firms in manufacturing industry (+20.8 per cent) and a more moderate increase in the number of employees (+12.3 per cent). The most dynamic branch of industry was metal goods, engineering, and vehicles, in which the increase both in the number of firms (+43.3 per cent) and in the number of employees (+23.8 per cent) was higher than the average for the manufacturing industries. Its proportional importance in terms of the workforce rose from 34.8 per cent in 1971 to 38.4 per cent in 1981. This is one of the key points to emerge from ISTAT's recent reappraisal of national accounting estimates for investment in machinery and tools. Within metal goods, engineering, and vehicles there were varying trends in the different economic sectors. The sectors which showed the highest employment growth were the manufacture of miscellaneous metal goods (not elsewhere specified in the classification), mechanical engineering, the manufacture of other transport equipment, and instrument engineering. There was negative employment growth rate, on the other hand, in the manufacture of office machinery and data-processing equipment, in which there was also a decrease in the number of firms, and in the manufacture of motor vehicles and parts, which, however, experienced a considerable increase in the number of firms.

In the other main branch of industry we are concerned with in this study, the manufacture of metals and extraction of minerals, there was a slight increase in the number of firms, but employment remained more or less stable, and thus there was a decrease in the proportional importance of the workforce over the ten-year period (from 17.3 to 15.4 per cent). There were slight increases in employment in the manufacture of non-metallic mineral products and in the chemical industry, but these were outweighed by the negative employment growth rates in the extraction and preparation of metalliferous ores, the extraction of minerals not elsewhere specified, and the production of man-made fibres.

In the 'traditional' industries (food and drink; textiles; leather and leather goods; footwear and clothing; timber and wooden furniture; paper, printing and publishing; rubber and plastics), in which are to be found the highest number of both firms and employees, there was an increase in both the number of firms (+13.8 per cent) and of employees (+8.3 per cent). These increases, however, were below the average for the manufacturing industries and thus there was a slight drop in the proportional importance of this sectoral aggregate (in terms of employment, from 47.9 per cent in 1971 to 46.2 per cent in 1981). It must be pointed out, however, that this relative decrease in employment is due exclusively to the negative employment growth rate experienced in the food and drink industries taken as a whole and in textiles, all other economic sectors recording a considerable increase in employment.

These modifications to the sectoral composition of Italian industry are relatively slight. By way of contrast, the size structure underwent a more significant change in the decade we are considering. The number of small and medium-sized firms (firms with a maximum of ninety-nine employees) increased by 21 per cent, and the corresponding employment figures rose by even more (+28.5 per cent). Increases were recorded in all branches and almost all sectors of economic activity, the only exception of note being footwear and clothing, in which there was a decrease of 5.8 per cent. Growth rates were particularly high in the various sectors of metal goods, engineering, and vehicles, and in paper, printing and publishing, rubber and plastics, and other manufacturing industries, the latter sectors recording growth rates of around 60 per cent.

There was only a slight increase in the number of firms with 100 employees or more (+5.8 per cent), and thus their proportional importance was further reduced. An analogous situation is to be found in all individual sectors and most notably so in those industries connected with the construction of transport and in the manufacture of office machinery and data-processing equipment.

The data we have presented here confirms, therefore, the considerable increase in importance of small-to-medium size firms from an overall demographic point of view, but clearly gives no indication of the relative importance of size of firm within individual classes of economic activity nor of the characteristic size of production units.

There was a decrease in the average size of firm in all industrial sectors between 1971 and 1981, though the situation in small-to-medium-sized firms (up to ninety-nine employees) was relatively stable in comparison with the firms of 100 employees or more. The average size of the former decreased from 5.53 employees in 1971 to 5.2 in 1981, while the latter decreased from 438 to 402. The overall average size of firms dropped from 10.6 employees to 9.85. The slight change in the average size of small-to-medium firm is also to be found in the individual industrial sectors. There are much more significant size changes in the large firms, most notably so in the production of man-made fibres and in the manufacture of vehicles.

There was therefore a general increase in the proportional importance of small-to-medium firms, slight in terms of the number of firms but more significant in terms of employment figures, the latter having risen from 48.5 per cent of the total workforce in 1971 to 55.5 per cent in 1981. This increase in employment in smaller firms is to be found above all in the traditional industries (almost 10 per cent), but is also noteworthy in metal goods, engineering and vehicles taken as a whole, and in instrument engineering in particular, the latter recording an increase of 12 per cent.

If we now subdivide the small and medium firms into smaller categories, we find that the highest growth rate in terms of both the size of the workforce and the number of firms is to be found in firms of between ten and nineteen employees. Within this subgroup, the most dynamic branch of industry was metal goods, engineering, and vehicles. Firms of between twenty and ninety-nine employees recorded a more modest growth rate, greater, however, than that recorded by the larger firms. Despite the high growth rate in firms of between ten and nineteen employees, it was the very smallest size category (up to nine employees) which in both 1971 and 1981 claimed the highest number of firms, though the proportional importance of this size category did decrease during this period.

We shall now look at the characteristic size of firm for particular industrial sectors in order to see where small and medium-sized firms were typically to be found and where they proved to be more dynamic. Within metal goods, engineering, and vehicles there was a typical size of firm of around thirty employees in the manufacture of metal goods not elsewhere specified and in instrument engineering, while for the other sectors of this branch of industry the characteristic size was well over 100 employees. Small and medium-sized firms were more typically found among the traditional industries, the only exception being sugar, drinks, and other foodstuffs. Lowest average sizes were found in timber and wooden furniture (10.8) and in leather and leather goods (18.1). The characteristic size of all economic sectors decreased between 1971 and 1981, though especially so in the production of man-made fibres, the manufacture of motor vehicles and parts, textiles, and rubber and plastics.

We may sum up by saying that small and medium-sized firms are still to be found above all in the traditional industries, and that there is a tendency for large firms, especially firms of 500 employees or more, to decrease in size. This is particularly true of the traditional industries but also applies to other branches of industry. In metal goods, engineering, and vehicles there is employment growth in both small-to-medium firms (between twenty and ninety-nine employees) and medium-to-large firms (between 100 and 499 employees), and thus there seems to be no clear evidence that technology determines an optimum size of firm.

2. The role of small and medium firms in the sectoral structure of Italian industry, 1983–85

Information obtained through the survey on gross product in firms of twenty employees or more allows us to judge whether in more recent years there has been a further change to the sectoral and size structures of Italian manufacturing industry. Firms with fewer than twenty employees cannot be taken into consideration since the results of the sample survey carried out on firms of ten to nineteen employees in the same period cannot be used for most comparative purposes.

The sectoral composition of the manufacturing industries did not undergo particularly noteworthy changes in the period we are considering. In 1983, 18.6 per cent of the workforce was employed in the manufacture of metals and extraction of minerals, 44.1 per cent in metal goods, engineering and vehicles, and 37.3 per cent in the traditional industries. The negative employment growth rate experienced in the various sectors of industry in the following two years led to a situation where the proportional importance of metal goods, engineering and vehicles dropped by 1 per cent and that of the traditional industries increased by a similar amount. This change may be attributed to the decreases in employment, albeit slight, in large firms, especially in the manufacture of miscellaneous metal goods (not elsewhere specified in the classification) and electrical and electronic engineering, and to the increase in importance of medium-to-large firms in the traditional industries.

In the period 1983–5 the number of small-to-medium firms (between twenty and ninety-nine employees) decreased by 2.3 per cent, a slightly smaller decrease than the average for the manufacturing industries (−2.5 per cent). The corresponding number of employees decreased by 2.4 per cent, a decrease which was also found in almost all individual sectors of economic activity. The fall in employment experienced by the manufacturing industries as a whole, however, was considerably higher (−7.1 per cent). The proportional importance of small-to-medium firms increased, therefore, in terms of both the number of firms and the size of the workforce. In the latter case the increase was of 1.6 per cent, with higher than average increases recorded in the manufacture of metal goods not elsewhere specified, mechanical engineering, and instrument engineering. In the traditional industries there was a further shift towards small-to-medium-sized firms in those sectors connected with the fashion industry.

In short, the data provided by the surveys on gross product in 1983 and 1985 tend to confirm the overall dynamics of small and medium-sized firms observed during the period 1971–81. Their importance increased in almost all the industrial sectors analysed, though there were also slight modifications in the sectoral structure, together with some interesting changes at the level of the individual employment sector.

If we now consider Italian manufacturing industry from the point of view of turnover, we find that a quarter of the turnover came from the manufacture of metals and extraction of minerals, more than a third from metal goods, engineering, and vehicles, and 40 per cent from the traditional industries. These percentages remain unaltered for the two years we are considering. If we now also take the size of firm into consideration, we find that in 1985 over half the turnover from small-to-medium firms came from the traditional industries, with over 10 per cent coming from both food processing and textiles. More than 10 per cent also came from both mechanical engineering and the manufacture of metal goods not elsewhere specified, which together accounted for almost all the turnover of this size of firm in metal goods, engineering, and vehicles. The economic sectors we have mentioned here are also those in which the small-to-medium firms have the strongest presence, together with leather and leather goods, timber and wooden furniture, and other manufacturing industries, in which sectors small-to-medium firms account for 60 per cent or more of the turnover.

Finally, the percentage of turnover accounted for by small-to-medium firms increased by more than 1 per cent between 1983 and 1985. This increase occurred in almost all the sectors of industry considered and was considerably higher than average in metal goods, engineering and vehicles. Decreases occurred in food processing, leather and leather goods, timber and wooden furniture, and, most noticeably, in other manufacturing industries, where the decrease was of more than 4 per cent.

3. Technological innovation and the size of firm

It is often held that the traditional industries have relatively small need of technological innovation, at least when compared with other factors such as taste and design. The strong presence of small and medium-sized firms in these industries does not necessarily mean, however, that such firms can automatically be classed as technologically backward. The ability and willingness to innovate must be verified directly at the firm itself.

The ISTAT-CNR (National Research Council) survey on technological innovation has enabled us to estimate the degree to which firms have reaped the benefits of technological progress and to relate these findings to the size of firm. The survey was carried out on a sample of firms of twenty employees or more. Out of the 34,042 firms which were contacted, 24,104 (70.8 per cent) replied, though in the case of firms of 500 employees or more the proportion which replied was as high as 86 per cent. Firms were asked whether they had introduced innovation in any or all of the following three areas: (a) products manufactured, (b) the production process, and (c) organization. They were also asked how innovation had made its entry into the firm and, most important of all, what factors tended to stand in the way of technological innovation. The results of the survey are to be treated with a certain amount of caution in that the survey took the form of a postal questionnaire sent out to the individual firm, and no form of objective checking has been carried out. ISTAT has very recently begun a survey based on interviews which will allow a more thorough investigation of the topic.

Of the 24,104 firms who replied to the questionnaire, 69.3 per cent stated that they had introduced technological innovation. These firms accounted for 85.2 per cent of employees and 86.7 per cent of the turnover. If we first consider the results of the survey from the point of view of the size of the firm, we find that technological innovation had taken place in 88.9 per cent of firms with 500 employees or more. These firms account for only 2.9 per cent of the total number of firms which took part, but for 46.1 per cent of the employees and 54.4 per cent of the turnover. Of firms with between twenty and forty-nine employees, 63.3 per cent stated that they had introduced new technology. These accounted for 61.8 per cent of firms participating in the survey.

If we take turnover as our defining parameter instead of the size of the workforce, we find that innovation has occurred in 93 per cent of firms with a turnover of at least 500 billion lire. These firms, however, represent only 0.2 per cent of the total. Of firms with a turnover of less than 500 million lire, only 37.5 per cent had introduced new technology. In this case, however, the figures should be treated with a certain amount of caution on account of the low value of the turnover. The category where the highest number of firms are to be found, that is firms with a turnover of between 1 billion and 5 billion lire, recorded innovation in 68.9 per cent of cases. These account for 51.9 per cent of firms involved in the survey.

The survey also allows us to examine the spread of technology from a geographical point of view. In this case we find that there is a substantial difference between the industrialized areas of the north and the less industrialized south. Some 71.6 per cent of firms in north-west Italy stated that technological innovation had taken place, while the same is true for only 59.7 per cent of firms in the islands. An analogous situation is found within individual size categories. With regard to firms of 500 employees or more, 90.7 per cent of firms in the north-west had introduced new technology, while in the islands the figure was 71.4 per cent. The figures for the size category twenty to forty-nine employees were 65.6 and 58.5 per cent respectively. It should be noted that 46.3 per cent of firms which had been involved with techological innovation are located in the north-west, while only 6.7 per cent are located in the south and 1.7 per cent in the islands.

If we now analyse the data from the point of view of sector of economic activity, we find that the highest percentage of innovative firms are to be found in the manufacture of office machinery and data-processing equipment (95.2 per cent), followed by the production of man-made fibres (94.1 per cent) and mechanical engineering (82.5 per cent). A high degree of innovation is also to be found in the chemical industries (80.7 per cent), within which there is a notable 89.8 per cent in pharmaceuticals. The lowest values are recorded in footwear and clothing (19.7 per cent), which accounts for 11.7 per cent of firms taking part in the survey.

Let us now turn our attention to the type of innovation which has been introduced. First, it should be pointed out that although it is possible to place different interpretations on the three types of innovation mentioned (innovation as regards products manufactured, production process, and organization), it is clear, nevertheless, that wherever a firm has introduced innovation into two, or indeed all three of these areas, then that firm has chosen to involve key aspects of its operations in the process of innovation. The results of the survey are as follows: 14.6 per cent of firms stated that they had been involved in all three types of innovation, while 22.4 per cent had introduced innovation as regards the products manufactured and the production process. Some 9.6 per cent of firms had introduced innovation only as regards the products manufactured and 15.7 per cent in the production process, though in the latter two cases more precise details are needed from the firms in question. The above figures undergo only slight changes when the data is considered from a geographical point of view. Another interesting fact to emerge is that 16.2 per cent of innovative firms stated that they were involved in research and development. Finally, it is important to mention that the most common channel through which technological innovation makes its way into firms is through relations with other firms at an earlier or later stage in the production process. Some 69.2 per cent of innovative firms stated that innovation took the form of the acquisition of tools and equipment or the purchasing of raw materials from other firms.

4. Information systems and the size of firm

Economic theory has often held that the use of information is in its own right a factor capable of increasing the efficiency, and therefore the profitability, of a firm, especially when the elements of uncertainty within the firm, and therefore of risk, are taken into account. It has been demonstrated that the value of information increases with the increase in size of the firm, and that large firms not only have more information at their disposal but also manage to grow larger by virtue of this extra information. Intelligent use of the information sources at one's disposal allows one to have knowledge of markets, products and technologies, and above all, to discover new markets, products, and technologies.

Making the best use of information, however, also involves carrying out in-depth cost–benefit analyses; the acquiring and processing of information costs money. It is essential to be able to place the acquired information into a decision-making process which none the less remains accessible to the entrepreneur or manager. Firms must be of a certain minimum size in order to have access to information which might be of use to the decision-making process. Important economies of scale exist, despite the fact that technological progress, and the higher standards of managerial training have reduced the minimum scale and reduced the cost of the information and increased the speed with which it becomes available. It seems likely that the acquisition of information is becoming more and more important as a guiding force in the decision-making process and as a factor in the growth and efficiency of firms.

Following on from the 1983 survey on gross product, ISTAT carried out an *ad hoc* survey into the organization of information within firms. This latter survey allows comparisons to be made between the size of firms and the type of information considered to be important by that firm. Firms were asked whether they drew up one or more of the following planning documents: budget, financial plan, demand forecast, production programme, supplies programme. They were also asked whether, in the preparation of these plans, they made use of quantitative models, outside consultants, or any other particular planning methodology. We will make only brief comment on the results of this survey, noting that the survey covered not only manufacturing industry but also the energy and construction industries, and that the size of firm is based on turnover and not on the number of employees.

Some 24.9 per cent of the firms interviewed were seen to have a well-developed information system, though there was no necessary correlation between this and their production technology. These firms accounted for 59.6 per cent of the total number of employees, and 65.1 per cent of the gross product. Within this category 14.4 per cent were judged to have a very advanced information system in that they stated that they always made use of quantitative models; these firms accounted for 49.8 per cent of the total gross product. The percentage of firms belonging to this category increases in proportion to the increase in turnover, reaching 73.3 per cent in the case of firms with a turnover of more than 500 billion lire.

Some 28.6 per cent of firms, although not having an extensive range of financial planning reports, did at least have a minimal information system. These firms accounted for 15.6 per cent of the total gross product. They are typically small-to-medium sized firms, and it would be interesting to see over a period of time whether they are coming closer to the firms with a more advanced information system or whether they are regressing towards the group of firms with no planning documentation. The latter group account for 46.4 per cent of the total number of firms, 22.9 per cent of the employees, and 19.3 per cent of the gross product. The percentage of firms belonging to this group decreases in proportion to the increase in turnover, in direct contrast to what was seen to happen in firms with a highly developed information system. We can confirm, therefore, that the need for an information system grows with the increase in the size of firm; this trend is also confirmed when one views the data from the point of view of individual economic sectors.

5. Labour costs, productivity, and profits

In a market economy the only index of a firm's success is the profit rate, and it is on the basis of this index that we now evaluate the performance of small and medium-sized firms and compare it with that of medium-to-large firms. The information at our disposal will not allow us to make a deeper analysis and take into account indebtedness and depreciation. Despite these limitations, the ratio of profits to value added is by no means without interest, in that it brings together labour productivity, wages, the amount of inputs in the production cycle, and finally the degree of flexibility, as measured by comparing variable costs with total costs.

It should also be noted that in order to carry out meaningful comparisons, it will be necessary to take into consideration production which is carried out as a result of subcontracting agreements. These may be the result of the various expressions of decentralization of production brought about by technological, organizational, or institutional factors.

In order to identify the relationships which underlie the behaviour of small and medium-sized firms and of large firms, it is first necessary to state a number of hypotheses:

(1) The maximization of profits is an objective of both large firms and small-to-medium sized firms.
(2) The various forms of technology in existence are available to both large firms and smaller firms; the choice of technology will affect the size of the production environment, and vice versa.

(3) Technological innovation is related to the size of firm, but the latter is not the only conditioning factor. Theoretical debate has not been able to resolve this question completely, though it has shown that the factors which stimulate innovation are also related to the firm's position in the production cycle, to features of the firm's organization structure, and to the entrepreneur's or management's attitude towards innovation.

(4) The relationship between variable costs and fixed costs changes according to the scale of production; it affects profit rate and, above all, degree of risk.

(5) An increase in the size of firm is accompanied by a change in the composition of its workforce, a stronger union presence, and more complex industrial relations. These variables will mean different salary levels for the same level of productivity.

(6) For each economic sector the market is the same, and therefore the price is the same for all producers. In the absence of such a hypothesis, monetary variables would have to be adjusted to take into account the different prices for the same product to be found on different markets.

(7) Credit access varies with the size of the firm (we will not, however, be able to take this variable into account).

The analysis of the distribution of gross product between wages and gross profits is in apparent contradiction with a theoretical picture which, on the whole, leads to a different interpretation. It confirms the vitality of small-to-medium firms and the difficulties large firms are encountering in Italy. Figures for the period 1983–5 clearly indicate in fact an inverse relationship between profitability and size of firm. This relationship was found to exist in each year considered and in very many different sectors of economic activity. However, medium and large firms saw their profits grow by 3 to 4 per cent, and in some sectors this growth was very considerable indeed, leading to a reduction in the advantage the small firms had over the medium-to-large firms. There are a number of variables which account for this phenomenon.

First, we must consider the composition of the workforce from the point of view of number of employees versus number of self-employed persons. All other things being equal, the greater the number of self-employed workers, the lower will be the salary costs; this is because the remuneration of the self-employed is included, for accounting purposes, in gross profits. In the period we are considering, the small firms had about 12 per cent more self-employed workers than the medium-to-large firms. The distortion created through the presence of a smaller or larger proportion of self-employed workers may be alleviated to a considerable extent if one attributes to each self-employed worker a salary equal to the average salary of management and white-collar workers in that sector. The difference between value added and the new total of wages thus obtained accounts for almost all the gross profits, excluding therefore the remuneration paid to self-employed workers. Since the latter are to be found mainly in the smaller firms, this adjustment chiefly affects this size of firm, and increases the wage totals attributable to it. This increase was of around 6 per cent in both 1983 and 1985 in firms of less than twenty employees. The corrected profits are still seen to decrease as the size of the firm increases, however the difference between small and large firms is reduced.

In 1985 the largest profits in over half the industrial sectors were recorded in the size category of fifteen to nineteen employees, while a similar proportion of the lowest profits were to be found in the largest size category (more than 999 employees). Interesting exceptions to this are the sectors of footwear and clothing and the production of man-made fibres, in which the highest profit margins are to be found in the size category 200–499 employees. Also of interest is the fact that between 1983 and 1985 there was a clear drop in the profit rate of the size category of ten to fourteen employees. This caused largest profits to be shifted upwards to other size categories, especially to the next category (fifteen to nineteen employees), and also to the category thirty to forty-nine employees.

The cost of labour is one factor which helps to explain the relative disadvantage of the medium-to-large firms. In 1983 the labour cost per employee was on average about 40 per cent higher in large firms than in smaller firms, with the greatest differences being found in food and drink, textiles, and footwear and clothing, followed by the extraction industries, chemicals, and the various sectors of metal goods, engineering and vehicles. This is true despite the presence of an unemployment benefit system (*Cassa Integrazione Guadagni*) which, according to the ISTAT survey, tends to bring about a decrease in labour costs per employee, and whose effects are felt above all in large firms. If we adjust the labour costs per hour in order to take this factor into consideration, the differences between large firms and small firms are even greater.

The cost of labour increases, then, in proportion to the increase in size of the firm. If we analyse the two major contributors to labour costs – gross wages and compulsory contributions – it is found that the major differences between size categories relate to salary levels and not the payment of social security contributions. It is also to be noted that, although the difference in average labour costs between small and large firms remained unaltered between

1983 and 1985, there was a considerable increase in the compulsory contributions paid out by small firms and in gross salaries paid out by large firms. In fact, while the scatter rate for labour costs increased by 3 per cent in 1985, for gross wages the same index increased by 12 per cent. The difference in labour costs between the size categories diminished, therefore, but the same cannot be said for remuneration. These considerable salary differences can be explained by the fact that in the larger firms there is a higher proportion (almost double) of management and white-collar workers among the employees than there is in the smaller firms. This leads to higher average labour costs, given the salary differences between white-collar workers and manual workers.

The percentage of white-collar workers and management in the workforce increases with the size of the firm. The highest proportions of non-manual labour are found in iron and steel and chemicals, followed by metal goods, engineering, and vehicles, while the lowest proportions are found in food and drink, textiles, and footwear and clothing. Between 1983 and 1985 there was a more or less general increase in the ratio of white-collar workers to manual workers, higher than average in the small-to-medium firms and in the traditional industries (food and drink; textiles; leather and leather goods; footwear and clothing; timber and wooden furniture; paper, printing and publishing; rubber and plastics). There was also a reduction in the differences between the value of this ratio in the various size categories.

This confirms, on the one hand, the considerable organizational costs sustained by large firms, for example the cost of information management and the cost of keeping up with technological change. At the same time, it is a confirmation that this process of organizational change also involves small and medium-sized firms by virtue of the growing complexity of management whether in marketing, finance, or personnel, not to mention the increasing complexity of the production process as a result of technological innovation.

Another factor is the greater pressure applied by trade unions within the larger firms. This may be seen by comparing the hourly rates of manual workers in different sizes of firms, though other factors are also at work here (seniority, degree of skill, cost of overtime). The hourly wage paid by large firms is, on average, 50 per cent higher than that of small firms and increases in proportion to the size of the firm. This differential increased in 1985 because of salary increases 4 per cent higher in large firms than in small firms.

There also seems to be a high correspondence between the number of hours worked by manual workers and the size of the firm in which they are employed. In 1983 manual working hours were more or less the same for the smaller-size categories but began to decrease in firms of fifty employees or more. Manual workers in smaller firms worked an average of 12 per cent more than those in large firms. It should here be remembered that use of the unemployment benefit system was higher in the larger firms, and that this might have contributed to a lowering of the average number of hours worked. However, it would also seem that the tendency towards a reduction in the number of hours worked indicates that the distorting effect of the unemployment benefit system is not enough to account for the notable differences found in all sectors of economic activity. In 1985 the tendency was even stronger. The average hours for the manual worker begin to decrease even sooner, in the size category of twenty to twenty-nine employees, and the difference between the smallest firms and the largest firms increases by 4 per cent. The number of hours worked are highest, on average, in the manufacture of metal goods not elsewhere specified, in iron and steel, and in chemicals. The average variation recorded between 1983 and 1985 is about 5.8 per cent in firms of less than twenty employees, 2.8 per cent in firms of twenty to ninety-nine employees, and 2.9 per cent in the remainder, with an increase in the scatter rate per size category of around 10 per cent.

The information available on labour costs expressed in terms of both cost per hour and cost per employee help to explain, therefore, the tendency for gross profits to decrease in the various size categories. At the same time, however, labour productivity is seen to correspond to a high degree to the size of firm. We have a situation, therefore, where the relative degree of productivity does not correspond to the relative wage level. An econometric estimation of the relationship between wages and productivity in 1983 offers results which are satisfactory in 75 per cent of cases, and especially in those sectors where labour-intensive processes are used, above all in the traditional industries (with the exception of sugar, drinks, and other foodstuffs). These tendencies become even stronger in 1985.

In 1983 the gross product per employee in small firms was approximately 80 per cent of the analogous figure in larger firms. This proportion decreases to about 60 per cent in 1985, when there is also a higher correspondence between productivity and size of firm, and a considerable increase (+27 per cent) in the degree of variation within the various size categories. The results are much the same if an estimated index of hourly productivity is used. In this case the progress over the three-year period by the larger production units is seen even more clearly.

It is interesting to compare profit levels for 1983 with those for 1985. In the latter year the profit boom was seen above all in the larger firms. This did not, however, remove the differences in profitability between size categories. It would seem, therefore, that the economies of scale to be found in the larger production units lead, marginally, to profit growth which increases as production increases. The increase in productivity achieved between 1983 and 1985 (+35 per cent) underlines the very successful performance of the medium-to-large firms, which brought about a significant reduction in the relative cost per unit produced. It still remains to be explained, however, why profit margins continue to be a factor indicative of size of firm. Between 1983 and 1985 there was a 40 per cent decrease in the average difference of profitability between size categories, and this change is to found especially in large firms, above all in food and drink, textiles, footwear and clothing, and in metal goods, engineering, and vehicles.

A suitable explanation for the differences in profitability between different size categories might be sought in the different ratios between variable costs (manual workers' wages and cost of intermediate goods) and total costs. This ratio decreases proportionately as the size of firm increases in almost all sectors of economic activity. The greatest differences between small and large production units are to be found in the traditional sectors, followed by metal goods, engineering, and vehicles, iron and steel, and then chemicals. The average difference between small and large production units was around 7 per cent in 1983 and 5 per cent in 1985. During the three-year period there was a general decrease in all sectors of economic activity of the difference in the ratio of variable costs to fixed costs, with a decrease in the scatter rate of around 7 per cent.

Assuming that labour costs, actual productivity, and gross profit margins remain constant, a higher incidence of fixed costs is a constraint which will bring about a reduction in profits; this becomes less true as the level of production increases. This relationship has been examined in econometric terms with satisfying results both for individual economic sectors and for industry as a whole. In fact the negative relationship between profitability and fixed costs is relatively stable during the period 1983–5, and has been verified in about 70 per cent of cases. The best results were obtained from regressions carried out on metal goods, engineering, and vehicles, while the relative worsening of the correlation recorded in 1985 is due above all to the results for food and drink, textiles, and footwear and clothing.

Another useful piece of information is provided by the sectoral scatter of the variables we have considered (labour cost, productivity, profits, etc.) within each of the size categories. The intersectoral variability of many of these factors seems in some way related to the size of firm. In particular, we may differentiate the smallest firms (up to thirty employees), medium sized firms (thirty to 200 employees) and larger firms. The indices of intersectoral variability of the cost of labour are U-shaped, whether calculated in terms of labour costs per employee or average wage per employee. The scatter rate for productivity is found to be similar, though less regular, while that of profits and of hours worked increases regularly with the size of firm.

6. Interdependence within the production system

In the latter part of the 1970s there was an increase in the degree of interdependence between firms, not only within the industrial system itself but also between the latter and the service industries. This was a consequence of the decrease in size of the large firm, the tendency towards more specialization in individual phases of the production process, and an increase in the use of subcontracting. We may use the ratio of intermediate costs to turnover as a fairly simple index to the importance of exchange between economic sectors. In the manufacturing industries, intermediate costs account for, on average, over 65 per cent of the total turnover. The importance of intermediate goods obviously varies from one industrial sector to another. It is higher than average in the case of industries involved with the processing of raw materials. This is the case in, for example, the manufacture of metals and extraction of minerals, especially in chemicals and the production of man-made fibres, and, within the traditional industries, in food and drink and leather and leather goods. Within the various sectors of metal goods and engineering, characterized by a much higher than average level of value added, one sector clearly stands out from the rest. This is the manufacture of motor vehicles and parts, in which the decentralization of production has led to an increase in the importance of exchange with other sectors.

If we examine the ratio of intermediate goods to turnover from the point of view of the size of firm, we see that there is a more or less stable situation when the manufacturing industries are taken as a whole, but that there are more notable differences between the individual sectors. In the manufacture of metal goods and extraction of minerals, there is a positive correlation, albeit slight, between the value of intermediate goods and the size of firm. This correlation is also found in two sectors within the metal goods and engineering aggregate – mechanical engineering and the manufacture of office machinery and data-processing equipment. In the traditional

87

industries, the lowest values for the ratio intermediate costs to turnover are recorded in the lowest and highest size categories (ten to nineteen employees, and 500 employees or more).

During the three-year period 1983–5, there was a slight increase in the importance of intermediate goods both in the manufacturing industries taken as a whole and in the majority of the individual sectors of economic activity. This is true of all size categories with the exception of the very smallest production units (ten to fourteen employees) and the very largest (over 999 employees). In order to understand more fully the reasons for this increase in the value of exchange between sectors, we must break down intermediate costs into their component parts. A further factor which might have influenced the relationship between intermediate costs and turnover is the rates of exchange between sectors; but, in the present discussion we will not be able to take this factor into consideration.

There was an increase, albeit very slight, in the combined value of 'various expenditure' and 'expenditure on non-industrial services' when considered in relation to the value of sales. This was true for the manufacturing industries taken as a whole and also for the three sectoral aggregates, where in fact the increase was very similar for all three branches of industrial activity. This factor seems to confirm the consolidation of the tendency to decentralize certain services linked to the production process, services which had previously formed part of the firm's internal activities. If we now consider this ratio from the point of view of size of firm, we find that in the very small firms (up to nineteen employees) the proportional value of the two types of expenditure mentioned is clearly and systematically lower than in the other size categories, and that this value tends to grow, even if somewhat irregularly, as the size of firm increases, until the largest size category is reached (more than 999 employees), at which point there is a reduction in the importance of expenditure on non-industrial services. These trends are true for all three sectoral aggregates, but especially so for the traditional industries. The manufacture of office machinery and data-processing equipment forms an exception to these trends, in that the value of the variable in question is inversely proportional to the size of the firm.

Turning to expenditure incurred through the purchasing of raw materials and of intermediate products and through work subcontracted to other firms, we will consider this in relation to turnover, a ratio which measures the extent of exchange with other economic sectors which are themselves producers of goods. It is found that in the years 1983–5 there is a slight increase in this ratio, attributable both to the increased use of intermediate products and to the increased use of subcontractors to carry out phases of the production process using raw materials provided by the firm. These increases were most notable in small and small-to-medium firms (up to ninety-nine employees), which size categories had already been seen to be more disposed towards subcontracting in 1983. The medium-to-large firms would seem, then, less disposed towards the use of sub-contracting and more inclined towards internal production or the direct purchasing from outside firms of semi-manufactured material to be used in the production process. The sectors in which the use of subcontracting seems more common are, within metal goods and engineering, the manufacture of office machinery and data-processing equipment, electrical and electronic engineering, and other transport equipment, and, within the traditional industries, textiles, footwear and clothing, and paper, printing, and publishing. In these sectors there was also the greatest increase between 1983 and 1985.

Next we will consider the ratio between manufacturing work carried out by firms as the result of subcontracting agreements and total turnover. This also provides a measure of the extent of the decentralization of production, this time, however, seen from the point of view of the producer and not the commissioning firm. We find that as the size of firm increases, this ratio tends to decrease rapidly, and almost disappear in the case of the largest firms. This was expected to be the case, and confirms beyond any doubt that there is a higher incidence of interdependence between firms in the small and medium size categories. In the manufacture of office machinery and data-processing equipment, firms which subcontract work to other firms are found above all in the medium-to-large firms (up to 499 employees). In the same sector, firms which have been subcontracted to provide semi-manufactured products tend to be either very small (ten to fourteen employees) or medium sized (fifty to ninety-nine employees).

It is difficult to interpret fully the increase in the value of exchange between economic sectors or, to look at it from another point of view, the increase in the amount of value added in the manufacturing industries. There are too many differences between the individual economic sectors. The figures we have presented above, however, would seem to confirm the opinion that the increase in importance of the small and medium firms is a result of the splitting-up of the production process into distinct phases, and also of the tendency of medium-to-large firms to substitute intermediate inputs for internal labour. These inputs either take the form of products purchased directly on the market, or of work given over to other, generally smaller firms which remain dependent on the commissioning firm, for example, through subcontracting agreements.

The larger firms (which in most cases means firms of 500 employees or more) appear, however, to maintain a high degree of vertical integration, especially in the traditional industries, though it must be added that in the latter sectors the larger size category is less important. In metal goods and engineering the only more or less systematic picture offered is the lesser importance of the work sub-contracted to other firms and of expenditure on non-industrial services, and, in contrast, a higher incidence of purchase of raw materials and semi-manufactured products.

Access to international markets

We have calculated the extent to which companies have access to international markets by measuring the ratio of value of exports to total turnover for each of the size categories. In both 1983 and 1985 the figure is around 24 per cent for the manufacturing industries as a whole.

Of the three main branches of industry, the highest value for this ratio is recorded by metal goods and engineering, where there is an average of around 33 per cent, with particularly high values in the manufacture of office machinery and data-processing equipment, and mechanical engineering. The lowest average value is that of the traditional industries, in which the average is 19 per cent. The true picture for the traditional sectors, however, is very complex, with figures ranging from below 10 per cent in the case of food and drink, the lowest percentage of all for the manufacturing industries, to over 30 per cent in the case of leather and leather goods and footwear and clothing, which are found to be among the most export-oriented sectors.

Naturally, if only exporting firms are taken into consideration, the degree of penetration into international markets is higher, around 30 per cent for the manufacturing industries taken as a whole. However, the degree of relative importance of the three main branches of industry remains unaltered.

If we analyse the data with regard to the size category, we find that the highest degree of penetration into international markets is found in the largest firms. Whereas this is true for the manufacturing industries as a whole, it is not true for the aggregate of traditional industries; here there seems to be a more important role played by the small and medium-sized firms than by the large firms. In 1985 firms with a maximum of ninety-nine employees accounted for 26 per cent of the total foreign sales of the manufacturing industries, while in the traditional industries the same size category provided 44.4 per cent of the total.

If the turnover through exports is a measure of the overall degree of penetration into international markets, the proportion of individual firms which export measures the extent to which home industry is integrated with the rest of the world. According to the data provided by the survey on gross product, more than 67 per cent of manufacturing firms are to some degree involved in exporting, and again there is a positive correlation in all three sectoral aggregates between the involvement in exports and the size of firm. The values for small firms are particularly high. The information at our disposal, however, does not allow us to verify whether or not the contribution to exports of the various size categories remains constant over a period of time. In particular, it does not allow us to decide whether smaller firms have only an occasional role to play in the export market and therefore come and go with greater frequency than the larger firms. It is generally held that the ability of a firm to remain on the international market is linked to that firm's ability to overcome certain barriers which divide the home market from the international market, for example the higher degree of organization and information. The fact that there are a large number of exporting firms among the smaller-sized firms could indicate that this size of firm has gained a stable place on the international market.

Finally, we should mention that the characteristics of competitiveness on the international market seem to have an influence on the dynamics of productivity. There is a higher level of value added per employee among the exporting firms than among the non-exporting firms in the various sectors of all three major branches of the manufacturing industries, with the exception of certain size categories of 'other manufacturing industries'.

8. Conclusions

It is always difficult to present concise conclusions when the research which has been carried out is concerned with the analysis of complex phenomena. We have tried to draw attention to factors which form a part not only of the structure but also of the dynamics of industry. We have tried to separate underlying tendencies, which will be confirmed in the near future, from more ephemeral phenomena which may no longer be present in the next survey carried out.

A first observation is that it is not possible to universalize the statement 'small is beautiful'. At the risk of being banal, we would suggest that the statement should read, 'small is beautiful, but only in those employment sectors where it is possible for the small and medium-sized firms to expand'. The small and medium-sized firms

Small firms and industrial districts in Italy

are to be found above all in the traditional industries and in mechanical engineering and manufacture of miscellaneous metal goods. However, these sectors account for less than a third of the total industrial output. The concept 'small is beautiful' is useful, therefore, but should not be overgeneralized.

Second, with regard to the dynamics of industry, the 1980s seem to confirm the tendencies which appeared during the 1970s, especially with regard to the decrease in size of the large production units. In addition, the information currently available indicates a clear comeback by the medium-to-large firms, which gain considerable ground in relation to the small-to-medium firms. This improvement takes the form, above all, of the increase in productivity per employee, which is linked to technological innovation and to reductions in staff.

A third observation is the fact that the ratio of profits to value added is higher in small and medium-sized firms than in large firms, and this is true for all sectors of the manufacturing industries. The reason for this is that labour costs in small and medium-sized firms are lower than those in medium-to-large firms, and a higher degree of productivity per employee in the medium-to-large firms is not enough to compensate for this difference in labour costs. There are many factors which bring about this situation, for example the great flexibility of the small and medium-sized firms, the higher degree of selectivity of the market when dealing with small and medium-sized firms, and the greater speed with which small firms are penalized by the market. With regard to the latter point, difficulties encountered by large firms are endured much longer, and since the statistical information for the period we are dealing with does not exclude firms in difficulties, the result is that average values are lower than they would otherwise have been.

Our next consideration concerns the level of organizational costs and degree of technological complexity resulting from the increase in importance of management and white-collar workers in relation to manual workers, in its turn a result of the profound innovative changes occurring throughout the whole production system. At the same time we must consider the difficulties relating to management in the large industrial firms. Small and medium-sized firms are often slow to acquire and process information and to use this information for managerial purposes. This fact, together with the continuing existence of technologically backward firms whose management is based solely on traditional methods, should act as a warning to the small and medium-sized firms in question. It has also been shown that the medium-to-large firm which has not kept up with the times, both technologically and organizationally, and which does not possess a well-developed information system, is not capable of survival, because labour costs are very heavy and demand a sustained increase in productivity.

The debate on the decentralization of production showed up the decline in importance of economies of scale in determining the optimum size of firm, and the consequent dominant role of a production cycle divided into many different phases. The facts at our disposal show that subcontracting is an organizational choice within the small and medium-sized firms, in that this form of dependence between firms tends to decrease as the size of the firm increases; this is true both for work subcontracted to other firms, and, especially so, for work carried out on behalf of other firms.

Finally, the presence of firms on the international market offers a very interesting example of how inappropriate it is to view the degree of penetration into the foreign market from a global, aggregate standpoint instead of adopting a more analytical stance. In those sectors in which both technology and tradition favour flexibility, design, and a direct relationship with the customer, the small and medium-sized firms are present in significant numbers on the international market. In those sectors in which technological progress, the cost of installation, and the continuity of supply are important factors for a continuing presence on the international market, we find instead that the medium-to-large firms are more favoured.

Appendix 4

Table A4.1 Industrial census 1971, 1981: firms and employees

Divisions and classes	Firms 1971	Firms 1981	% change	Employees 1971	Employees 1981	% change	Average size 1971	Average size 1981
Extraction and manufacture of minerals other than fuels, chemicals	32,646	37,000	+13.36	900,863	903,493	+0.29	27.59	24.41
Extraction and preparation of metalliferous ores	57	68	+1.75	11,080	7,594	−31.46	194.39	130.93
Metal manufacturing	2,198	2,198	—	205,053	203,627	−0.70	93.29	92.63
Extraction of minerals not elsewhere specified	4,203	4,363	+3.81	45,897	42,947	−6.43	10.92	9.84
Non-metallic mineral products	21,282	24,171	+13.57	326,540	339,604	+4.00	15.34	14.05
Chemical industry	4,874	6,116	+25.48	270,480	276,313	+2.16	55.49	45.18
Man-made fibres	32	100	+212.50	41,813	33,408	−20.10	1,306.66	334.08
Metal goods, engineering and vehicles	117,766	168,774	+43.31	1,811,948	2,243,594	+23.82	15.39	13.29
Metal goods not elsewhere specified	76,275	98,902	+29.67	527,404	680,562	+29.04	6.91	6.88
Mechanical engineering	19,876	30,708	+54.50	376,852	524,214	+39.10	18.96	17.07
Office machinery and data processing equipment	1,748	1,486	−14.99	54,056	48,531	10.22	30.92	32.66
Electric and electronic engineering	13,890	21,600	+55.51	406,462	498,022	+22.53	29.26	23.06
Manufacture of motor vehicles	1,274	2,291	−79.83	305,221	287,891	−5.68	239.58	125.66
Other transport equipment	1,049	2,258	−115.25	89,720	131,988	+47.11	85.53	58.45
Instrument making	3,654	11,529	−215.25	52,233	72,386	+38.58	14.29	6.28
Other manufacturing industries	340,571	387,403	+13.75	2,490,632	2,697,954	+8.32	7.31	6.94
Food	37,589	41,215	+9.65	264,575	281,813	+6.52	7.04	6.84
Drink and tobacco	7,755	7,222	−6.87	159,096	132,462	−16.74	20.52	13.33
Textiles	47,839	48,536	+21.98	553,080	495,421	−10.43	11.56	8.29
Manufacture of leather	6,821	11,833	+73.48	59,307	85,754	+44.59	8.69	7.75
Leather goods	103,893	97,871	−5.80	543,534	649,657	+19.52	5.23	6.64
Timber and wooden furniture	99,799	110,819	−11.04	401,451	451,981	+12.59	4.02	4.08
Paper, printing and publishing	15,295	24,275	−58.71	237,073	284,172	+10.87	16.50	11.71
Rubber and plastics	11,557	18,650	−61.37	191,295	221,162	+15.61	16.36	11.86
Other manufacturing	10,023	17,162	+71.23	81,221	95,532	+17.62	4.10	9.87

Table A4.2 Industrial census 1981: firms by numbers of employees

Divisions and classes	Up to 99 employees			100 and over		
	Firms	Employees	Average size	Firms	Employees	Average size
Extraction and manufacture of minerals other than fuels, chemicals	35,867	333,706	9.30	1,139	569,787	500.25
Extraction and preparation of metalliferous ores	53	607	11.45	5	6,987	1,397.40
Metal manufacturing	2,010	28,197	14.03	188	175,400	933.14
Extraction of minerals not elsewhere specified	4,334	36,494	8.42	29	6,453	222.52
Non-metallic mineral products	23,695	199,101	8.40	476	140,503	295.17
Chemical industry	5,703	67,546	11.84	413	208,767	505.49
Man-made fibres	727	1,761	24.46	28	31,647	1,130.25
Metal goods, engineering and vehicles	166,305	1,015,230	6.10	2,469	1,228,364	497.51
Metal goods not elsewhere specified	98,210	500,434	5.10	692	180,128	260.30
Mechanical engineering	29,942	260,534	8.70	766	263,680	344.23
Office machinery and data processing equipment	1,464	5,983	4.09	22	42,548	1,934.00
Electric and electronic engineering	21,020	152,595	7.26	580	345,427	595.56
Manufacture of motor vehicles	2,104	29,446	14.00	187	258,445	1,382.06
Other transport equipment	2,126	21,745	10.23	132	110,243	835.17
Instrument making	11,439	44,493	3.89	90	27,893	309.87
Other manufacturing industries	384,533	1,892,730	4.92	2,870	805,224	280.57
Food	40,940	194,623	4.75	275	87,190	317.05
Drink and tobacco	7,039	53,765	7.64	183	78,697	430.04
Textiles	57,630	306,395	5.32	726	189,026	260.37
Manufacture of leather	11,759	72,618	6.18	74	13,136	177.51
Leather goods	97,199	490,983	5.05	672	158,674	236.12
Timber and wooden furniture	110,589	405,548	3.87	250	46,433	185.73
Paper, printing and publishing	23,937	163,922	6.85	338	120,250	355.77
Rubber and plastics	18,381	127,596	6.94	269	93,566	347.83
Other manufacturing	17,079	77,280	4.52	83	18,252	219.90
Total	588,705	3,241,668	5.53	6,478	2,603,375	401.88

Table A4.3 Industrial census 1981: firms by employee number categories (%)

Divisions and classes	Up to 9 Firms	Up to 9 Employees	10-19 Firms	10-19 Employees	20-99 Firms	20-99 Employees	Total up to 99 Firms	Total up to 99 Employees	100 and over Firms	100 and over Employees
Extraction and manufacture of minerals other than fuels, chemicals	71.00	9.62	13.89	7.61	12.03	19.70	96.92	36.94	3.08	63.06
Extraction and preparation of metalliferous ores	62.07	1.78	12.07	1.15	17.24	5.07	91.38	7.99	8.62	92.01
Metal manufacturing	53.59	2.23	18.74	2.76	19.11	8.85	91.45	13.85	8.55	89.15
Extraction of minerals not elsewhere specified	72.01	27.77	18.04	24.05	9.28	33.15	99.34	84.97	0.66	15.03
Non-metallic mineral products	75.01	16.55	12.10	11.54	10.93	30.53	98.03	58.63	1.97	41.37
Chemical industry	61.48	5.05	16.25	4.82	15.52	14.58	93.25	24.45	6.75	75.55
Man-made fibres	30.00	0.46	17.00	0.74	25.00	4.07	72.00	5.27	28.00	94.73
Metal goods, engineering and vehicles	82.32	16.72	9.98	9.93	6.24	18.60	98.54	45.25	1.46	54.75
Metal goods not elsewhere specified	86.32	32.40	8.52	16.24	4.45	24.89	99.30	73.53	0.70	26.47
Mechanical engineering	72.95	13.27	13.73	10.75	10.83	25.68	97.51	49.70	2.49	50.30
Office machinery and data processing equipment	90.71	8.21	6.46	2.49	1.35	1.63	98.52	12.33	1.48	87.67
Electric and electronic engineering	77.13	9.80	12.41	7.18	7.78	13.87	97.31	30.64	2.69	69.36
Manufacture of motor vehicles	51.42	1.66	21.34	2.29	19.07	6.28	91.84	10.23	8.16	89.77
Other transport equipment	64.48	3.51	16.12	3.70	13.55	9.27	94.15	16.47	5.85	83.53
Instrument making	91.22	31.45	4.89	10.45	3.11	19.56	99.22	61.47	0.78	38.53
Other manufacturing industries	86.76	29.94	7.97	15.17	4.53	25.04	99.26	70.15	0.74	29.85
Food	90.50	39.28	5.41	10.38	3.42	19.40	99.33	69.06	0.67	30.94
Drink and tobacco	77.29	14.10	11.78	8.59	8.42	17.90	97.47	40.59	2.53	69.41
Textiles	84.80	22.30	8.58	13.35	5.59	26.20	98.76	61.85	1.24	38.15
Manufacture of leather	81.62	34.00	12.09	21.82	5.66	28.87	99.37	84.68	0.63	15.32
Leather goods	84.75	27.41	9.52	19.33	5.04	28.84	99.31	75.58	0.69	24.42
Timber and wooden furniture	92.05	48.81	5.04	16.13	2.69	24.79	99.77	89.73	0.23	10.27
Paper, printing and publishing	79.35	21.36	12.64	14.22	6.61	22.11	98.61	57.68	1.39	42.32
Rubber and plastics	79.27	19.32	11.70	13.07	7.59	25.31	98.56	57.69	1.44	42.31
Other manufacturing	88.66	38.49	7.09	16.70	3.77	25.70	99.52	80.89	0.48	19.11
	84.52	21.72	8.91	11.99	5.48	21.75	98.91	66.44	1.09	44.54

Table A4.4 Survey of GNP and small firms 1985: employee-number categories (%)

Divisions and classes	Employee-numbers categories		
	20–99	100 and over	Total
Extraction and manufacture of minerals other than fuels, chemicals	23.284	76.716	100.000
Extraction and preparation of metalliferous ores	9.908	90.092	100.000
Extraction of minerals not elsewhere specified	59.979	40.021	100.000
Non-metallic mineral products	41.876	58.124	100.000
Chemical industry	15.617	84.383	100.000
Man-made fibres	3.400	96.600	100.000
Metal goods, engineering and vehicles	25.436	74.564	100.000
Metal goods not elsewhere specified	50.714	49.286	100.000
Mechanical engineering	35.196	64.804	100.000
Office machinery and data processing equipment	3.027	96.973	100.000
Electric and electronic engineering	16.122	83.878	100.000
Manufacture of motor vehicles	7.280	92.720	100.000
Other transport equipment	7.387	92.613	100.000
Instrument making	33.747	66.253	100.000
Other manufacturing industries	45.075	54.925	100.000
Food	36.760	63.240	100.000
Drink and tobacco	20.288	79.712	100.000
Textiles	43.776	56.224	100.000
Manufacture of leather	66.294	33.706	100.000
Leather goods	53.370	46.830	100.000
Timber and wooden furniture	72.324	27.676	100.000
Paper, printing and publishing	33.344	66.656	100.000
Rubber and plastics	39.094	60.906	100.000
Other manufacturing	61.662	38.338	100.000
Total	32.587	67.403	100.000

Table A4.5 1985 GNP survey: employee-number categories (% of total manufacturing industry)

Divisions and classes	Employee-numbers categories		
	20–99	100 and over	Total
Extraction and manufacture of minerals other than fuels, chemicals	13.292	21.180	18.809
Extraction and preparation of metalliferous ores	1.561	6.865	5.136
Extraction of minerals not elsewhere specified	1.053	0.340	0.572
Non-metallic mineral products	7.493	5.030	5.833
Chemical industry	3.129	8.176	6.531
Man-made fibres	0.056	0.769	0.537
Metal goods, engineering and vehicles	33.467	47.448	42.889
Metal goods not elsewhere specified	12.820	6.025	8.240
Mechanical engineering	11.605	10.333	10.747
Office machinery and data processing equipment	0.091	1.416	0.984
Electric and electronic engineering	5.371	13.514	10.860
Manufacture of motor vehicles	1.545	9.518	6.919
Other transport equipment	0.921	5.582	4.063
Instrument making	1.113	1.057	1.075
Other manufacturing industries	53.241	31.374	38.502
Food	4.484	3.730	3.976
Drink and tobacco	2.118	4.025	3.403
Textiles	10.323	6.412	7.687
Manufacture of leather	1.894	0.466	0.931
Leather goods	13.774	5.820	8.413
Timber and wooden furniture	8.463	1.566	3.814
Paper, printing and publishing	5.061	4.893	4.948
Rubber and plastics	5.124	3.861	4.272
Other manufacturing	1.999	0.601	1.057
Total	100.000	100.000	100.000

Table A4.6 1985 GNP survey: turnover (%)

Divisions and classes	Employee-numbers categories		
	20–99	100 and over	Total
Extraction and manufacture of minerals other than fuels, chemicals	19.940	80.060	100.000
Extraction and preparation of metalliferous ores	16.034	83.966	100.000
Extraction of minerals not elsewhere specified	64.468	35.532	100.000
Non-metallic mineral products	37.647	62.353	100.000
Chemical industry	15.017	84.983	100.000
Man-made fibres	3.485	96.515	100.000
Metal goods, engineering and vehicles	25.135	74.865	100.000
Metal goods not elsewhere specified	51.514	48.486	100.000
Mechanical engineering	33.685	66.315	100.000
Office machinery and data processing equipment	1.882	98.118	100.000
Electric and electronic engineering	18.012	81.988	100.000
Manufacture of motor vehicles	6.284	93.716	100.000
Other transport equipment	8.248	91.752	100.000
Instrument making	33.205	66.795	100.000
Other manufacturing industries	41.511	58.489	100.000
Food	41.321	58.679	100.000
Drink and tobacco	21.812	78.188	100.000
Textiles	46.321	53.679	100.000
Manufacture of leather	67.426	32.574	100.000
Leather goods	48.625	51.375	100.000
Timber and wooden furniture	67.483	32.517	100.000
Paper, printing and publishing	30.068	69.932	100.000
Rubber and plastics	42.907	57.093	100.000
Other manufacturing	56.547	43.453	100.000
Total	30.509	69.491	100.000

Table A4.7 1985 GNP survey: turnover (% of total manufacturing industry)

Divisions and classes	20–99	100 and over	Total
Extraction and manufacture of minerals other than fuels, chemicals	16.187	28.534	24.767
Extraction and preparation of metalliferous ores	4.012	9.225	7.635
Extraction of minerals not elsewhere specified	0.784	0.190	0.371
Non-metallic mineral products	5.688	4.136	4.609
Chemical industry	5.619	13.962	11.417
Man-made fibres	0.084	1.021	0.735
Metal goods, engineering and vehicles	28.469	37.230	34.557
Metal goods not elsewhere specified	10.484	4.332	6.209
Mechanical engineering	10.364	8.958	9.387
Office machinery and data processing equipment	0.092	2.105	1.491
Electric and electronic engineering	4.849	9.692	8.214
Manufacture of motor vehicles	1.267	8.296	6.151
Other transport equipment	0.650	3.173	2.403
Instrument making	0.762	0.673	0.700
Other manufacturing industries	55.344	34.236	40.676
Food	10.695	6.668	7.897
Drink and tobacco	4.757	7.487	6.654
Textiles	10.286	5.234	6.775
Manufacture of leather	2.461	0.522	1.114
Leather goods	8.066	3.742	5.061
Timber and wooden furniture	6.247	1.322	2.824
Paper, printing and publishing	5.253	5.364	5.330
Rubber and plastics	5.437	3.176	3.866
Other manufacturing	2.141	0.722	1.555
Total	100.000	100.000	100.000

Column header spanning "20–99" and "100 and over": **Employee-numbers categories**

Table A4.8 1985 GNP survey: turnover per employee (million lire)

Divisions and classes	10–14	15–19	20–29	30–49	50–99	100–199	200–499	500–999	1,000 and over
Extraction and manufacture of minerals other than fuels, chemicals	114.000	126.904	137.082	148.520	172.655	177.329	214.475	191.954	185.036
Extraction and preparation of metalliferous ores	207.744	170.926	297.017	273.778	374.874	311.208	250.299	211.281	164.958
Extraction of minerals not elsewhere specified	78.546	102.523	97.799	95.150	93.865	97.581	79.799	27.499	67.494
Non-metallic mineral products	90.875	102.850	95.999	94.706	100.721	117.443	125.074	112.842	110.067
Chemical industry	180.369	206.690	218.230	245.819	226.186	207.597	259.059	236.610	245.007
Man-made fibres	211.630	109.576	362.174	269.806	148.718	101.739	280.489	103.856	188.027
Metal goods, engineering and vehicles	76.049	84.861	102.876	107.928	113.349	113.388	106.870	108.410	112.214
Metal goods not elsewhere specified	72.085	77.011	99.187	102.699	110.193	105.466	95.496	100.361	106.714
Mechanical engineering	81.396	82.799	105.651	115.307	118.428	118.054	133.667	98.091	127.953
Office machinery and data processing equipment	108.839	119.786	185.575	155.754	95.295	97.476	106.185	153.877	223.052
Electric and electronic engineering	80.302	103.625	109.094	114.975	119.491	125.941	96.848	125.198	92.303
Manufacture of motor vehicles	71.643	108.998	112.492	95.337	109.070	119.361	103.192	110.667	125.632
Other transport equipment	73.325	98.055	94.871	89.860	89.013	73.260	96.416	86.574	77.870
Instrument making	79.505	81.893	87.885	84.787	90.566	89.431	90.110	102.344	79.420
Other manufacturing industries	84.669	103.621	130.323	137.212	132.333	148.890	149.472	141.504	173.829
Food	167.404	306.716	325.376	330.193	274.151	279.942	228.732	292.958	229.345
Drink and tobacco	233.523	275.351	301.136	288.852	281.413	279.890	251.121	234.230	268.699
Textiles	84.614	103.719	131.315	136.721	119.684	122.430	113.502	110.263	107.855
Manufacture of leather	105.348	141.535	153.614	171.636	171.448	191.844	122.032	–	87.221
Leather goods	50.674	47.696	69.300	73.175	80.655	82.955	113.624	76.215	79.558
Timber and wooden furniture	62.849	72.436	89.282	96.306	97.548	129.310	114.516	86.176	–
Paper, printing and publishing	94.310	109.583	118.243	132.587	142.374	133.471	165.941	154.468	160.539
Rubber and plastics	100.476	112.941	139.934	135.051	135.206	132.484	132.667	113.132	92.452
Other manufacturing	91.170	126.037	132.515	145.454	133.592	273.941	75.135	162.230	125.663
Total	84.630	100.027	122.549	129.177	131.097	140.352	144.304	140.852	140.738

Table A4.9 1985 GNP survey: gross product per employee (million lire)

Divisions and classes	10–14	15–19	20–29	30–49	50–99	100–199	200–499	500–999	1,000 and over
Extraction and manufacture of minerals other than fuels, chemicals	39.659	42.013	42.781	44.639	49.113	51.548	56.998	52.290	43.741
Extraction and preparation of metalliferous ores	46.397	46.369	54.079	54.464	60.911	57.948	49.971	46.621	35.063
Extraction of minerals not elsewhere specified	41.083	50.153	45.776	46.154	44.082	42.442	34.419	21.862	22.541
Non-metallic mineral products	33.732	37.179	35.530	36.056	39.054	43.600	50.477	45.917	39.135
Chemical industry	54.304	50.879	58.775	61.779	63.806	59.916	64.970	58.489	56.602
Man-made fibres	54.741	34.258	57.783	54.006	45.542	37.297	77.015	36.473	51.606
Metal goods, engineering and vehicles	32.048	34.534	39.212	40.779	42.822	41.819	40.662	40.155	41.670
Metal goods not elsewhere specified	30.897	32.011	37.607	38.733	40.777	39.171	37.239	38.124	41.902
Mechanical engineering	35.255	35.243	41.529	43.385	45.129	45.056	45.783	38.709	45.343
Office machinery and data processing equipment	47.855	60.453	74.011	80.428	42.112	44.934	38.913	54.689	78.597
Electric and electronic engineering	31.069	39.903	40.255	42.111	45.249	44.270	38.437	42.376	41.121
Manufacture of motor vehicles	28.205	33.067	37.165	35.300	39.398	39.373	38.189	36.678	37.800
Other transport equipment	33.401	34.089	33.624	36.987	34.507	23.938	43.328	38.097	36.234
Instrument making	31.811	39.798	37.128	37.825	40.853	39.050	43.555	44.704	33.635
Other manufacturing industries	27.689	30.021	34.924	35.931	37.827	38.102	42.847	41.058	44.190
Food	33.162	40.780	43.387	41.349	40.241	36.665	38.121	50.077	46.833
Drink and tobacco	48.234	56.413	48.809	50.224	58.371	51.604	55.972	60.377	40.762
Textiles	29.529	32.622	41.194	42.537	39.972	40.446	40.097	38.098	37.858
Manufacture of leather	28.186	33.702	36.758	38.703	41.714	41.154	31.800	–	19.825
Leather goods	19.760	19.271	23.237	24.413	27.643	27.049	35.624	27.707	32.281
Timber and wooden furniture	24.856	27.111	31.112	31.942	33.861	39.000	36.222	33.856	–
Paper, printing and publishing	35.637	39.282	41.860	44.001	47.164	44.908	54.905	54.063	60.109
Rubber and plastics	34.940	37.714	43.636	42.375	43.251	44.853	46.504	37.433	35.017
Other manufacturing	27.712	33.181	34.429	34.801	37.742	24.944	29.150	28.580	52.735
Total	30.208	32.678	34.298	38.654	41.118	41.542	44.515	43.498	42.618

Table A4.10 1985 GNP survey: hourly productivity (corrected, thousand lire)

Divisions and classes	10–14	15–19	20–29	30–49	Size classes 50–99	100–199	200–499	500–999	1,000 and over
Extraction and manufacture of minerals other than fuels, chemicals	26.073	25.946	25.798	26.444	29.329	31.430	35.523	32.557	27.658
Extraction and preparation of metalliferous ores	31.080	28.762	31.916	31.924	35.450	34.614	31.367	30.798	21.753
Extraction of minerals not elsewhere specified	26.256	30.858	28.710	27.251	26.419	24.817	29.980	22.327	13.347
Non-metallic mineral products	22.623	23.382	21.465	21.708	23.658	26.073	31.706	29.444	26.604
Chemical industry	33.583	29.427	34.724	35.182	37.213	38.771	39.137	26.701	35.793
Man-made fibres	31.407	18.245	38.945	23.756	28.369	19.017	46.264	26.715	32.745
Metal goods, engineering and vehicles	21.514	21.757	23.204	24.083	25.629	26.084	27.228	26.780	29.750
Metal goods not elsewhere specified	20.734	20.395	22.361	23.034	24.459	24.296	24.249	24.940	26.845
Mechanical engineering	23.654	22.081	24.066	25.045	26.777	27.171	28.777	32.165	29.446
Office machinery and data processing equipment	30.522	48.223	40.932	48.493	24.664	27.600	24.191	28.069	47.771
Electric and electronic engineering	20.852	24.550	24.383	25.777	27.041	27.999	28.301	26.629	29.463
Manufacture of motor vehicles	19.621	19.977	21.898	20.700	24.551	25.060	35.405	24.621	29.413
Other transport equipment	22.054	21.985	21.314	22.218	21.408	19.908	28.260	29.625	25.133
Instrument making	21.164	24.978	21.819	22.109	23.634	23.572	27.140	27.963	21.024
Other manufacturing industries	18.712	19.293	21.391	21.935	23.065	23.756	27.123	30.601	29.017
Food	21.808	25.929	25.654	24.392	22.564	21.659	23.662	38.722	28.557
Drink and tobacco	30.933	34.140	29.191	29.699	34.758	31.899	34.511	25.481	27.262
Textiles	19.728	20.939	25.075	25.707	24.197	25.085	25.817	–	24.885
Manufacture of leather	19.408	21.417	22.721	23.462	25.500	24.078	21.442	20.159	–
Leather goods	13.543	12.682	15.231	15.887	20.514	17.893	23.451	24.022	20.572
Timber and wooden furniture	17.190	17.597	18.819	19.114	27.586	23.923	21.975	34.506	–
Paper, printing and publishing	23.648	24.100	23.958	25.519	25.707	27.168	33.803	27.003	37.131
Rubber and plastics	22.959	23.526	25.080	24.691	24.937	27.193	28.972	26.035	24.921
Other manufacturing	18.419	21.618	22.287	21.928		17.407	19.981		24.773
Total	20.322	20.790	22.557	23.260	24.848	25.820	28.790	28.731	29.076

Table A4.11 1985 GNP survey: hourly gross pay per worker (thousand lire)

Divisions and classes	10–14	15–19	20–29	30–49	50–99	100–199	200–499	500–999	1,000 and over
Extraction and manufacture of minerals other than fuels, chemicals	7.913	8.150	8.936	9.278	10.034	10.869	11.571	11.465	12.294
Extraction and preparation of metalliferous ores	8.598	8.860	9.769	10.089	10.734	11.066	11.418	11.397	12.495
Extraction of minerals not elsewhere specified	8.393	8.463	9.565	9.358	9.902	10.143	17.074	10.863	11.502
Non-metallic mineral products	7.571	7.993	8.540	8.923	9.669	10.304	10.844	10.920	10.715
Chemical industry	8.285	8.210	9.648	9.964	10.574	11.968	12.176	12.018	12.659
Man-made fibres	7.503	8.943	11.115	8.860	9.667	11.398	11.895	11.142	12.768
Metal goods, engineering and vehicles	7.887	7.976	9.163	9.375	9.891	10.465	10.850	10.918	11.442
Metal goods not elsewhere specified	7.768	7.747	9.032	9.233	9.762	10.363	10.958	11.090	11.874
Mechanical engineering	8.349	8.350	9.369	9.652	10.239	10.527	10.781	11.143	11.335
Office machinery and data processing equipment	8.129	8.171	9.817	10.413	9.350	10.049	11.554	10.359	10.929
Electric and electronic engineering	7.678	8.328	9.142	9.386	9.608	10.613	11.069	10.627	11.375
Manufacture of motor vehicles	7.704	7.131	9.026	8.881	10.005	10.373	10.289	10.670	11.289
Other transport equipment	7.833	7.791	9.118	9.321	9.883	11.311	10.586	11.393	11.914
Instrument making	7.649	7.802	9.250	8.928	9.083	9.455	10.439	10.181	10.413
Other manufacturing industries	7.050	7.124	8.189	8.400	8.929	9.494	10.010	10.789	11.899
Food	8.088	8.449	9.051	9.217	9.701	9.816	10.139	11.582	11.755
Drink and tobacco	8.059	8.807	9.710	9.542	10.094	10.320	10.502	11.665	12.378
Textiles	7.052	7.517	8.589	8.680	8.833	9.310	9.750	9.962	9.999
Manufacture of leather	6.906	7.070	8.023	8.133	9.368	9.266	10.319	–	–
Leather goods	6.226	6.092	7.235	7.380	7.930	8.248	8.676	9.382	9.337
Timber and wooden furniture	7.042	7.054	7.950	8.307	8.721	9.404	9.501	10.679	–
Paper, printing and publishing	7.865	8.240	8.856	9.210	10.160	11.183	12.401	12.807	13.525
Rubber and plastics	7.806	7.451	8.643	8.893	9.485	10.337	10.722	11.538	11.699
Other manufacturing	8.523	7.434	8.471	8.770	9.457	10.930	9.216	9.225	14.852
Total	7.391	7.490	8.583	8.820	9.397	10.031	10.602	11.006	11.746

Table A4.12 1985 GNP survey: gross profits (%)

Divisions and classes	Size classes								
	10–14	15–19	20–29	30–49	50–99	100–199	200–499	500–999	1,000 and over
Extraction and manufacture of minerals other than fuels, chemicals	45.630	46.501	42.642	42.559	43.305	42.634	42.879	40.055	26.990
Extraction and preparation of metalliferous ores	50.113	47.772	50.352	49.567	51.345	48.665	41.932	40.674	8.660
Extraction of minerals not elsewhere specified	44.039	52.811	45.390	44.057	38.492	31.460	-0.161	4.649	-20.420
Non-metallic mineral products	40.982	43.004	36.395	34.905	35.294	36.509	42.639	41.705	30.516
Chemical industry	55.097	51.292	50.588	50.951	49.607	46.879	43.557	39.474	39.668
Man-made fibres	53.451	-20.507	54.101	49.832	45.165	13.260	59.472	29.056	41.402
Metal goods, engineering and vehicles	35.878	37.101	35.703	36.842	36.352	32.848	32.665	30.313	32.015
Metal goods not elsewhere specified	35.720	36.299	35.516	36.252	35.188	31.230	26.619	30.325	25.536
Mechanical engineering	37.406	35.114	35.933	36.884	36.305	33.391	34.113	24.781	33.473
Office machinery and data processing equipment	44.522	62.398	59.045	59.992	33.809	44.928	34.631	38.714	52.249
Electric and electronic engineering	34.000	39.775	37.521	39.525	40.916	36.308	33.725	33.289	30.286
Manufacture of motor vehicles	32.692	39.468	34.074	32.147	33.794	33.984	33.130	31.325	34.346
Other transport equipment	38.882	41.174	28.347	32.146	27.085	7.156	38.943	28.202	19.155
Instrument making	37.333	45.079	31.482	35.555	37.595	30.366	32.710	37.694	13.004
Other manufacturing industries	35.077	38.340	39.640	39.923	38.358	35.671	37.836	34.127	31.150
Food	35.867	44.804	44.872	41.476	33.006	29.565	30.606	35.549	31.085
Drink and tobacco	53.280	55.719	45.173	47.138	50.483	44.957	46.062	43.634	30.430
Textiles	39.825	41.693	45.965	46.959	42.822	41.500	39.763	37.209	32.582
Manufacture of leather	38.441	46.298	45.845	46.469	43.358	41.799	24.368	–	42.209
Leather goods	25.956	24.615	29.257	30.933	32.642	30.921	40.485	27.205	23.649
Timber and wooden furniture	29.884	32.818	32.650	32.187	32.758	35.219	28.311	22.081	–
Paper, printing and publishing	40.646	40.926	40.088	41.342	38.374	38.511	34.514	34.383	36.066
Rubber and plastics	40.785	46.369	45.997	43.515	40.823	39.516	37.897	30.048	22.297
Other manufacturing	29.189	43.218	38.995	36.332	38.403	0.141	26.351	36.009	27.125
Total	36.548	38.946	38.743	39.237	38.415	35.973	37.123	34.496	30.615

Table A4.13 1985 GNP survey: ratio between subcontracting and value added

Divisions and classes	Size classes								
	10–14	15–19	20–29	30–49	50–99	100–199	200–499	500–999	1,000 and over
Extraction and manufacture of minerals other than fuels, chemicals	6.659	8.274	6.602	7.196	9.129	9.063	5.954	15.526	5.680
Extraction and preparation of metalliferous ores	11.455	13.362	26.413	22.987	32.659	17.645	21.658	23.484	11.233
Extraction of minerals not elsewhere specified	3.638	1.400	0.723	0.560	0.070	7.016	2.134	0.016	-
Non-metallic mineral products	7.936	5.520	3.800	4.424	2.943	1.629	2.283	20.306	3.571
Chemical industry	4.088	17.720	6.769	6.261	6.390	12.678	2.826	12.214	0.043
Man-made fibres	-	-	0.677	2.801	1.678	-	-	-	-
Metal goods, engineering and vehicles	23.157	17.753	15.260	14.750	10.841	6.362	7.438	4.203	3.800
Metal goods not elsewhere specified	31.584	26.773	21.192	22.290	18.081	7.893	10.201	5.778	4.727
Mechanical engineering	13.446	9.509	8.032	7.343	5.347	3.887	3.440	3.814	5.753
Office machinery and data processing equipment	14.582	1.526	-	-	31.386	-	2.601	-	0.202
Electric and electronic engineering	14.023	12.306	15.681	12.749	7.727	8.869	9.096	4.629	4.803
Manufacture of motor vehicles	29.175	9.444	17.333	23.388	10.982	5.692	2.389	1.975	1.641
Other transport equipment	27.779	17.289	15.360	31.882	12.749	13.984	15.260	2.871	6.040
Instrument making	11.315	12.411	14.277	7.417	9.773	4.418	7.015	5.205	2.765
Other manufacturing industries	25.810	25.043	21.636	19.776	22.240	14.965	11.469	11.592	5.621
Food	2.790	2.130	5.022	7.173	6.894	7.904	3.774	2.177	0.041
Drink and tobacco	4.858	1.957	3.488	1.493	13.124	2.040	3.043	1.637	0.014
Textiles	61.815	51.241	48.119	47.349	48.967	33.327	21.455	31.371	1.658
Manufacture of leather	38.296	31.921	35.381	15.156	25.889	7.282	24.820	-	-
Leather goods	40.703	49.954	-	26.780	22.100	20.588	11.569	9.460	0.128
Timber and wooden furniture	4.826	4.674	3.984	3.976	3.959	0.204	0.732	0.084	-
Paper, printing and publishing	10.116	12.191	14.164	8.972	22.845	11.315	18.266	9.915	16.779
Rubber and plastics	14.325	3.844	6.052	5.390	4.375	1.166	1.845	9.045	-
Other manufacturing	24.771	25.446	32.934	20.621	32.063	34.867	-	30.459	-
Total	22.549	20.389	17.280	16.139	15.930	10.672	8.662	10.044	4.601

Table A4.14 1985 GNP survey: ratio between subcontracting work and production costs

Divisions and classes	Size classes								
	10–14	15–19	20–29	30–49	50–99	100–199	200–499	500–999	1,000 and over
Extraction and manufacture of minerals other than fuels, chemicals	3.276	5.461	6.579	5.563	5.633	5.652	4.446	4.973	8.455
Extraction and preparation of metalliferous ores	2.452	4.596	4.278	4.179	3.698	3.184	3.992	4.773	9.563
Extraction of minerals not elsewhere specified	7.027	7.032	16.716	15.131	13.851	9.153	14.204	23.410	24.720
Non-metallic mineral products	4.621	7.991	9.547	9.073	9.087	11.574	9.589	10.485	7.912
Chemical industry	0.934	1.867	3.034	2.664	4.800	3.792	3.044	3.756	7.423
Man-made fibres	–	1.145	1.663	5.786	3.426	2.074	10.240	9.128	7.717
Metal goods, engineering and vehicles	12.387	12.891	12.649	13.733	14.794	12.678	11.045	13.401	8.653
Metal goods not elsewhere specified	10.663	14.475	12.823	14.515	15.710	13.227	13.089	22.897	15.672
Mechanical engineering	15.803	12.574	13.151	13.853	13.839	12.338	10.481	11.012	12.940
Office machinery and data processing equipment	6.237	6.752	1.935	11.809	14.907	33.122	4.617	3.000	6.478
Electric and electronic engineering	12.004	11.522	12.180	11.326	13.150	10.402	11.165	11.007	8.192
Manufacture of motor vehicles	9.658	7.430	8.447	13.532	13.374	11.994	7.877	18.567	3.629
Other transport equipment	16.226	12.139	16.636	21.402	29.288	34.045	11.499	10.008	22.375
Instrument making	15.271	14.478	10.700	11.030	18.013	10.183	12.132	17.716	6.510
Other manufacturing industries	11.247	11.427	11.370	11.188	11.726	10.799	11.757	10.525	7.566
Food	0.540	0.606	1.377	1.692	1.973	1.654	2.396	2.854	2.357
Drink and tobacco	0.746	0.215	2.185	1.535	2.485	1.847	5.372	3.310	3.825
Textiles	26.946	27.752	29.194	27.828	23.780	23.344	17.155	25.660	15.913
Manufacture of leather	13.576	11.924	10.123	8.810	8.565	11.023	6.625	–	13.699
Leather goods	21.049	26.737	20.583	20.948	22.012	23.668	25.996	22.921	13.704
Timber and wooden furniture	5.559	5.850	7.646	8.134	6.652	6.707	8.243	5.879	–
Paper, printing and publishing	10.824	11.336	16.240	12.814	19.047	19.692	17.436	11.291	15.786
Rubber and plastics	6.293	7.668	6.535	7.118	6.684	8.212	6.189	5.745	2.237
Other manufacturing	8.312	11.620	9.719	6.259	7.244	2.898	6.810	6.422	–
Total	10.565	11.031	10.988	10.955	11.442	10.281	9.391	9.348	8.381

Table A4.15 1985 GNP survey: exports as % of total production

Divisions and classes	Size classes							Total
	20–29	30–49	50–99	100–199	200–499	500–999	1,000 and over	
Extraction and manufacture of minerals other than fuels, chemicals	13.808	13.993	19.154	20.054	22.729	24.209	23.710	21.735
Extraction and preparation of metalliferous ores	8.650	13.440	17.250	16.231	24.961	25.756	23.581	21.903
Extraction of minerals not elsewhere specified	6.049	10.076	7.737	21.590	33.662	–	5.665	12.006
Non-metallic mineral products	17.455	16.583	22.889	22.049	20.537	17.335	16.253	19.319
Chemical industry	13.549	11.764	18.253	20.537	20.549	25.533	21.847	21.034
Man-made fibres	40.744	38.261	41.917	63.749	59.544	31.797	50.534	50.914
Metal goods, engineering and vehicles	21.461	24.824	28.866	32.599	33.567	35.663	37.605	33.380
Metal goods not elsewhere specified	13.674	16.606	21.225	23.070	28.946	28.876	24.141	21.796
Mechanical engineering	30.020	33.495	39.555	46.433	46.426	50.215	58.674	46.127
Office machinery and data processing equipment	6.740	4.198	10.819	46.036	29.892	3.322	54.617	51.425
Electric and electronic engineering	19.701	20.414	22.893	22.664	25.353	38.097	32.407	28.898
Manufacture of motor vehicles	27.973	24.192	27.488	24.381	19.722	15.157	28.393	27.243
Other transport equipment	39.509	36.115	20.194	26.444	21.686	12.876	37.781	32.432
Instrument making	22.129	33.288	34.869	36.645	53.837	38.999	20.500	36.520
Other manufacturing industries	19.488	20.550	21.911	22.501	21.669	18.198	11.493	19.512
Food	6.263	6.961	10.542	12.968	10.199	10.434	6.747	9.337
Drink and tobacco	9.715	9.663	9.545	5.563	10.786	11.049	2.745	6.571
Textiles	27.730	27.677	25.450	28.952	27.289	22.125	29.675	27.196
Manufacture of leather	27.278	30.571	33.893	44.896	24.674	–	88.295	34.747
Leather goods	33.944	39.506	38.347	37.227	32.457	34.325	33.287	36.086
Timber and wooden furniture	17.350	18.596	18.456	20.463	32.847	19.202	–	19.942
Paper, printing and publishing	6.592	7.030	6.537	9.529	14.996	11.200	12.633	10.720
Rubber and plastics	17.726	19.465	26.620	36.034	38.356	31.094	31.530	29.439
Other manufacturing	52.121	38.349	46.595	24.815	39.659	28.360	23.690	37.537
Total	19.183	20.724	23.540	24.997	25.535	25.614	27.446	24.855

Table A4.16 1985 GNP survey: exporting and non-exporting firms (absolute values)

Divisions and classes	Size classes 20–29	30–49	50–99	100–199	200–499	500–999	1,000 and over	Total
Exporting firms								
Extraction of minerals, manufacture of metals, mineral products, and chemicals	629	669	571	353	222	85	85	2,614
– of which, chemicals	162	174	187	135	103	44	34	839
Manufacture of metal goods	1,903	2,018	1,713	946	489	135	159	7,363
– of which, mechanical engineering	773	876	677	392	162	41	47	2,968
Food, textiles, leather, wood, etc.	3,012	3,000	2,266	1,192	517	113	70	10,170
– of which, footwear and clothing	793	825	615	292	109	27	6	2,667
– miscellaneous manufacturing	170	153	97	35	16	3	1	475
Non-exporting firms								
Extraction of minerals, manufacture of metals, metal products and chemicals	638	487	252	121	44	15	9	1,566
– of which, chemicals	86	72	30	30	13	3	2	236
Manufacture of metal goods	1,168	847	447	166	86	32	15	2,761
– of which, mechanical engineering	227	140	78	22	7	9	2	485
Food, textiles, leather, wood, etc.	2,417	1,785	873	295	107	22	14	5,513
– of which, footwear and clothing	657	412	183	57	18	4	–	1,331
– miscellaneous manufacturing	44	38	13	3	1	–	–	99

Table A4.17 1985 GNP survey: value added per employee (million lire)

Divisions and classes	Size classes							Total
	20–29	30–49	50–99	100–199	200–499	500–999	1,000 and over	
Exporting firms								
Extraction of minerals, manufacture of metals, mineral products, and chemicals	41.4	46.3	52.6	53.8	57.4	52.9	43.9	49.0
– of which, chemicals	59.9	63.6	65.3	63.2	65.2	60.0	56.2	60.3
Manufacture of metal goods	41.4	42.5	44.2	43.1	43.1	40.7	42.3	42.6
– of which, mechanical engineering	43.0	44.5	45.6	45.4	46.3	40.0	45.5	44.9
Food, textiles, leather, wood, etc.	32.7	37.9	38.4	38.5	42.8	41.5	40.0	40.1
– of which, footwear and clothing	26.9	27.1	29.6	28.1	37.0	29.1	32.5	30.0
– miscellaneous manufacturing	34.9	34.7	38.6	24.0	29.0	28.6	52.7	32.9
Non-exporting firms								
Extraction of minerals, manufacture of metals, metal products and chemicals	41.2	42.2	40.9	44.8	54.4	47.8	34.1	43.4
– of which, chemicals	56.6	57.4	54.1	47.5	63.1	26.7	69.8	54.7
Manufacture of metal goods	35.7	36.7	37.4	34.7	29.7	37.89	35.9	35.3
– of which, mechanical engineering	36.4	36.5	40.3	37.7	33.5	31.0	41.6	36.9
Food, textiles, leather, wood, etc.	31.4	32.5	36.4	36.3	41.8	38.8	51.8	36.5
– of which, footwear and clothing	18.7	19.0	20.9	21.8	27.3	21.0	–	20.5
– miscellaneous manufacturing	32.7	35.2	30.9	33.0	32.0	–	–	33.2

Chapter 3

A model of the small firm in Italy

Ash Amin

Italy
6110

111 - 22

The recent revival of small firms in the OECD countries has been characterized by very different forms of growth. For instance, areas in the United States such as Boston have experienced an economic revitalization led by the growth of high-tech industry, generating new employment in small businesses outside manufacturing. In some of the large cities in the UK experiencing deindustrialization (e.g. Birmingham), the growth of small firms has been a response to mass unemployment, as well as the effect of large firms putting out peripheral production tasks.

The phenomenon characterizing central and north-eastern Italy is altogether different. The model chosen for this exposition might be termed the Bologna model, since it typifies the kind of small-firm economy in and around Bologna and other areas of Emilia. But it is in some ways an 'ideal type'. Other kinds of small business exist in Italy.

The Bologna model is an example of a development in Italy which must be almost unique in the advanced industrial economies, in that certain areas of the country have been able to achieve relatively high growth rates in manufacturing – by value and in employment terms – through the production by small firms of so-called low-tech goods (e.g. specialized light engineering, shoes, clothing, furniture, musical instruments, jewellery). That such firms can continue not only to survive, but actually grow in recessionary times, in mature product markets dominated (at least in the case of the UK) by large corporations which are fiercely competing against each other and against cheaper imports from Third World countries, comes as quite a challenge to analysts of small-firm competitiveness.

One of the striking features of Italy is the existence of a number of types of small firms, reflecting the enormous difference between the social and economic structures of the various regions. For instance, in the south, there is still, owing to the lack of stable waged employment opportunities, a noticeable presence of artisans

111

and small firms which manage to survive because of local demand for their goods and because of their ability to reduce costs through tax avoidance and minimum unit labour costs.[1] Often they are not registered, as required by law.

However the south has also seen the development of small and medium-sized firms stimulated by the wave, between 1969 and 1974, of private and public sector investment from the north, in industries such as motor vehicles, mechanical engineering, and electronics.[2] The growth of this type of small firm has also been helped by regional policy and other small incentives.[3]

Yet another type of small firm development in Italy which resembles but is much more extensive than that in the UK, is the use of subcontracting by large firms, in Piedmont and Lombardy, as a means of reducing direct labour costs and risks and rendering the production process more flexible. There are a number of different forms of this type of subcontracting in Italy, ranging from the putting-out of various production tasks to already existing small firms and domestic outworkers, to the giving of incentives to workers at different levels of the large firm's hierarchy to become entrepreneurs.

What is most interesting about the small firms in the model I have chosen is that they do not conform to the assumptions made, notably by external observers, about small firm formation in Italy being related to the decentralization of production by large firms, or the existence of market niches which do not interest large firms because of insufficient or unstable demand, or the ready availability of a cheap and flexible workforce drawn from Italy's large secondary labour market. The small firms in the central and north-eastern regions (Trentino-Alto Adige, Veneto, Friuli, Emilia-Romagna, Tuscany, Umbria, and Marche) are not in general subcontractors for large firms, nor is their price competitiveness owed to a single factor such as low wages or the intensive exploitation of labour. However, it must be stated that many now flourishing independent firms actually started off as subcontractors.

Schiattarella demonstrates that the strength of small firms in Italy as a whole during the 1970s had more to do with increases in productivity than with the ability of firms to rely upon a 'deregulated' labour market. First, he shows that while the share of national output by firms employing between twenty and 100 workers rose from 31 per cent in 1972 to 34 per cent in 1980, in the group of traditional sectors featuring a high level of small-firm activity (textiles, clothing, shoes, leather and fur goods), their share of employment actually dropped marginally from 36.1 per cent in 1972 to 35.8 per cent in 1979. Labour productivity among these small firms in 1972 was only marginally lower than that within firms employing more than 500 workers and rose at the same time within both groups during the 1970s. Interestingly, however, productivity remains comparable between the two groups at a time when, owing to higher wage increases among the smaller firms, the differential in the cost of labour between the two is virtually halved from about 40 per cent to 20 per cent in 1980. The competitiveness of these small firms therefore does not appear to derive from low wages.[4]

It could of course derive from a higher level of labour utilization, although this does not appear to be confirmed by the evidence on the rates of investment within the two size groups in the sectors mentioned above. The level of per capita investment in tools and machinery among the small firms grew by 59 per cent between 1968 and 1973 and rose dramatically by 169 per cent between 1973 and 1978, whereas among the large firms it grew by 91 per cent in the first period and only by 64 per cent in the second – recessionary – period. Thus, while in 1972 the fixed-investment-per-employee ratio in the small firms was 3 per cent lower than the ratio for the large firms, by 1980 it was actually 16 per cent higher. This evidence, in contrast to the traditional view, suggests that the basis for Italian small firm competitiveness during the 1970s is modernization and new investment. Given the enormous variation that exists between small firms, this observation, drawn from aggregate data, is of course no substitute for detailed analysis, but it does nevertheless raise certain doubts about small firm survival in the traditional 'low-tech' industries being solely a function of low wages and a deregulated labour market.

The model

The small firms in the central and north-eastern regions of Italy are a visible expression of the novel form of growth in traditional industries described above. In 1951 agriculture was the principal source of employment in the seven regions in question, but by 1971 manufacturing industry had become the principal source. In the course of the 1970s industrial output in all these regions grew at a higher rate than the national average, well above that of Piedmont, Italy's oldest and most industrialized region.[5] In 1971, 37 per cent of the firms and 35 per cent of the employment in Italian secondary manufacturing industry (i.e. excluding energy, mining, chemicals, and construction) was located in these regions, rising respectively to 42 and 38 per cent by 1981. While the stock of firms and employment at national level in secondary manufacturing grew respectively by 22 and 15 per cent during the 1970s, their increase in the seven regions was 38 and 28 per cent respectively.

Both in 1971 and in 1981, over 70 per cent of the manufacturing firms in these regions were in the low 'value-added' and 'traditional' sectors such as food, textiles, clothing, shoes, leather goods, furniture, paper, jewellery, musical instruments, and toys. Nationally, the number of firms and employment in these traditional sectors (taken as a whole) grew respectively by 13 and 8 per cent, while the rate of increase in these seven regions was significantly higher – 32 and 21 per cent respectively. The majority of the firms in each region (75 per cent in Emilia-Romagna and 85 per cent in Tuscany) are tiny, employing less than ten workers; and between 60 and 70 per cent of total secondary manufacturing employment in each region occurs in firms employing less than 100 workers.

These are startling results confirming that the regions in Italy with the highest growth rates are those dominated by a myriad of very small firms producing traditional-sector consumer goods. Moreover, the goods are highly competitive in international markets: the share of these products (excluding the food industry) in Italy's export of manufacturing rose from 20.5 per cent in 1968 to 27.7 per cent in 1977. Perhaps even more interesting is the fact that this growth phenomenon covers about a third of the national territory and has occurred in regions which were scarcely industrialized thirty years ago. Clearly not all of the regions have developed along the same lines and not at the same pace, but there are nevertheless three characteristics which have produced a reasonably homogeneous form of small-firm development. These characteristics, one exogenous and the other two endogenous, in combination isolate the essence of this model.

Fluctuating markets

The first factor relates to the nature of the market niche for the commodities which is such that it requires and permits small-scale production. The goods which are produced in central and north-eastern Italy are of medium-to-high quality, often trading on a brand name or even the 'Made in Italy' label, which conjures up various images of style or craftsmanship. They are not the cheap, mass-produced and standardized goods which usually characterize the traditional consumer industries. On this point it is interesting to observe that Italy's exports in these industries to the OECD countries remained quite stable during the 1970s despite the onslaught by much cheaper products from the less-developed countries (LDCs).[6] For example, between 1968–9 and 1977, the share of the LDCs in OECD imports grew from 22.6 to 29.5 per cent for leather and skin goods, 28.7 to 35.9 per cent for wood manufacturers, 13.7 to 17.0 per cent for textiles, 25.6 to 42.8 per cent for clothing, 21.0 to 45.1 per cent for travel goods and 9.8 to 29.4 per cent for footwear. In the same period, Italy's share in the respective industries changed from 7.7 to 11.4 per cent (leather), 15.1 to 19.1 (wood), 9.1 to 9.3 per cent (textiles), 17.9 to 12.6 per cent (clothing), 18.5 to 23.5 per cent (travel), 42.4 to 36.1 per cent (footwear). The stability of Italian exports without doubt reflects the shift towards the higher-quality end of the product market by the Italian producers.

The first advantage drawn by the small firms selling in the upper tiers of the market is that because the demand for the product depends less on its price than its quality, the competitiveness of the firms is not entirely determined by their ability to minimize unit costs. Under these circumstances small firms with production costs that are marginally higher than those of large firms able to exploit scale economies, can nevertheless continue to compete in the market. Of course, competition on the basis of price is not eliminated, and in fact the maintenance by the Italian authorities of an undervalued lira throughout the 1970s gave the small firms in question a significant price-competitive advantage in export markets. The second advantage which the small firms possess in the market is their ability to meet demand for non-standardized goods: a demand which is erratic and subject to major seasonal fluctuations. This ability derives from possessing shorter production runs which can cope with short-term demand. But the firms in the Italian model also possess, as we shall see below, a unique production structure which is highly sensitive to the peculiarities of the market.

Flexible production and the division of labour between firms

The second condition which explains the economic buoyancy of the small firms in central and north-eastern Italy concerns the organization of production on a highly flexible basis. Since the 1970s, large-factory production, organized along the Fordist lines of continuous flow and mass integrated production, and along the Taylorist principles of scientific management, has undergone a series of transformations towards achieving more flexibility in the use of labour and machinery. The search by large firms for new economies in production through rationalization, the introduction of numerically controlled machinery, changes in the internal division of labour (e.g. the putting-out of certain tasks to independent subcontractors and in-house specialization of other tasks), and changes in the external division of labour (e.g. just-on-time delivery of supplies), have dramatically altered the face of manufacturing industry. In simple terms, this reorganization of the labour process has sought to eliminate the rigidities of large-scale production which includes restrictive labour practices, management and organizational diseconomies of scale, stockpiling in the event of demand fluctuations, and mismatches in the time and flow of goods between different phases of the production process.

The economies in production achieved by the small firms in the central and north-eastern regions closely resemble those related to new forms of flexible production within the large firms. While many of the small firms may originally have begun as subcontractors because of the vertical disintegration of production among the large firms, now, owing to the evolution and consolidation of a particular industrial structure in the individual areas, they trade with other local small firms and small merchants. It is this latter development which has made possible the emergence of a form of flexible production which is different from and not tied to the new experiments taking place within large industry.

The distinctive feature of the industrial districts which have developed around the provincial towns of central and north-eastern Italy is that each one specializes in the production of a particular commodity.[7] The real strength of the areas, however, derives from the way in which production is organized within and between the small firms. Clusters of small firms are productively integrated with each other on a subcontracting basis. Strategic entrepreneurs, usually merchants or small businessmen from the provincial cities, purchase the finished goods on a contractual basis from a number of small firms which in turn subcontract to several smaller family firms and domestic outworkers.

This system of complex subcontracting allows costs and risks to be spread out between a number of firms, but it also allows production to be based upon short-term contracts which can be rapidly adjusted to market requirements by switching between subcontractors when a particular type of good is required or by raising or reducing subcontracting when the level of demand fluctuates.

The producers themselves vary in the degree of autonomy they possess *vis-à-vis* the subcontracting firms. Very often the domestic outworkers and the small family units carrying out deskilled production tasks are caught in the clutches of one or two buyers, while firms specializing in certain skilled operations will tend to attract many more customers. However, common to all the producers is the lack of any real contact with the market mechanism: the purchase and sale of goods does not occur through the free market but through a series of direct contracts, between the buyer and the seller. The replacement of formal ties with the market by reciprocal arrangements introduces a measure of flexibility (quite often forced)

116

in the exchange relations between the entrepreneurs which the market would not normally permit. Direct negotiations on issues related to prices, delivery, payment, credit and even the cost of materials and technologies, ensure, through the principle of reciprocal benefits, the survival of both parties entering into the contract. The flow of goods and information between the economic actors occurs outside the open market.

The division of the full production cycle required to make a product into its constituent parts and their separation between producers, has generated new economies, reflected in the final price of the finished goods. First, it eliminates many of the bottlenecks and inelasticities associated with the fully integrated production process in which the production times and the flow of the line in the different stages of production must always be in consonance with each other. The fragmentation of the labour process into separate units allows each one to set its own pace of work and its own level of output, and in synchrony with the immediate market rather than with another phase in the production process. Fragmentation does of course require the efficient circulation of goods and information between the producers. In the Italian industrial district this is guaranteed by geographical proximity between the firms as well as the frequent use of microcomputers to communicate information sometimes even to domestic out-workers.

Built into this system of production, there is also an enormous pressure to reduce costs. In the case of a large firm deciding to fragment its production process, the firm continues to maintain control over and co-ordinate the separate stages in production: the exchange of parts between the different stages is not governed by the laws of the market. In the case which we are examining, there is no overall co-ordinating body and the production of the finished commodity takes place on the basis of competitive exchange relations between separate entrepreneurs. What may have once been the different parts of one production process are now separate commodities bought and sold on the basis of contractual agreements and competition between separate owners. Each firm therefore seeks to minimize costs either through the use of the most appropriate production technologies (e.g. multi-purpose tools and machinery which can be put to a number of different uses), or through the depression of wage costs and the flexible use of labour (especially within the rural firms and family units at the lower end of the production hierarchy). There is, however, also an important technical factor related to fragmentation which has facilitated the lowering of unit prices. The small firms, through production specialization and contracts with a number of clients, can achieve scale economies which other small firms cannot normally achieve.

117

The most interesting feature of small firm competitiveness in this Italian model is the limited relevance of an explanation based upon the peculiarities of the individual firm, such as the way in which labour is recruited, used and remunerated, or the form of the technologies adapted, or the marketing skills of the entrepreneurs. It would be misguided to give emphasis to the economic and social organization of production within the individual firms. This is because the firms are not free operators in a free market but one part of a complex and integrated system of production, deriving their strength from the economies and the stability achieved by the system as a whole. We are not talking about independent small firms in the traditional sense, nor about subcontractors for large firms, but about the development of an industrial system (almost a corporation) composed of inter-linked but independently owned production units. The uniqueness of the industrial districts derives more from the economics of the vertical disintegration of the production process resulting in a new set of inter-firm relationships, than from the small firms themselves.[8]

Uniqueness of place

The third factor which explains this form of small firm development concerns the nature of the local, social, and institutional traditions which have enabled the growth of the industrial systems. These are traditions which are unique and cannot be reproduced elsewhere. This second endogenous factor is related to the establishment of a peculiar but dynamic rapport between the modern market town and the once agricultural countryside.[9]

The producers are located in the rural areas which surround the provincial towns of the central and north-eastern regions of Italy. These are areas with a long-standing tradition of peasant farming. The origins of the new industrial entrepreneurship are to be found in the dynamics of a recent agricultural history in which a large number of small peasant households were farming not only for subsistence but also producing cash crops for the market. They are areas embracing an entrepreneurial and not a proletarian culture, and accustomed to market transactions. This is the ready mechanism which has generated the new entrepreneurship which in its social organization of production is virtually identical to the old: family units (which may even hire-in or hire-out labour) capable of working flexible hours, of saving by reducing wage costs and family expenditure, of coping with fluctuations in demand for the product because of income derived from other interests, and of entering into market transactions. In other words, it is the unique social structure of these areas which has produced this kind of small-firm development. Of course, the transition from peasants to artisans is not simple, especially in the formation of the appropriate skills. Brusco has in fact noted that the specialization of an industrial district in a particular trade originates in most cases from the presence, at some point in time, of a large firm in the same product sector, which enabled the diffusion of skills in the area through its workforce and also acted as a seed-bed for the development of specialist supply firms.[10]

The producers in the countryside have limited marketing outlets of their own, and this is where the towns have played a crucial role. The 'strategic' entrepreneurs of the city are not just the merchants who buy the goods from the direct producers, but like the middle-men of pre-capitalist economies, they constitute the main bridge between town and country, between production and distribution. These individuals co-ordinate production in the small units by supplying them with information on market trends and also orders from the larger merchandising houses. But as merchants from towns which have for centuries been independent trading and financial centres, they are also responsible for marketing the product to an international audience at the frequently held trade fairs.

In the 1980s each industrial district, in symbolizing a single trade, has come to assume a corporate identity which facilitates the reproduction of the system. This is not only because it provides a series of structures and functions suited to local industrial requirements, such as the specialized production goods, machinery, and skills. It also, through product specialization, offers a host of producer, marketing, and financial services which facilitate the survival of the small firms.

Conclusion

In the Italian model there appears to have been a widespread flowering of entrepreneurship, in the sense of a large number of new firms being born, but remaining small. However, the real strength of the model is that it is a production system controlled by relatively few merchants in the major towns and cities of central and north-eastern Italy. It is the merchants who have determined the products of this system as well as their penetration potential into quality-based export markets. Furthermore, the model's economic power lies in it approximating, as it were, to a corporation with its labour divided between many spontaneous centres of production, whose relationship with each other is nevertheless competitive – a corporation without a roof. The single elements of the system flourish as a result of their interdependence; not because any one of them, however competent, is capable of playing on the stage alone.

Acknowledgements

This chapter is based on a longer article, 'Small firms and the process of economic development: explanation and illustration from Britain, Italy and the United States', by A. Amin, S. Johnson and D. Storey, Centre for Urban and Regional Development Studies, University of Newcastle upon Tyne, 1986.

Notes

1. A. Del Monte and A. Giannola, *Il Mezzogiorno nell'Economia Italiana*, Bologna: Il Mulino. A. Graziani, E. Pugliese (eds) *Investimenti E Disoccupazione nel Mezzogiorno*, Bologna: Il Mulino, 1979.
2. A. Del Monte and M. Raffa (eds) *Tecnologia e Decentramento Produttivo*, Turin: Rosenberg and Sellier, 1977.
3. A. Del Monte, 'The effects of regional policy on the industrial development of the south of Italy', *Mezzogiorno d'Europa* 4 (1984): 563–83.
4. R. Schiattarella, *Mercato del lavoro e Struttura Produttiva*, Milan: Franco Angeli, 1984.
5. As we are concerned to explain the current situation, which is to some extent an ideal type, the analysis underplays the importance of chance and dynamism among the small firms, for instance the move away from subcontracting for large firms during the 1960s and to different forms of market penetration in the 1970s.
6. F. Onida, 'Italian exports and industrial structure in the 1970s', *Banco di Roma: Review of Economic Conditions in Italy*, February 1980.
7. S. Brusco, 'Small firms and industrial districts', mimeo, University of Modena, 1985.
8. A. Giannola, 'Il rapporto fra imprese, analisi del dibattito teorico e risultati di una ricerca empirica: dal decentramento ad un nuovo modello di relazioni interindustriali', in *Grande Impresa e Artigianato*, Milan: Franco Angeli, 1985.
9. A. Bagnasco, 'La costruzione sociale del mercato: strategie di impresa e esperimenti di scala in Italia', *Stato e Mercato* 13 (1985): 9–45.
10. Brusco op. cit.

Appendix 5

Emilia-Romagna is often seen as a paradigm of the small firm economy, and the following is a note giving the basic facts on manufacturing industry in the region. It has been supplied by Dr Enrico Giovannetti of the University of Modena and by Dr Adriana Zini of ERVET, to whom grateful acknowledgements are due.

Emilia-Romagna has a high level of industrialization, particularly in the three central provinces of Bologna, Modena, and Reggio-Emilia, but its salient feature is the very large number of production units in manufacturing: more than 67,000 in a region with fewer than 4 million inhabitants. In other words, there is a firm for every sixty inhabitants, compared with an average of one for ninety in Italy as a whole. Most of the establishments are extremely small: only 2 per cent of firms have more than fifty employees while 58,000 do not have as many as ten. Moreover, the range of products is very diverse. The existence of sectors of industry usually considered traditional (clothing, ceramics, furniture, food) alongside more modern sectors (machine tools and electronic equipment) demonstrates great industrial flexibility.

The engineering industry accounts for 42 per cent of manufacturing employment in the region, and its largest segment is the manufacture of machines (including agricultural machinery, machine tools, precision instruments, and electronic equipment). Textiles, clothing, food, leather, furniture, rubber, and plastics account for another 42 per cent, with ceramics, glass, chemicals, and construction materials making up the remaining 16 per cent. Analysing the output in another way, a rough approximation might show about 50 per cent in the traditional industries, 35 per cent in mechanical and electrical engineering, and about 15 per cent in high technology. A striking example of innovation is the creation of a completely new biomedical industry in the area of Mirandola, which started twenty years ago with one very small firm taking components from other

121

Small firms and industrial districts in Italy

small manufacturers in Emilia and which has grown into one of the world's main centres for the production of advanced equipment for the medical profession.

Table A5.1 summarizes the statistics.

Table A5.1 Manufacturing industry in Emilia-Romagna

	Production units	Employees
Extraction of minerals, mineral products and chemicals	*3,694*	*88,745*
of which: ceramics	442	35,659
chemicals	697	18,745
construction materials	734	10,459
glass	157	5,900
others	1,664	17,982
Engineering and metal products	*23,574*	*232,139*
of which: manufacture of machines	5,921	96,481
metal-working	12,267	74,828
industrial plant, machine tools, electronics	3,077	31,067
vehicle manufacture	813	22,656
precision instruments	1,496	7,097
Other manufacturing industries	*40,613*	*233,845*
of which: textiles, clothing and knitwear	18,814	79,454
food	5,154	52,634
wood and furniture	8,541	37,258
printing and publishing	2,259	20,600
leather and footwear	2,217	19,266
plastics and rubber	2,244	18,033
others	1,384	6,600
Total manufacturing industry	*67,881*	*554,729*

Source: Industrial Census, ISTAT, *VI Cens. dell'industria, dell commercio, dei servizi e dell'artigianato*, Rome, 1981.

Chapter 4

Sectors and/or districts: some remarks on the conceptual foundations of industrial economics

Giacomo Becattini

123-35 *Italy*
6110
9412

The economist who embarks on an enquiry into industrial activity at a level between the system as a whole and the single productive process is faced even before he begins with the problem of identifying an intermediate entity capable of presenting an object of meaningful study. By meaningful study I mean the possibility of identifying definite, stable regularities which can provide a rational basis both for the behaviour of the economic agent and for government action.

The problem of defining an industry or a sector lies precisely in the need to circumscribe one portion of the industrial system so that it can be studied in relative isolation from the rest. Such a study can start, however, only after a clear and stable boundary has been drawn, and so it is necessary to define what is inside the boundary as well as what remains outside. It would be undesirable for the boundary to shift in the course of the period considered, so that a certain entity could be first included, then excluded. The ideal would be to establish, therefore, a clear and unchangeable demarcation line.[1]

Of course, it is always possible to obtain clear and unchanging demarcation lines by relating the phenomenon under investigation to some totally independent entity which is in itself unchanging. For example, it is easy to distinguish a sector or industry according to whether it is totally or largely (the latter case being more complicated) dependent on the use of a certain raw material. Thus it is possible to speak, in a clearly defined way, of the iron, wood, and leather industries, and so on.

But if our chief concern is to fix economically meaningful dividing lines in our classification, we must shun aseptic and unproblematical classifications based on parameters which lie outside the process we wish to examine.

Indeed it is not a question of classifying dead forms, which are incapable of further transformation, but of probing a living, continually changing reality. The fact that we are trying to anatomize a living process means above all that any hope of identifying rigorously defined and firmly settled boundaries is illusory. The most one can hope for is a *reasonable* degree of demarcation and stability, in which the term 'reasonable' cannot be defined once and for all, but must be established case by case, according to the aim of the research.

I should like to illustrate the considerations stated above by re-examining – though with completely different ends – some of the sets of reference criteria for defining industries which I put forward in a book published several years ago[2] and which a number of industrial economists have found useful in their field of applied research.[3] The first group of definitions I wish to examine is that which hinges upon the satisfaction of needs.

All productive processes which contribute to the satisfaction of a need by providing goods or services and which are substitutable or complementary in relation to the need, comprise the corresponding industry. Where there is, let us say, a basic need for liquid nourishment, we can assign to it the whole of the processes which satisfy it.[4] In a very general way, these make up the drinks industry.

It should be noted that on this very general level all processes of drinks production, whether carried out by businesses or independently by consumers, fall within the boundaries of the industry.[5]

One important advantage of such a conception is that it allows the search for a fundamental relationship between intensity of a given basic need and some synthetic indicator of the average living conditions of a particular group of people, as in the case of Engels' or Schwabe's laws.[6]

The chief limitations of this set of definitions of industry seem to be the following. First, the extreme degree of technological, organizational, and cultural heterogeneity characterizing the various components of an industry defined in this way. This variation neutralizes most of the economist's investigative tools; for example, any average structural datum becomes meaningless in such a context. Second, there is, in my opinion, something of a clash between the ideological premises underlying this classification and the logic which governs the functioning of any capitalist society. The 'specific meaning' of capitalism – as distinct from the role which it objectively plays – lies not in the satisfaction of human needs but in the use of those very needs to favour the accumulation of capital. In this sense, capitalism, as an economic and cultural whole, continually defines and redefines men's needs, first arousing and then trampling them down in an unceasing and endless cycle.

I do not mean that the conscious use of a definition of sector based on eternal and unchanging basic needs necessarily leads to an ideological mystification which presents capitalism as being directed towards the satisfaction of genuine and authentic needs. What I do mean is that such a definition does not conform to the true nature of the capitalist process: it is, so to speak, external and not intrinsic to it.[7]

In other words, if you want to study the economy of an industry within the framework of the capitalist process of development, you cannot look at the need for liquid nourishment, or for transport, or similar generalities; what you must focus on is the need, let us say, for alcoholic drinks, or better, a specific subgroup of those, which might even mean one particular brand name.

But the further one goes along this road, the vaguer and more implausible any functional connection between the level of consumption and a synthetic indicator of people's economic conditions becomes; and it is the latter which is the chief virtue of this kind of definition. It does not make any sense to posit a definite, stable relationship between, let us say, the average level of income and the demand for a very specific commodity. Even if the class of goods considered were actually unchanged, their significance for people would change continually.[8]

From a practical point of view, the most successful set of definitions of industry is that based on technological similarity. This attempts to group together productive processes which are in some sense similar, either in the skills involved or in the technical organization of the productive process (which to a large degree reproduces skills); or in the type of raw material used (this last is often a convenient proxy for a similarity of the previous two types), regardless of the use to which the products of the industry defined in this way, are to be put.

This type of definition hits the nail on the head: it often reveals a sufficient degree of homogeneity between the processes of production so grouped as to allow the use of some of the economist's favourite analytical tools. Without the economist's instinctive acceptance of this kind of division of the industrial field, the input–output analysis would never come into being. Yet this instinctive acceptance of technological similarities poses far more problems than it seems to solve by apparently cutting the Gordian knot of definition.[9]

In an unchanging situation this kind of classification would be the most applicable, since it conforms best to the need to derive the taxonomy from the inside, so to speak, of production in itself. Its great weakness lies in the fact that technology is one of the fastest-changing aspects of modern production. Today's technological grouping of processes is no longer valid tomorrow: a whole block of firms can shift from one sector, defined in technological terms, to another, while continuing to serve the same markets. Rapid change in both raw materials and processes is in fact one of the main features of industrial development.

Statisticians continually change their classification, but this should be seen not as steps towards a perfect classification, but as keeping up with changes in technology and shifts in research paradigms. The gains obtained in terms of the technological homogeneity of process, by the use of this criterion, are offset by the heterogeneity of the product in relation to consumer needs, however defined.

One of the groups of definitions analysed in my earlier study may be rather more relevant to the problem. This is the group of definitions which I labelled sociological, where the dominant feature is the subject's awareness of belonging to a particular industry. It seems to me that these definitions can be useful for our present purpose. The sense of belonging is difficult to measure but none the less real for that, and when it exists it is a social force of the first order. The role it plays in workers' political and social organization is sufficient to show how a given situation changes once that feeling of belonging has come into play. I believe it is impossible to study a developmental process without considering aspects of collective psychology alongside the more strictly economic relationships.

The sense of belonging – like rivalry, emulation, imitation, and so on – is one of the factors which unify and separate groups of people: such factors are not necessarily ephemeral and indeed are often deeply rooted and capable of exerting considerable influence upon responses to externally determined conjunctures. Any subdivision of production which fails to take account of this, is doomed to explain away the complexity and richness of social reality. For this reason I have a strong fellow-feeling with those industrial economists who, either implicitly or explicitly, adopt sociological definitions as the basis of their work.[10]

Sociological definitions capture people's sense of belonging to a certain industry, a feeling which arises from within the social process and which, because habits of mind tend to lag behind, fails to keep pace with change in the external circumstances.

Let us now take a quick look at the different needs of the maker of theoretical models of industry on the one hand and of the field worker on the other. I wish to do this in order to encourage more fruitful exchanges between them. In Italy at least, the relationship is predominantly one way: from the theorist to the applied economist; with the former providing the latter with schemes to try out in the field. I have no desire to underrate theory, nor to encourage the extrapolation of hasty generalizations from particular research experiences; what I do want to do is to point out that some of the approaches commonly adopted by economic theorists make many of the models they propose, not accidentally or marginally, but essentially, unsuitable for field studies.

One of the dominant methodological tendencies to be found among theorists of industrial activity is what one might call the structuralist approach. Exponents of this approach try to trace the behaviour of members of a particular industry back to certain so-called structural features of the industry itself: technology, degree of concentration, and so on. Once these structural features have been identified, the behaviour which counts for the researcher is already clearly defined. If firms behave rationally, they cannot help but lead to a given situation.

Some methodologists have coined the term 'situational determinism' to describe the methodological approach which tends to construct theoretical models in which the agent, while in theory free to do what he wants, is in fact obliged by a combination of the psychology attributed to him and the situation postulated around him to make one and only one decision (single-exit situation).[11] Certainly the entrepreneur operating in an industry characterized by perfect competition will find himself in this situation; but, *mutatis mutandis*, the entrepreneur in Sylos Labini's oligopolistic model finds himself in a very similar situation. In this case too the behaviour which counts for the theorist is, to a large degree, determined by the assumed situation. What better premise could there be, it has been observed, for empirical studies, which will not have to concern themselves with the intangible personality traits or level of information of the entrepreneur, or pursue ephemeral, elusive, expectations, but can concentrate on structural data, which are easily obtained and the same for everybody?

I believe that the questions raised here touch at the heart of the economist's methodological problems, and this does not seem to me an appropriate occasion to deal with them: I shall therefore limit myself to a couple of peripheral observations which seem to me, nevertheless, relevant to the subject.

The first observation concerns the fact that a structural model may perhaps be of some use in studying an established industry which is just ticking over, but cannot help us in the study of an industry undergoing rapid growth.

The expansion strategies of firms which are part of a rapidly growing industry, clearly go beyond the explanatory power of a structural model, whether competitive or oligopolistic. I believe that studies of expanding industries should follow interpretative schemes close to those of Schumpeter (and Marshall and Young, as we are going to see) and should take particular account of the principle that much of the most successful investment would never have been made on the basis of a rigorous analysis of the prospects for profitability which existed in the initial situation. I realize that this last hint is extremely inconvenient for a scientific approach to industrial activity, but I believe it contains the essential kernel of truth about capitalist expansion.

A second consideration, connected with the first, concerns the broad range of decisions not vindicated by successful results, which surrounds the much smaller nucleus of decisions which led to a successful outcome. Theorists tend to disregard these unsuccessful decisions, considering them accidental errors which more or less cancel one another out. D.H. Robertson used a highly expressive metaphor to describe second-rate entrepreneurs who do not know that they are second-rate, calling them hawthorn seeds which think they are acorns.[12] Only time will tell: the oaks will grow tall and last for centuries, while the hawthorns will never emerge from the undergrowth and will live for a much shorter period. Industrial development is determined not only by the oak-tree entrepreneurs but also by a never-ending stream of hawthorn entrepreneurs. And where there are hawthorns, the acorns which drop from the oaks may never reach the ground.

Briefly, decisions which do not fit into accepted schemes, like firms which should not exist, are an essential part of an ever-changing reality, and any theoretical model which ignores them will have a restricting and reductive effect on applied research. What is the moral to be drawn from this digression? In my opinion, it offers a warning against too rigid interpretations of theoretical models of industry and suggests that findings of field work should be used to create rigorous but imaginative typologies. In short, Keynes's dictum should be transferred into this field of enquiry: 'The specialist in the manufacture of models will not be successful unless he is constantly correcting his judgement by intimate and *messy* acquaintance with the facts to which his model has to be applied.'[13]

But it is time to end this digression and return to the central theme: the various ways of aggregating productive units. As it has a long history, I hope I may be permitted to put it into context.

Some hundred years have passed since Alfred Marshall first defined the twin concepts of external and internal economies. Since then they have had a rich and varied existence. The main problem whose effects are still felt today, at least in some quarters, was brought about by Sraffa in 1925–30.

In the course of a deservedly famous attempt at a radical critique

128

of neoclassical economics, Piero Sraffa took it upon himself to declare that economies external to the individual business but internal to the industry as a whole, were extremely rare, not to say non-existent, and used this conclusion to try to demolish that part of the Marshallian analysis relying upon increasing returns.[14]

This expulsion of internal–external economies from neoclassical theory of value (i.e. the theory of relative prices) was taken, by careless readers, to be a demonstration of the non-existence in the real world of external economies in general. Fortunately, the banishment of the latter by some theorists did not affect scholars concerned with economic development and localization, who continued to use the concept of external economies and diseconomies, and indeed to define and refine it further.

It seems to me that the time is now ripe to take up the question where Sraffa left it in 1926. In fact, nothing could be further from Sraffa's intentions in the studies mentioned above than to deny the existence or the practical importance of external economies: he simply observed that they develop in such a way as not to fit the boundaries of any single industry (defined, however, in terms which are not free from ambiguity)[15] so that they cannot be used to explain increasing returns in a given industry. He does not say that they cannot be used to explain increasing returns at a super-industrial level, but on the contrary he quotes – with implicit approval – the passage in *Industry and Trade* where Marshall declares that 'the economies of production on a large scale can seldom be allocated exactly to any one industry: they are in great measure attached to groups, often large groups, of correlated industries'.[16]

On closer examination, Marshall's statement reveals an extremely interesting background, both for the researcher in economics and for the historian of economic thought.

In *Industry and Trade*, which in some ways stands to the *Principles* in the same relation as an advanced course to an elementary one, Marshall explains clearly – assuming his audience to have mastered the techniques of economic reasoning – that the concept of cost of production presented in the *Principles* has absolutely nothing to do with the real world. 'We must go far from the facts of life to get a case, in which the cost of production of a single thing can be exactly deduced from the total cost of the business in which it is made'.[17]

In the real world, which here is set against the imaginary world of the textbooks, 'the cost of any one thing – a bale of cloth, a lawn-mower, or an engraving – cannot be definitely isolated from that of similar things made in the same process with it'[18]. As a consequence, the tendency of market prices to approach the cost of production, including normal profits, of a representative firm (representative of what? one might ask), is to a great extent obscured.

These quotations suffice to show that Marshall does not assign any theoretical status to the concepts of industry and representative firm beyond that of the total cost of a single product. As far as he is concerned they are didactic expedients for conveying, in an intelligible and, if possible, illuminating way, the idea of the varying relationships (variations which are partly regular, partly casual) between continually changing entities to students embarking on their first study of economic reality; expedients which are to be abandoned as soon as one passes from the abstract world of textbooks to the true work of the economist, that is the disentanglement of the complexities of social reality.

At this point, the question which comes to mind is this: is it possible that Marshall (the theorist of partial equilibrium!) contented himself with a sort of contemplation of the complexity of the web of interconnections between different processes, renouncing any attempt to categorize an intermediate entity between the individual firm and the system? The reflection that the epigraph to *Industry and Trade* invokes not only 'the many in the one' but also 'the one in the many' should be enough – apart from Marshall's well-known industrial analysis – to convince us that at least some attempt at such a categorization must exist in some corner of Marshall's works.

Indeed, there are two attempts of this kind, albeit at an embryonic level. The first – on which the young Marshall pinned some hopes of a radical renewal of economics – merits only a brief mention here since it concerns the subject only tangentially. It is the idea, already dear to Marshall before 1877, but hovering at the back of his mind for the rest of his life, of a subdivision of society into distinct and opposing 'economic nations', made up of workers' unions and confederations of industrialists, trading the composite goods at their disposal (work and various kinds of goods) among themselves. The aspect of this project which I should like to emphasize here is the fact that the cement which binds together these intermediate bodies (which he calls compact industrial groups) – quite different from Jevons's trading bodies and difficult to relate either to Marx's spheres of production or special classes – is a sense of belonging, in which components of material interest and of loyalty to a social group are welded together. So infatuated was Marshall with this idea that he tried to apply his international trade curves to these peculiar 'economic nations':

Much is to be learnt from the application of the pure theory of foreign trade to the circumstances of the relations between the supply and the demand for the wares produced or the services rendered by any unorganized industrial group. But this application becomes of vital moment in the case of those industrial groups which are formally organised and which set themselves deliberately to regulate the supply of their wares or of their services so as to dispose of them on terms as advantageous as possible to themselves.[19]

This line of thought, which originated in J.E. Cairnes' and Cliffe Leslie's theory of 'non-competing groups', was not pursued by Marshall in his *Principles of Economics*, but we have good reasons to think that it did not disappear from his teaching in Cambridge. A second line of thought runs through the whole of Marshall's work and plays a significant role in it. The young Marshall, somewhat annoyed by the blithe optimism of latter-day exponents of classical thought about economics of scale and the efficiency of big business, wrote:

the customary method of treating the advantages of division of labour and of production on a large scale appears to me to be in one respect defective. For the manner in which these advantages are discussed in most economic treatises is such as to imply that the most important of them can as a rule be obtained only by the concentration of large masses of workmen in vast establishments.[20]

In Marshall's view, however, at least in some manufacturing sectors, 'the advantages of production on a large scale can in general be as well attained by the aggregation of a large number of small masters into one district as by the erection of a few large works.'[21] In fact,

with regard to many classes of commodities it is possible to divide the process of production into several stages, each of which can be performed with the maximum of economy in a small establishment. . . . If there exist a large number of such small establishments specialised for the performance of a particular stage of the process of production, there will be room for the profitable investment of capital in the organising of subsidiary industries adapted for meeting their special wants.[22]

He envisages two kinds of subsidiary industry engaged in the manufacture of the machine tools needed for each separate phase of production, and also in those engaged in buying and distributing the various materials needed by small factories and buying and distributing the latter's products.

To this set of advantages deriving from localized industry should be added others regarding the training of skilled workers and the rapid circulation of ideas:

> when the total number of men interested in the matter is very large there are to be found among them many who, by their intellect and temper, are fitted to originate new ideas. Each new idea is canvassed and improved upon by many minds; each new accidental experience and each deliberate experiment will afford food for reflection and for new suggestions, not to a few persons but many.[23]

This *ante litteram* description of recent features of industrial development in certain areas of Italy will not surprise those who know, as Marshall did, the kind of development which took place in the metallurgical and textile-producing areas of Great Britain in the nineteenth century.

What I should like to stress here is that the unit to which Marshall referred even then is not that of technologically defined industries, but that of an industrial district or area. The conditions of population density, presence of infrastructure, industrial atmosphere, which are both the source and the result, the cause and the effect, of that part of returns which cannot be explained either by internal economies of scale or by R & D, apply to the industrial district. It is this extra-element of productivity which made Lancashire, the Ruhr and Lombardy yesterday, and the so-called Third Italy today, stand out against the rest.

What holds together the firms which make up the Marshallian industrial district, much diminishing the meaning of the cost of production of each single product, is a complex and tangled web of external economies and diseconomies, of joint and associated costs, of historical and cultural vestiges, which envelops both inter-firm and interpersonal relationships.

The Marshallian industrial district is a localized 'thickening' (and its strength and weakness both lie in this spatial limitation) of inter-industrial relationships which is reasonably stable over time. Its composite nature, tending towards the multisectorial, gives it, even in the midst of intense change, a stability which a unit such as a single industry, in the technological sense of the term, lacks; it is therefore possible to study it, in order to ascertain its permanent characteristics, the laws which govern its formation, its maintenance and its decline. Paradoxically, the greater the ability of the district to renew itself, to graft new sectors on to old, to develop its original industry in ever more specialized ways – in accordance with Allyn Young's celebrated model –[24] the more it retains its identity as an industrial district.

132

As regards the concept's capacity to foster empirical research and endow it with 'social depth' and 'cultural outreach', I need only mention the fact that, initially, in the delimitation, and subsequently in the close examination, of this reality, where geography and society form a seamless robe, the individual skills of the historian, the geographer, the economist, the sociologist, and so on, necessarily come together. Many of the differences in organization and terminology which currently divide the various social sciences, could be, if not resolved, at least seriously faced in the course of an ever more thorough study of this Janus-like entity – on the one hand the unique and unrepeatable result of a natural environment and a history which has run its course, and on the other a particular case of possible laws of social evolution.

Of course, the industrial district does not yield all external economies; on the contrary, as society moves on, precisely those which are least tied to spatial proximity are strengthened. For this reason I do not propose a single frame for the interpretation of economic reality in terms of compact industrial districts but rather a grid: both in terms of technologically defined sectors and of industrial districts wherever the conditions are favourable.

A final remark. An industrial policy which attempts to understand not only the visible exogenous conditions but also the hidden endogenous reasons for the formation, development, and decline of existing industrial districts, and which gives them judicious encouragement, promoting their geographical spread, their completion and technological evolution, along lines which correct their inner tendencies without frustrating them, would obtain, I guess, better results than the one founded on industrial sectors, the internal logic of whose development is, for the reasons I have tried to set out above, often difficult to grasp.

Acknowledgement

This paper is a new version of an article published in the January 1979 issue of *Rivista di Economia e Politica Industriale* 'Dal "settore industriale" al "distretto industriale" Alcune considerazioni sull'unità d'indagine del'economia industriale'.

Notes

1. On the general problem of process boundary delimitation, barely touched on here, see the key treatment by N. Georgescu-Roegen, *The Entropy Law and the Economic Process*, Cambridge, Mass.: Harvard University Press, 1971, Ch. 9.

2. *Il concetto di industria e la teoria del valore*, Turin: Boringhieri, 1962.
3. For example, F. Momigliano, *Economia industriale e teoria dell'impresa*, Bologna: Il Mulino, 1975, pp. 56–60; V. Balloni, *L'industria italiana degli elettrodomestici*, Bologna: Il Mulino, 1978, p. 13.
4. It may be objected that the need for liquid nourishment is partially satisfied by solid nourishment. This simply underlines the difficulty of setting out definite dividing lines in a subject such as this.
5. A concept such as 'industry' or 'productive sector' can be of some importance in a planned economy, which should take account of the fact that not all goods and services are produced by the 'social machine' and that people make up what the 'social machine' fails to provide, by means of complex, but not completely unpredictable, mechanisms.
6. The explanatory value of these empirical laws is analysed in S. Zamagni's *L'analisi neo-classica della domanda: un'esposizione critica*, Bologna: Patron, 1977, pp. 128–36.
7. One current of contemporary economic thought tends to interpret the growing fragmentation of the means of consumption as an ever more complicated means of satisfying *given* needs. Its most typical exponent is K. Lancaster; see his 'A new approach to consumer theory', *Journal of Political Economy*, 1966: 132–7.
8. Think of how the 'cultural meaning' of certain items of clothing (e.g. shoes) or food (e.g. chicken or turkey) has changed for large sections of the population since the war.
9. Some of the resulting difficulties as regards fieldwork are dealt with in the essay by M. Rispoli, 'L'analisi del processo industriale' in P. Saraceno (ed.) *Economia e direzione dell'impresa industriale*, Milan: Isedi, 1978.
10. For example, Balloni op. cit., p. 1.
11. See S.J. Latsis, 'A Research Programme in Economics', in S.J. Latsis (ed.) *Method and Appraisal in Economics*, Cambridge: Cambridge University Press, 1976, pp. 16–39.
12. See D.H. Robertson, 'The Colwyn Committee, the income tax, and the price level', *Economic Journal*, December 1927.
13. D. Moggridge (ed.) *The Collected Writings of J.M. Keynes*, London: Macmillan, 1973, Vol. XIV, p. 300.
14. See P. Sraffa, 'Sulle relazioni tra costo e quantità prodotta', *Annali di Economia*, 1925; 'The Laws of Returns under Competitive Conditions', *Economic Journal*, December 1926.
15. If I am not mistaken, he implicitly accepts the usual definition: 'the group of firms which produce a given type of consumable *goods*, for example fruit or nails', where what is meant by goods is 'something with regard to which it is possible if not to draw up at least to imagine a demand list which is *tolerably* homogeneous and independent of supply conditions'. See Sraffa, *The Laws*.
16. See A. Marshall, *Industry and Trade*, London: Macmillan, 1919, p. 18.
17. Ibid., p. 190.

18. Ibid., p. 191.
19. See J.K. Whitaker (ed.) *The Early Economic Writings of Alfred Marshall, 1867–1890*, London: Macmillan, 1975, Vol. 2, p. 123.
20. See Whitaker, Vol. 2, p. 195.
21. Ibid., p. 196.
22. Ibid., p. 196–7.
23. Ibid., p. 198.
24. See A. Young, 'Increasing Returns and Economic Progress', *Economic Journal*, December 1928.

Chapter 5

The industrial district in Marshall

Marco Bellandi

136 - 52

During the last few years a debate has developed around the factors which might explain the competitive capacities which the proliferating small and medium-sized firms in certain Italian regions have shown.[1] The still widespread belief that only large firms take full advantage of the economies which characterize modern industry does not encourage the search for independent factors of efficiency at the root of such competitive capacities. However, the evidence regarding groups of spatially agglomerated small firms points toward explanations which involve factors of efficiency. Support for this approach is to be found within the works of Alfred Marshall.[2]

Many decades ago Marshall, arguing against the idea of efficiency being found only in large firms, identified and analysed the peculiar characteristics of efficiency in small firms concentrated in particular localities or districts: the 'industrial districts' which he discovered in England, Germany, and other countries. We propose to review the conceptual aspects of the Marshallian industrial district.

This is not to imply that the proliferation of small firms in some Italian regions can be related solely to the growth of industrial districts; nor that such growth can be fully explained by the efficiency aspects stressed by Marshall. However, these aspects should not be ignored.

Localization of industry, industrial districts, and external economies

Some preliminary qualifications are needed on the definition of an industrial district and the nature of Marshall's analysis. In the first place we have to face a geographical problem. When Marshall writes on the 'localization of industry', sometimes he distinguishes between a 'manufacturing town' and an 'industrial district'. The difference is expounded in *Industry and Trade*:

Almost every industrial district has been focused in one or more large towns. Each such large town, or city, has been at first the leader in the technique of industry, as well as in trade: and the greater part of its inhabitants have been artisans. After a time factories, requiring more space than was easily to be had where ground values were high, tended to move to the outskirts of the city; and new factories grew up increasingly in the surrounding rural districts and small towns. Meanwhile the trading functions of the city developed.[3]

An industrial district can include one or more small towns, its tertiary functions are often poor, and the industrial structures are sparser than in a manufacturing town. Marshall, however, generally leaves this distinction aside in his analysis of the advantages of the 'localized industries'. Thus it is possibly better to use one term for both: the more generic 'industrial district'.

In the second place it is worth noting that this analysis often concerns districts which are each strongly characterized by one particular industry, such as textiles, cutlery, or shoes. These industries typically cover various 'sub-industries'. The firms of a district can be linked in three ways: (1) vertically or convergently, when different stages of a process are involved, as in the case of spinning or weaving or where assembly lines are fed by different sub-processes; (2) laterally, where the same stage in a like process is involved, as in the case of men's clothing and women's clothing; and (3) diagonally, when service processes are involved, such as repairing, trading, collecting, etc.[4]

In the third place we must recall the relationship between competition and efficiency, which characterizes Marshall's approach to the study of industrial organization. He considers economic efficiency – 'the effectiveness in the production of wealth' – to have a wide influence in modern industry in determining competitive capacities and survival. However, he also warns against an exaggerated and simplistic assessment of this factor. This is because economic efficiency may have different manifestations – 'economies' in Marshall's loose terminology – with different times and degrees of application; and that could imply, for example, that organizations which are characterized by high but slowly growing potentialities, are not able to survive against more precocious organizations which may be weaker in the long-run.[5]

Marshall assigns great importance 'to the economies arising from an increase in the scale of production in any kind of goods', according to the Smithian thesis that the wealth of nations depends on the division of labour, which in turn depends on the extension of

137

the market.[6] He introduces 'two technical terms' in order to classify the economies of scale, and to mark the possibility of such advantages in the absence of large firms: economies 'dependent on the resources of the industrial houses of business engaged in it [the industry], on their organisation and the efficiency of the management' are called *internal economies*; while 'these dependent on the general development of the industry' are called *external economies*.[7]

Marshall does not strictly define the industrial district in relation to small or medium-sized firms (henceforth we will refer to them as small firms). However, it is these firms which most interest him when discussing industrial districts. He points to 'those very important external economies which can often be secured by the concentration of many small businesses of a similar character in particular localities: or, as is commonly said, by the localisation of industry'.[8] They are an agglomeration of local, external economies, that is the economies of production and transaction costs which a firm enjoys and which derive from the size of the system to which it belongs.[9] More precisely, in Marshall's thought, the economies come from the working of the firm within the thick local texture of interdependencies which bind together the small firms and the local population.

These local economies do not exhaust the range of external economies: Marshall refers to 'others, especially those connected with the growth of knowledge and the progress of the arts, depend chiefly on the aggregate volume of production in the whole civilized world'.[10] External economies, both local and non-local, and internal economies are basic tools of Marshall's discussion of industrial organization. As R. Jenner points out, we might add to them two others, that is the internal constraints and the demand limitations on internal economies.[11] Here we will ignore the full framework and simply try to understand the external economies within the industrial district.

Division of labour among manufacturing firms

A system of small firms can achieve the full utilization of highly specialized instruments of production (and of specialized labour) if the production process is decomposable and its components are conveniently divided among the firms of the system:

the economic use of expensive machinery can sometimes be attained in a very high degree in a district in which there is a large aggregate production of the same kind, even though no individual capital employed in the trade will be very large. For subsidiary industries devoting themselves each to one small branch of the process of production, and working it for a great many of their neighbours, are able to keep in constant use machinery of the most highly specialized character, and to make it pay its expenses, though its original cost may have been high, and its rate of depreciation very rapid.[12]

The specialized firms can have, as in Marshall's explanation, a common localization; here we would say the industry takes advantage of the economies of scale which arise from the use of specialized means of production. This is one of the most important factors in explaining the efficiency of the industrial system of a district; but it does not explain the advantages of the agglomeration. We are in a field of external economies; not yet in the field of agglomeration economies. The same is true for the subsidiary industries in a district which are 'occupied with collecting and distributing the various materials and other commodities which are required by the small establishments in question, and with collecting and distributing the produce of their work'.[13] Marshall asserts their positive, specialized function. Although he does not point out explicitly a relevant agglomeration advantage, he seems to relate the keeping of these advantages of scale to the fact that small firms are nearly as spatially concentrated as a big integrated plant is. Why? Might it be to reduce the transport costs of semi-finished goods? In fact, Marshall seems not to assign general validity to an explanation of the agglomeration of successive stages of production based on the need to reduce transport costs of semi-finished goods.[14] Of course, there are cases in which this explanation applies. For example, it may be that the very specific transportation needs of some intermediate goods can be dealt with by types of trucks which are not efficient for long hauls. There is also the principle of pooled or massed reserves, according to which the pooling of the supply of similar items involves a relative decrease of the reserves necessary to meet the fluctuations of demand in each item – when these fluctuations are of independent random variable type. This principle brings about an agglomeration effect when, for example, a very fast supply is needed and proximity enables fast exchange to take place.[15]

It is clear from scattered passages that Marshall does not ignore this principle and other agglomeration effects of transport differentiation. There are, however, other agglomeration factors on which he focuses, in particular those connected to transaction, skill and innovation problems.

Transaction problems

Let us consider, first, some reflections of Marshall on dealings:

> [The customer] will go to the nearest shop for a trifling
> purchase; but for an important purchase he will take the trouble
> of visiting any part of the town where he knows that there are
> specially good shops for his purpose. Consequently shops which
> deal in expensive and choice objects tend to congregate together;
> and those which supply ordinary domestic needs do not.[16]

When someone wants to buy a product which is a novelty to him and
is highly priced and has quality variations, he can profit by paying
attention to various price–quality combinations. This often involves
personal research among dealers. Costs of the research grow fast if
the buyer has relatively little available time. Thus it can be profitable
to him to find, within a narrow area, the various types of goods
from which to select. Of course, the advantage depends also on the
relative accessibility of the area from the buyer's home.

The advantages to the customer can be seen as an economy on
some costs of dealers' activity. This is a particular agglomeration
economy, achievable either by a large store or by a concentrated set
of smaller stores. It also applies to costs for wholesale or industrial
transactions; for example, an industrial firm needs information in
order to find industrial and service firms to satisfy its input
requirements. The informational needs are reduced when the transaction involves either the reiteration of past transactions or the
exchange of highly standardized inputs. In these cases they can be
easily met by telephone, correspondence, and so on. Otherwise,
direct personal contact among agents is often the most efficient or
even a necessary means of overcoming the difficulties and achieving
the transaction:

> personal contact is most needed, (i) in trade between allied
> branches of production, at all events in regard to things which
> have not yet been brought completely under the dominion of
> either General or Particular standardisation; and (ii) in all
> dealings, especially retail, connected with dress, ornaments and
> other goods, which need to be adapted to individual requirements
> and idiosyncrasies.[17]

These conditions explain advantages deriving from the agglomeration
of similar activities. They can also help to explain agglomeration of
different activities with input–output linkages; for example when the
problem arises of frequently adjusting or setting up new input–output
relations to fit unpredictable or not easily definable demand quickly.

And the more frequent the necessity of speedy contact, the more profitable that agglomeration becomes.

An important aspect of the transaction problem brought about by non-routine activities on non-standardized objects is that it is difficult, almost by definition, to organize them by means of pure market transactions. The want of repetition and standardization amplifies information asymmetries and non-competitive conditions, thus increasing the costs of market transacting. Marshall does not ignore these problems, which nowadays are at the centre of transaction cost theories.[18] It would be possible to connect these problems with Marshall's reflections on custom and competition, business confidence and industrial groups, automatic and deliberate organization, standardization, and change.[19] First, Marshall recalls the existence of 'mutual knowledge and trust', that is of personal confidence, underlying the 'normal arrangements of many transactions' in the markets:

> the normal arrangement of many transactions in retail and wholesale trade, and on Stock and Cotton Exchanges, rests on the assumption that verbal contracts, made without witness, will be honourably discharged

Or even:

> Some [commodities] are adapted to special tastes, and can never have a very large market; and some have merits that are not easily tested, and must win their way to general favour slowly. In all such cases the sales of each business are limited, more or less according to circumstances, to the particular market which it has slowly and expensively acquired

Where:

> nearly everyone has also some particular markets; that is, some people or groups of people within whom he is in a somewhat close touch: mutual knowledge and trust lead him to approach them and them to approach him, in preference to strangers.[20]

And neighbourhood relations may help the development of 'mutual knowledge and trust', according to processes such as those referred to in the next paragraph.

It seems worth noting Marshall's interest in the continuous development of standardization in modern industry, which of course diminishes the relevance of transaction costs. To Marshall such a development is neither pervasive nor unconstrained: standardization is often only 'particular' to an individual producer or to a group of producers. Marshall points out that some large established industrial districts take great advantage of standardization which has been developed internally, shared, and handed down: 'Some British textile industries have developed efficient standardization and specialization almost automatically.' In particular, 'The high automatic organization of these industries is in great measure due to the fact that their plant is made in their own districts, with constant intercommunication of ideas between machine makers and machine users.'[21] When a group of firms shares some standardization of processes, for example, it is easier for them to adjust or set up a mutual network of transactions, even without personal contacts or without specific personal confidence. In this case the agglomeration effect results from the fact that standardizations are particular to local producers.

Finally, we can infer, as a variation on the theme of 'particular markets', that even the effective realization of other external economies of agglomeration depends on the possibility of easy adjustment or setting up of networks of transactions among firms. Without this possibility, for example, it is obviously difficult to turn the presence of pooled reserves at hand into an advantage of quick availability of inputs.

The accumulation of skills

An important group of factors connected with an established industrial district is referred to by Marshall as the 'industrial atmosphere'. In the *Theory of Foreign Trade*, in the *Economics of Industry*, and in *Principles of Economics*, Marshall has a metaphor which suggests the term 'industrial atmosphere' introduced in his later *Industry and Trade*. In an industrial district, where a mass of skilled workers is concentrated, the mysteries of the industry 'become no mysteries; but are as it were in the air, and children learn many of them unconsciously'.[22]

So, for example:

> It is to be remembered that a man can generally pass easily from one machine to another; but that the manual handling of a material often requires a fine skill that is not easily acquired in middle age: for that is characteristic of a special industrial atmosphere.[23]

Process of mutual training, learning by doing, and incentive to work, are favoured by proximity. 'When large masses of men in the same locality are employed in similar tasks, it is found that, by associating with one another, they educate one another.'[24] Such processes could be simply attributed to the experiences on the job. But for Marshall their scope is broader: 'in districts in which manufacturers have long been domiciled, a habit of responsibility, of carefulness and promptitude in handling expensive machinery and materials becomes the common property of all'.[25]

Thus the agglomeration of industry in a district generates, in time, an aptitude for industrial work, and this aptitude communicates itself to most of the people who live in the district. Marshall's words suggest the presence of a cultural process connected to the needs of the industry. Greater strength is attributed to this process if the population involved lives in a relatively confined area, where there is an established concentration of several firms. Of course, the skills to which these processes apply are not necessarily only manual.[26]

Marshall does not fail to note that technical progress and scientific management can reduce the importance of those advantages, and hence increase the power of big firms, which are less tied to local aid:

> partly under American influence, machinery has covered so large a range of work that a comparatively short training enables a youth, who is naturally alert, to control a manufacturing process that not long ago would have required the work of a great number of artisans. . . . There are few industries in which a considerable supply of skill of this kind [which requires special training from boyhood upwards] is as imperatively necessary as ever.[27]

For these 'few industries', however, it is still true that any attempt to start them 'in a new home has great difficulties and risks'.[28] In any case, when an industry needs a large supply of skills, not necessarily 'industrial atmosphere rooted', a specialized industrial district represents a large specialized labour market for such skills. This is the source of other true examples of external agglomeration economies:

> Again, in all but the earliest stages of economic development a localized industry gains a great advantage from the fact that it offers a constant market for skill. Employers are apt to resort to any place where they are likely to find a good choice of workers with the specialized skill which they require; while men seeking employment naturally go to places where there are many employers who need such skill as theirs and where therefore it is likely they will find a good market.[29]

An ample labour market is not effective if the market extends over too large an area. Not only might there be problems for housing and commuting, but there is also likely to be a problem in the diffusion of information about the demand and supply of skilled labour. Here

again we see an agglomeration economy arising from the combination of pooled reserves and transaction advantages.[30]

Innovation

Marshall is most conscious of the advantages of large firms as
regards innovation. He often recalls that full account has to be taken
of their concentrated power of study and experimentation on a vast
scale, of advertising to create new wants, of appropriation of innovation profits.[31] So, 'the small manufacturer can seldom be in the
front of the race of progress'. Nevertheless, 'he need not be far from
it, if he has the time and the ability for availing himself of the
modern facilities for obtaining knowledge'.[32]

The availability of 'modern facilities for obtaining knowledge' is
enhanced when the small firm works within an industrial district:

> an established centre of specialised skill, unless dominated by a
> guild or trade union of an exceptionally obstructive character, is
> generally in a position to turn to account quickly any new
> departure affecting its work; and if the change comes gradually,
> there is no particular time at which strong incitement is applied
> to open up the industry elsewhere. . . . Even the changeful
> conditions of America show a surprising permanence of many
> localised industries[33]

This passage requires some comment. The first concerns the diffusion of innovation when the industrial district 'turns to account
quickly any new departure'. We have seen the application of this to
a shopping-centre economy. But a similar principle also applies when
the district is considered as a concentration of demand, and not only
as a concentration of supply. So, for example, an outside supplier
of a patented innovation for the processes which characterize a
specialized district, is probably well aware of that market for its own
innovation; moreover, the concentration favours the sale when the
promotion requires some exchange of know-how through personal
contacts, and when speedy after-sales service is requested. The
accumulation of specialized skill improves the chances of acquiring
new techniques, if these are not too innovative, since such an
accumulation involves the mastery of the actual know-how of an
industry. That potentially may depend on an industrial atmosphere
for the 'production' of not easily acquired skills and also for other
manifestations of the cultural orientation imparted by the life of
'localized industry'.

One of these manifestations could be an unfavourable one: the growth of 'a guild or a trade union of an exceptionally obstructive character', while – as Marshall remarks – 'even a little obstinacy or inertia may ruin an old home of industry whose conditions are changing.'[34] Of course, there are counterbalancing forces: 'yet history shows that a strong centre of specialized industry often attracts much new shrewd energy to supplement that of native origin, and is thus able to expand and maintain its lead'.[35]

Thus the attraction of labour, which previously I have discussed in simple economic terms, is coupled with a sociological force. But Marshall prefers not to further his investigation on this matter, and hence he refers simply to history. When the 'new shrewd energy' appears and is successful, it is easy to associate the industrial atmosphere with a continuous and constructive attention of businessmen and manufacturers to any change that could affect their industry:

> good work is rightly appreciated, inventions and improvements in
> machinery, in processes and the general organisation of the
> business have their merits promptly discussed: if one man starts
> a new idea, it is taken up by others and combined with
> suggestions of their own; and thus it becomes the source of
> further new ideas.[36]

This seems to indicate processes of imitation and emulation, such as those discussed in some modern theories on the diffusion of innovation, where spatial proximity and cultural homogeneity heavily condition the speed of transmission of new ideas and the frequency of their adoption.[37] A transactional problem arises with the transmission among competitive firms. Marshall is conscious of this type of problem, but his reflection on it is not straightforward. We find reference to innovative co-operation arranged within particular markets. An example of this is the 'intercommunication of ideas between machine makers and machine users', or the intercommunication between traders and producers:

> Traders not infrequently aid producers by direct hints as to
> customers' needs, and even by suggestions as to methods of
> meeting them: and various arrangements are sometimes made for
> the division of any gains that may thence arise.[38]

Business associations, whose scope is the 'constructive co-operation among kindred businesses' also help. The setting up of all these arrangements demands a relatively high degree of confidence, that can be generated within an established agglomeration.

However, when Marshall refers to the circulation of good ideas, it would seem that he is thinking implicitly of chance – even underground – processes of transmission of ideas; for example, through inter-firm mobility of skilled workers; the exchange of ideas within social institutions, like families, clubs, and so on; bandwagon effects – all of which are often spatially rooted. In any case, whether there are organized or spontaneous relationships, personal contact within the agglomeration encourages a constant intercommunication of ideas.

A problem remains with the premise that new and fruitful ideas can spring from relatively small manufacturing firms. How do they manage to do something new, when the 'concentrated power of study and experiment' of large teams is necessary to deal 'with the magnitude and complexity of modern industrial operations, and their intricate relations to and dependence on one another'?[39]

Discounting business associations, Marshall's answer is probably the one summarized in the dictum, 'No one is so wise as all the world'.[40] There is always some space for improvement and adjustment, even truly original ideas whose birth is generally hindered within the routine work of a large research team.[41] One source of such opportunities Marshall sees as the variation of one man's experience and thought, which results from contact with the experience and thought of others. In Marshall's opinion this contact also gives a sort of general stimulus, while a quite specific stimulus would be given by the prospect of improved status: 'the heads of an independent business may be willing to spend toilsome days and anxious nights in developing an idea, which holds out some promise of greatly raising its [sic] status'.[42] Moreover, such entrepreneurs can easily avail themselves of the 'independent and creative thought' of skilled and alert workers.[43]

Multisectoral industrial districts and industrial regions

Marshall refers to two factors which are characteristic of 'those large towns or large industrial districts in which several distinct industries are strongly developed'. The first refers to the normal employment of the differentiated labour capabilities of the members of each family, and hence to the economic advantages resulting from the unification of the household's budget:

> In those iron districts in which there are no textile or other factories to give employment to women and children, wages are high and the cost of labour dear to the employer, while the average money earnings of each family are low. But the remedy for this evil is obvious, and is found in the growth in the same neighbourhood of industries of a supplementary character.[44]

A second advantage also relates to the labour market, and has a broader scope:

> A district which is dependent chiefly on one industry is liable to extreme depression, in case of a falling-off in the demand for its produce, or of a failure in the supply of the raw material which it uses. This evil again is in a great measure avoided by those large towns or large industrial districts in which several distinct industries are strongly developed. If one of them fails for a time, the others are likely to support it indirectly; and they enable local shopkeepers to continue their assistance to work people in it.[45]

Of course, we may argue, there are other local means through which the support of a depressed industry by a buoyant one would work. The multisectoral nature of these agglomeration advantages is not always clear, and even when multisectoral economies are easily distinguishable they may not necessarily outweigh the economies deriving from monosectoral patterns.

On the subject of specialization in particular towns or districts, Marshall writes:

> It is generally recognised that the chief economy in production, as distinguished from marketing, that can be effected by a cartel or other associations of producers, is that of so parcelling out the demand of various sorts of the same class of product that each business can specialize its plant on a narrow range of work, and yet keep it running with but little interruption. This specialisation is however thoroughly effected without conscious effort in the Lancashire cotton industry; and especially in those branches of it, which are mainly in the hands of a multitude of independent businesses of moderate size. As is well known, fine spinning, coarse spinning, and weaving are localized separately. Individual firms frequently specialize on a narrow range of counts for spinning. Blackburn, Preston, Nelson and Oldham are centres of four different classes of staple cotton cloth, and so on.[46]

The process of geographical specialization can also maintain or possibly increase some external transaction economies if the 'industrial region' is endowed with specialized trading activities, in particular import–export activities, concentrated for example in central towns. This framework represents only one type of industrial region, even if an important one.

Marshall does not investigate such questions further; he refers to Hobson's *Evolution of Capitalism* as regards 'mutual influences of the localization of industry, the growth of towns and habits of town life, and the development of machinery'.[47] But the previous quotation plainly indicates the importance of considering the possibility of a broader regional framework. All the more so if one tries to apply that analysis to contemporary industries.

Conclusion

The relevance of Marshall's reflections on industrial districts is demonstrated by the appearance and development of similar ideas in the more recent work in industrial and spatial economics and urban sociology. It does not concern us here if these show a direct influence, or if they are independent revivals. We prefer to stress, in conclusion, some broader questions. We said at the beginning that the external agglomeration economies are a part of Marshall's approach to the problems of industrial organization. These apply particularly to the problem of whether the economies which characterize modern industry 'are attainable only by the aggregation of a large part of the business of the country into the hands of a comparatively small number of rich and powerful firms'.[48]

Even if, in Marshall's opinion, the 'compact centres of life and thought' are a historical starting-point for the progress of industry – 'for long ages industrial leadership depended mainly on the number and extent of centres of specialized skill in which these external economies abounded' – he cannot fail to note that things are changing.

> with the growth of capital, the development of machinery, and the improvement of the means of communication, the importance of internal economies has increased steadily and fast; while some of the old external economies have declined in importance; and many of those which have risen in their place are national, or even cosmopolitan, rather than local.[49]

However, Marshall holds that industrial progress is not measurable in a straight line; it is not an homogeneously advancing front. In the struggle for progress there are some old tools which lose their primacy, but somewhere, sometimes, they retain it or perhaps take a new lease of life.

Moreover, the vitality of groups of small, and hence seemingly weak, firms demonstrates a methodological point most clearly:

> Perhaps the earlier English economists confined their attention too much to the motives of individual action. But in fact economists, like all other students of social science, are concerned with individuals chiefly as members of the social

organism . . . economists study the actions of individuals, but study them in relation to social rather than individual life; and therefore concern themselves but little with personal peculiarities of temper and character. They watch carefully the conduct of a whole class of people, sometimes the whole of a nation, sometimes only those living in a certain district, more often those engaged in some particular trade at some time and place.[50]

That is, as G. Becattini has pointed out, Marshall maintains that the appropriate objects of research in economics have to be carefully chosen, all the more so in the applied area of industrial organization; often there are changing groups of people, and to detect them demands close attention to social and territorial features.

Acknowledgements

This is a new version of a paper published in *L'Industria* 3 (1982). The advice and stimulus of Professor Giacomo Becattini have been essential in this work. I am also grateful for Julia Bamford's help.

Notes

1. To quote only a few of the more recent books: R. Varaldo (ed.) *Ristrutturazioni industriali e rapporti fra imprese*, Milan: Franco Angeli, 1979; S. Goglio (ed.) *Italia: centri e periferie*, Milan: Franco Angeli, 1982; G. Fuà e C. Zacchia *Industrializzazione senza fratture*, Bologna: Il Mulino, 1983; M. Piore and C. Sabel, *The Second Industrial Divide*, New York: Basic Books, 1984.
2. See A. Marshall, *The Pure Theory of Foreign Trade: The Pure Theory of Domestic Values*, reprinted in J. Whitaker (ed.) *The Early Economic Writings of A. Marshall 1867–1890*, London: Macmillan, 1975; A. Marshall and M.P. Marshall, *The Economics of Industry*, London: Macmillan, 1879. A. Marshall, *Principles of Economics*, 8th edn, London: Macmillan, 1986 (1st edn, 1890); A. Marshall, *Industry and Trade*, 3rd edn, London: Macmillan, 1927 (1st edn, 1919).
3. Marshall, *Industry and Trade*, p. 285.
4. For more references to these relations in a Marshallian tradition see, for example: L. Lavington, 'Technical influences on vertical integration', *Economica*, March 1927; P.S. Florence, *The Logic of British and American Industry*, London: Routledge & Kegan Paul, 1961 (1st edn, 1953), p. 87.
5. 'Progress may be slow; but even from the merely material point of view it is to be remembered that changes, which add only a little to the immediate efficiency of production, may be worth having if they make mankind ready and fit for an organisation, which will be more effective in the production of wealth and more equal in its distribution; and that every system which allows the higher faculties of the lower grades of

industry to go to waste is open to grave suspicion.' Marshall, *Principles*, p. 207.

6. The connection with the Smithian theme is considered, for example, in A. Young, 'Increasing returns and economic progress', *Economic Journal*, December 1928; B. Loasby, 'Whatever happened to Marshall's theory of value', *Scottish Journal of Political Economy*, February 1978; and P. Mariti, *Sui rapporti fra imprese in una economia industriale moderna*, Milan: Franco Angeli, 1980.

7. Marshall, *Principles*, pp. 220–4. 'Many of these economies in the use of specialised skill and machinery which are commonly regarded as within the reach of very large establishments do not depend on the size of individual factories.' Marshall refers to economies of scale whether in relation to the plant or to the firm, as the case may be. According to Marshall, 'bigness' has to be understood as referring to the size of a firm that both demands a complex internal organization and has a significant part of the business of a national market.

8. Marshall, *Principles*, p. 221. See also *Industry and Trade*, p. 288.

9. For some applications of the concept of local external economies within the Marshallian tradition, see: Florence, p. 65 and 85; E.A.G. Robinson, *The Structure of Competitive Industry*, 4th edn, Cambridge: J. Nisbet, 1958 (1st edn, 1931), pp. 124–6. Quite recent comments in: R. Jenner, 'The dynamic factor in Marshall's economic system', *Western Economic Journal* 1, 1964; F. Forte, 'Le economie esterne marshalliane e la teoria contemporanea dello sviluppo', in *Rivista Internazionale di Scienze Sociali*, March–April 1971; G. Becattini, 'Dal "settore industriale" al "distretto industriale". Alcune considerazioni sull'unità di indagine dell'economia industriale', *Rivista di Economia e Politica Industriale* 1, 1979. (The concept is more or less independently used in *Regional Science and Urban Economics*, from A. Weber to F. Perroux and W. Isard.)

10. Marshall, *Principles*, p. 220. It needs to be stressed that: (a) the scale to which Marshall refers when speaking of economies of scale always has a strong time component, and hence has important irreversibilities (see, for comments, Forte, op. cit., and Loasby, op. cit.); (b) it seems that Marshall's applications of the concept of external economies to the problems of industrial organizations are not subject to the criticism by Sraffa on Marshallian external economies within the theory of value ('The laws of returns under competitive conditions', *Economic Journal*, December 1926): See Becattini, 'Dal "settore"', and more broadly, G. Becattini, 'L'interpretazione sraffiana di Marshall', *Economia e politica industriale* 47, 1985; (c) the external economies of agglomeration do not explain necessarily or directly, the birth of a district; (d) Marshall's terminology does not include 'agglomeration' or 'local' external economies, but here we will adopt those expressions – especially the first – since this adoption seems consistent with Marshall's intention.

11. See Jenner; Loasby; D. O'Brien, 'The evolution of the theory of the firm', in F. Stephen (ed.) *Firms, Organisation and Labour*, London: Macmillan, 1984.

12. Marshall, *Principles*, p. 225. Analytical models of the relation between vertical disaggregation and economies of specialisation are proposed for example in: G. Stigler, 'The division of labour is limited by the extent of the market', *Journal of Political Economy*, June 1951; P. Tani, 'La rappresentazione analitica del processo di produzione: alcune premesse teoriche', *Note Economiche* 4/5, 1976.

13. Marshall, *The Pure Theory*, p. 137.

14. Marshall, *Principles*, p. 227. See also: Florence, pp. 72–3 and 85.

15. Marshall, *Principles*, p. 241; *Industry and Trade*, pp. 277–8 and 600. See also Florence, pp. 50–1. This effect applies to a concentrated system of firms, as well as to a large plant. What is more worthy of note is that the implied economies of scale are important either when an economic organization relies on the perfect working of complex routines, or when a more flexible organization has to meet, by means of non-routine activities, an economic environment characterized by high degrees of change and idiosyncrasy.

16. Marshall, *Principles*, p. 227.

17. Marshall, *Industry and Trade*, p. 285. for a more recent illustration, see R. Vernon, 'External economies' (1960), reprinted in M. Edel and J. Rothenberg (eds) *Readings in Urban Economics*, New York: Macmillan, 1971.

18. Following the seminal paper by R. Coase on 'The nature of the firm', *Economica* 4, 1937, a rich literature has developed which brings to light the complex relationships between transaction costs and forms of organisation. In particular, for co-operation among firms, see G. Richardson, 'The organisation of industry', *Economic Journal*, 1972; and O. Williamson, 'Transaction costs economics: the governance of contractual relations', *Journal of Law and Economics*, 22, 1979.

19. The relation between custom and competition, and business confidence and industrial groups in Marshall's thought are investigated in G. Becattini, 'Invito a una rilettura di Marshall', introduzione a A. Marshall e M.P. Marshall, *Economia della Produzione*, Milan: ISEDI, 1975 (Italian publication of *Economics of Industry*), and M. Dardi, *Il giovane Marshall: mercato e accumulazione*, Bologna: Il Mulino, 1984.

20. Marshall, *Principles*, p. 29 and 239; *Industry and Trade*, p. 182; For comments on the relationship between Marshall's 'particular market' and the theories of imperfect and monopolistic competition, see Loasby, op. cit., and O'Brien, op. cit.

21. Marshall, *Industry and Trade*, pp. 599 and 603.

22. Marshall, *Principles*, p. 25. A reference on Marshallian industrial atmosphere is E. Lampard, 'The history of cities in the economically advanced areas', *Economic Development and Cultural Change*, January 1953. Implications and difficulties of economic studies based on 'industrial atmosphere'-like concepts are discussed, for example, in G. Becattini, 'L'economista e l'ambiente', *Giornale degli Economisti e Annali di Economia* 4, 1984.

23. Marshall, *Industry and Trade*, p. 287.

24. Marshall, *The Pure Theory*, p. 192.

25. Marshall, *Principles*, p. 171.
26. Marshall, *Industry and Trade*, p. 694.
27. Ibid., pp. 167–8.
28. What are these industries? Are they destined to disappear with the advance of mechanization and scientific management? We find an answer in Marshall that is naturally related and of the same kind as that regarding the development of standardization: the increase of the scale of manufacture that new methods allow can increase the demand for processes which are 'still done in the old ways', perhaps because they deal 'with materials which are very variable in characteristics', or with products which have to be finely customized. Ibid., pp. 118–19 and 246; *Principles*, p. 217.
29. Marshall, *Principles*, p. 225.
30. It is true that both types of problems are 'diminished by the railway, the printing press, and the telegraph', but here too the effects of progress are not pervasive nor uniform. Moreover, these means can work even within an industrial district, enlarging the area over which it extends but not lessening its identity of agglomeration.
31. Marshall, *Industry and Trade*, pp. 508, 593, 603; *Principles*, p. 234.
32. Marshall, *Principles*, p. 237.
33. Marshall, *Industry and Trade*, p. 287.
34. Ibid., p. 287. Some historical examples of corporative decline are reported and analysed in C. Sabel and J. Zeitlin, 'Historical alternatives to mass production: markets and technology in nineteenth-century industrialisation', *Past and Present*, August 1985. They also stress that appropriate local policies and external competitive pressures have sometimes been adopted to avoid the corporative decline.
35. Marshall, *Principles*, p. 225.
36. Ibid., p. 227.
37. See, for example, T. Hagerstrand, *Innovation Diffusion as a Spatial Process*, Chicago: University of Chicago, 1967 (1st edn, 1953).
38. Marshall, *Industry and Trade*, p. 279.
39. Ibid., p. 72.
40. Ibid., p. 174. Perhaps this dictum could be seen as a variation on the one written on the title page of *Industry and Trade*: 'The many in the one, the one in the many'.
41. Marshall, *Principles*, p. 232; *Industry and Trade*, pp. 601–7.
42. Marshall, *Industry and Trade*, p. 607.
43. Ibid., p, 247, 326. Some reflections on this theme are reported in S. Brusco, 'The Emilian Model: productive decentralisation and social integration', *Cambridge Journal of Economics* 6, 1982.
44. Marshall, *Principles*, pp. 226–7.
45. Marshall, *Industry and Trade*, p. 601.
46. Ibid., pp. 285–6.
47. Marshall, *Principles*, p. 226, footnote 1.
48. Ibid., p. 230.
49. Marshall, *Industry and Trade*, p. 167.
50. Marshall, *Principles*, pp. 20–1.

Chapter 6

The geography of industrial districts in Italy

Fabio Sforzi

(Translated by Julia Bamford)

Italy
6110
153 - 73
9412

The need for an objective approach to the empirical problem of determining the distribution over a geographical area of industrial districts in Italy has long been felt by many researchers in economics and geography. Nevertheless, there is neither a suitable method nor a reliable approach available for studying the problem. The following paragraphs propose the use of a multi-stage research approach using quantitative methods which constitute an attempt to fill the gap. The area studied to test the analysis is Tuscany, a region whose development has been characterized by light industry and small and very small firms. However, the main purpose of the research is to identify the spatial pattern of industrial districts in the Italian economy. This is undertaken in the second part of the chapter. The concept of industrial district emerges from Alfred Marshall's thought and has recently been proposed by Giacomo Becattini as the main framework for the interpretation of the economic reality of certain areas of Italy.[1] Other theoretical contributions have dealt with the same concept and have emphasized the need to examine the concept empirically. The following research aims to do this.

Methodological issues

In approaching the problem of spatially identifying the industrial district we are faced with a choice between two main alternative lines of research. The first and most ambitious approach would be to derive suitable criteria for the identification of the industrial district, tidying up what has been written hitherto on the subject; then an analytical methodology could be found, consistent with the theoretical premises we started out with, and a causal relation be established moving from theory to practice.

The second, simpler line of research would be to use a direct operational approach assuming that the body of theory already at our disposal enables us to define criteria and an analytical methodology for recognizing a spatial entity which could be considered an industrial district.

The first line of research has the advantage among others of tackling the subject-matter according to the canons of scientific method, establishing definitions which are unequivocal. It has in fact been pointed out that in the literature on industrial districts, various and sometimes dubious terminology has been employed for empirical evidence such as 'area-system', 'peripheral economy', 'diffused industrialization', which has sometimes been confused with categories like 'decentralization of production' or the pejorative 'black economy'.[2]

In this study the second line of research has been chosen because it is immediately operational. Nevertheless, some basic definitions must be clarified before they can be translated into empirical analysis. This is particularly so in the case of industrial districts, a term which Marshall used to describe the internal interactions of a system of small industrial firms involved in different phases of the same production process, closely linked to the population, spatially concentrated, and sharing a relatively restricted geographical area.

Empirical investigation

This comprehensive definition of the industrial district enables us to draw up the basic features of the research procedure. The purpose of this empirical exercise is to recognize industrial districts within a system of settlements whose boundaries do not necessarily coincide with those of a town or region. The research procedure used here consists of a multi-stage approach which gives rise to spatial patterns from which we can extrapolate if the local production systems of the area are merely specialized in industrial production or are a satisfactory empirical approximation of the concept of industrial district as defined above.

Economic patterns

The first stage is to classify the study area according to the economic characteristics of the plants located within it. The purpose is to identify the spatial pattern formed by the distribution and interdependence of production and to see if areas of industrial specialization emerge. The wealth of information which Italian industrial census data affords enables us to select a large number of variables capable of describing the characteristics of the plant at both regional and national level. The availability of spatial data referring to individual plants at enumeration district level enables us to go into fine spatial detail, thus reducing the type of ecological fallacy which inevitably arises when statistically and geographically meaningless basic data units like municipality are used. Through the application of powerful and appropriate multivariate statistical techniques, the enumeration district variables are processed to investigate the economic structure of the study area.[3] What we expect to find is the spatial pattern which is generated by the characteristics of each basic data unit constituting the economic space of the area under investigation as a specific combination of different parts of the production process. Map 1 in Appendix 6 (p. 166) shows the results obtained.[4]

As can be seen from the list of variables used, plants have not been discriminated by size class in terms of employees.[5] This is due to the fact that during preliminary analysis it was observed that variables defining size class were useless as discriminants between areas with the same product specialization. It does not mean, however, that size as part of the analysis is neglected in the research but that it is taken into account later, when single areas of specialization are identified. This can be undertaken for all the areas or just those of particular interest for the study.

In order to identify the spatial pattern of industrial districts it is useful to look at the spatial and economic characteristics of the Prato textile production system where plants are mostly small or very small. The question which arises is whether we can refer to this specialized industrial area as the Prato (textile) industrial district. According to our definition of industrial district, the answer is negative. Nevertheless, the results achieved by the more traditional studies on industrial districts would already be considered more than sufficient to conclude that Prato is an industrial district. Indeed, it would not be difficult to demonstrate that the form of production and organization of labour in the Prato area constitutes a 'spatially localized thickening of inter-industrial relationships' and that its development process is self-generating. At this point we could consider the identification search to be finished. However, our definition of industrial district does not easily lend itself to an alignment with this type of findings nor does it enable us to throw light on the social structure of the industrial area. Other researchers who have attempted classifications of different specialized industrial areas have recognized this as an essential element in the description of local spatial production systems.[6] The second stage of the research procedure is designed to solve this problem.

Social patterns

The second stage of the research repeats the procedure of the first with the study area now classified according to the social and demographic characteristics of its population.[7] This type of analysis of the social structure of the region allows us both to evaluate the social characteristics of the area and to see if there is a connection between social and economic identity. Map 2 in Appendix 6 shows the results.[8]

The local social structure of the Prato industrial area shows a preponderance of both the industrial working class and the entrepreneurial class together with a high proportion of working wives. This last characteristic is usually to be found only among white collar workers in the rest of Tuscany. The interpretation of the economic development of Tuscany in common with other regions in which light industry has been the driving force behind economic development has highlighted the role played by the family. The working life of members of the family often takes place in the same factory where the head of the household is entrepreneur and fellow worker also. This, however, does not imply that only family members are employed in small firms, because the phenomenon is to be found in industrial firms whose numbers far exceed family members.[9]

A strong interdependence has been confirmed between the social structure and the form of production which characterizes the system of firms making up the areas of industrial specialization.[10] This means that a system of firms which is spatially concentrated and industrially specialized and a population consistent with it and sharing the same geographical area has been found. It seems therefore that this spatial pattern can be considered as a geographical entity whose socialization process, values, and behaviour are oriented by the industry on which the community focuses its main interests.[11] This process of cultural transmission, which is the basis of 'industrial atmosphere', characterizes the industrial district and is one of the main requirements of small firm industry. The process assumes greater importance when the community involved exists in a restricted geographical area where a lasting and natural industrial concentration of firms is located. This leads us to the third conceptual element which defines the spatial component of the industrial district and which enables us to conclude our argument.

Geographical patterns

The third stage of the research procedure concentrates attention upon the concept of 'relative restrictedness', which is an essential element of the definition of industrial district used here. The meaning is that of 'self-containment', which in geography indicates a spatial system with the highest possible degree of interaction between its component parts, that is residential and production locations, defining thus its own functional boundaries.[12]

Starting from this assumption it is possible to identify spatial systems which are open systems interacting with the environment or with other systems at different order levels. It is well known that in reality all systems are open systems, even though some can be regarded as units, with smaller system interaction going on with each system, while others are configurations of lower-order elements interacting at lower levels.[13] On the basis of these considerations and using the behaviour of population, linking residence and workplace as variables generating networks of spatial interactions between the settlements of the study area, it is possible to develop the geographical pattern through which we can find the geographical system in which the economic and social system above is embedded. The applied research on the identification of spatial systems has called attention to quantitative methods able to provide meaningful results.[14] Using one of these functional regionalization algorithms, the spatial interaction data summarizing journey-to-work flows at municipality level were analysed for Tuscany in order to identify the daily urban systems constituting the region as a whole.

Map 3 in Appendix 6 shows that in the Prato area small industrial firms and local population have their functional boundaries fixed by a daily urban system, or in other words by a local labour market area.[15] This geographical system simply amounts to 'sharing a relatively restricted area', where there is a close social proximity between population and firms which extends to all social opportunities within the space–time dimension of a working day. Indeed, social opportunities go beyond contacts during working hours and with the other daily activities form a region in time and space, constrained by the accessibility of both residence and workplace.[16] Thus the research procedure can be considered complete, as also the geographical identity of the industrial district according to the original definition.

Interpretation of results

Recognition of the industrial district of Prato through the combined spatial patterns suggests that further investigation might reveal other geographical entities which could translate the concept of industrial district into reality. It is easy to foresee that other industrial districts will be discovered within Tuscany, especially if we consider the

157

IRPET interpretation of regional development and its urbanized countryside.[17] Hence the application of an operative approach to the task of spatially identifying the industrial district, involving analytical techniques and empirical enquiry, seems to have produced practical results. Moreover, the textile district of Prato presents the characteristic features described by the theoretical literature on the subject.[18]

It is obvious that to use the industrial district as a framework for the implementation of industrial policies we would need to investigate local interdependencies within the district. In this case research should aim at interpreting the behaviour of the main components of the district as a system: families, firms, and local government. Through the multiple-effect relations of the latter, various types of external economies are possible. These are at the heart of the formation and development of existing industrial districts but also of their possible decline.

Can the industrial district which has been identified here be considered a Marshallian industrial district? It seems to be the case since the Prato textile district is similar to Marshall's description of both the Lancashire cotton district and the Sheffield iron and steel district, all of them finding their *raison d'être* in that complex web of external economies and culture which envelop both inter-firm and interpersonal relations. In order to be able to answer the question a theory of empirical inquiry must be developed focusing on the industrial district as a real living system. The task of advancing knowledge on the industrial district seems at this point to be once more with theory according to the cycle of knowledge which goes from theory to practice and back again, re-elaborating what has been produced experimentally. Furthermore, when research is dealing with a spatially relevant object of study, it is crucial to know whether its behaviour is dependent at least in part on its components; only when the right things have been found to measure are measurements worthwhile.[19]

Although the multi-stage approach used here is complex, it presents relatively few difficulties from the analytical or interpretative point of view. The general availability of census and other official data means that these quantitative analytical methods can be extended to any Italian region or the country as a whole.

Industrial districts in Italy

Studies on the general spatial pattern of the Italian socio-economic system have recently become available, thus enabling us to extend the analytical approach used in Tuscany for identifying the industrial district of Prato to the whole of Italy. By this extension of the research we intend to identify Marshallian industrial districts elsewhere in Italy. The studies referred to here are the result of research on the spatial identification of local labour markets, economic and residential areas – an exhaustive investigation bringing to light the structure of human settlements, the same thing as the spatial patterns discussed above.[20]

The Italian geographical system

The multi-stage approach starts by identifying the geographical pattern of Italy using local labour market areas as spatial entities. These represent the geographical systems within which the relationships between families and firms take place. They have been identified as self-contained functional areas as far as the supply and demand of labour is concerned, where the majority of the local population can find or change their job without having to change their place of residence. This generates a complex web of journey-to-work flows which are the empirical and conceptual foundations of daily urban systems.[21]

In our analytical framework of research, this general spatial pattern of Italy and the geographical pattern of the Marshallian industrial district coincide. As we have seen above, for a geographical system to be recognized as a Marshallian industrial district, not only does it have to be organized as a 'system of interacting parts' but its population has to have a typical social structure, with a preponderance of the industrial working class and entrepreneurs, and its manufacturing sector forms a typical economic structure specialized in different phases of the same production process. However, the lack of functional boundaries delimiting single self-contained geographical entities prevents us from establishing the geographical system to which the social and economic structures correspond. This might lead us to assume that production and residential settlements make up a system merely because of their physical proximity rather than because they are components of the geographical system.[22] The general spatial pattern of local labour market areas (Map 4, Appendix 6) represents the first element in the identification of Marshallian industrial districts in Italy in the light of our multi-stage approach.

The social and economic structure

The next stage consists of investigating the social structure of the geographical systems which have been classified according to the characteristics of the resident population. The purpose is to select those systems whose structural characteristics are similar to those of a typical Marshallian industrial district. The combination of the presence of entrepreneurs, workers in small manufacturing firms, working wives and extended families with young people employed in industry seems to fit the typology. Map 5 in Appendix 6 shows the spatial social pattern of this typology within the Italian system. If we look at the social characteristics which were found by the 1975 IRPET study to accompany economic development based on light industry, then we see clearly that they coincide with those listed above. Geographical systems with these typical structural characteristics could be regarded, if mapped on a national scale, as a spatial pattern of light industrialization. The same phenomenon has been described as urbanized countryside in the interpretation of the development of light industry.[23]

This empirical evidence is significant in that it illustrates two-way links between the urbanized countryside and the Marshallian industrial district. The industrial district in as much as it is an 'organized complex of local interdependencies' could be considered a more advanced stage of industrial development than the urbanized countryside. The latter could be considered a transient form which evolves over time to increasing complexity and organization. This, however, is a subject which would be worth pursuing further elsewhere. As far as our current research is concerned the aim of describing the geography of Italy's industrial districts by the social identity of spatial systems is thus taken a step further. Looking at the analysis of their manufacturing characteristics which most closely resemble Marshall's definition of industrial district, seems to be the most direct way of reaching our goal. As a final stage the structure of economic production of the various spatial systems has been classified according to the characteristics of their plants, selecting those systems whose structural characteristics best correspond to definitions of the Marshallian industrial district.

Marshallian industrial districts

A first glance at the results (Maps 6 and 7, Appendix 6) shows that only very few of the geographical systems we have looked at can be considered industrial districts. It is also surprising that it is the social identity rather than the economic which reduces the chances of systems of specialized production being considered Marshallian industrial districts.

The systems of Biella (textiles), Cantù (furniture), Vigevano (footwear), Solofra (tanning) would have sufficient production specialization to be included, especially if we consider the important role each of these plays in the geography of the Italian economic system.[24] But their social structure, unlike that of geographical systems identified as industrial districts, is dominated by managerial and white-collar workers, by employment in services, although industrial employment is significant and there are consistent numbers of working wives. The real difference lies in the social status of the small industrial entrepreneur and the type of family he lives in.[25]

Some geographical systems, on the contrary, while having a social structure with the characteristics of the Marshallian industrial district, are not specialized enough in manufacturing production. Whilst Biella and Cantù have not the social structure of the typical industrial district, Faenza and Arezzo for example have an industrial structure which is not specialized enough.

Looking for a plausible explanation of these counter-intuitive empirical findings, we must remember that the specialization of the productive process within a single geographical system has been evaluated with reference to both the local and national system. Using the same quantitative methodology, another analyst may obtain the same results with the same data as ours, but their interpretation remains a matter of subjective insight.

There are three principal explanations of the results of the research: two are concerned with methodology, the third with interpretation. One explanation lies in the intrinsic nature of the unit of analysis which has been used to investigate the social and economic structure of the Italian geographical system. The geographical systems used as units of investigation are defined more by the functional relationships between their elements, residential and production settlements, than by their social and economic characteristics. Therefore they are heterogeneous entities in which the whole affects the measurement of the constituent parts; in other words, the whole is never simply the sum of the parts.

The furniture industry of Ponsacco, for example, will appear under a different light if we look at it isolated from its geographical system (the Val d'Era) or if we look at it as part of the production structure of the area as a whole. In this case it may be that the furniture industry, while being typical for Ponsacco, is no longer so in the Val d'Era. Another methodological explanation of the results of the research is brought to light when two industrial specializations, equally important for an area, co-exist without either being considered typical of the system.

As far as interpretation is concerned, the problem of identifying the Marshallian industrial district is tied up with that of the transformation of 'organized complexity' which characterizes them. When we talk about the 'process of transformation of organized complexity' we refer to a situation in which a geographical system passes from a stage where no one economic activity is predominant, to one of 'progressive differentiation', where some activities begin to predominate and eventually one emerges which involves and dominates the whole social and economic structure. This transition implies an increase in the internal complexity of the system and can evolve into a more advanced structure of production if interaction is developed with surrounding geographical systems. Economic activities in systems belonging to the same environment are located and relocated leading to the formation of different spatial patterns.[26]

Final remarks

The variety of forms which the area of small-firm production take poses problems for the definition of where the Marshallian industrial district stands with respect to the others within both a local framework of development and a national one. The local spatial production systems become increasingly complex and progress from undifferentiated stages to more specialized stages of production. Within this variety, where does the industrial district develop from, and which stage can it evolve into? A local socio-economic organism always remains a system, even though some of its parts have a more decisive role to play in the running of it than others. However, when it passes from an undifferentiated stage to a more differentiated, specialized one, it bears the seeds of its own disintegration. The more specialized the component parts are, the more difficult it is to substitute them, and their loss can be catastrophic for the system as a whole.

The capacity of self-regulation of the system decreases as its internal differentiation and specialization increases, thus increasing its relative dependence on relations with the surrounding environment. The Marshallian industrial district represents a 'state of progressive specialization' within that process of light industrialization which forms the basis of the urbanized countryside. Where it is going to depends both on its processes for internal regulation and its interaction with surrounding systems and their stages of development.

In the light of the empirical evidence at our disposal and the theoretical considerations made above, it is difficult to judge the Marshallian industrial district as it stands at the moment. It may be in a critical state ready to evolve to a more advanced state or it may be in a steady state with tendencies to stability. This all depends on the degree of potential conflict with the surrounding environment and the possible solutions which emerge.

Acknowledgements

This is a new version of a study which appeared in G. Becattini (ed.) *Mercato e forze locali, il distretto industriale*, Bologna: Il Mulino, 1987.

Notes

1. G. Becattini, 'Dal "settore industriale" al "distretto industriale".
   Alcune considerazioni sull' unità d'indagine dell'economia
   industriale', *Rivista di Economia e Politica Industriale* 1, 1979.
2. G. Bianchi, M. Bellandi, and F. Sforzi, *Analisi delle interdipendenze
   locali: alcune premesse teoriche*, Florence: IRPET, 1982.
3. S. Openshaw and F. Sforzi, *Metodologia per l'analisi della struttura
   sociale e produttiva urbana*, Florence: IRPET, 1983.
4. The pattern of the economic system which emerges from the analysis
   of the whole of Tuscany is reproduced here for the area between
   Florence and Pistoia, where Prato is the central place. As is obvious
   from Map 2, areas characterized by commercial activities (grocery
   stores, bars, haberdashery, furniture and car repairs, etc.) alternate
   with manufacturing areas characterized by light industry. Services to
   firms and government offices together with the other public and
   private services tend to be located in Prato's central business
   district. The rest of the area on the contrary consists of small
   settlements where manufacturing is carried out. If we exclude some
   areas of sparse manufacturing, textile production extends over a wide
   area. The contiguity of production areas is to be seen for other
   types of production, such as clothing, footwear, leather goods,
   furniture. The boundaries of these areas are well defined.
5. Rate variables of economic activities (as percentage of employees)
   used in the analysis: (1) Agriculture, (2) energy industries, (3)
   extraction of minerals, (4) metal manufacture, (5) manufacture of
   non-metallic mineral products, (6) glass and glassware, (7) ceramic
   goods, (8) chemical industries, (9) production of man-made fibres,
   (10) manufacture of metal goods, (11) mechanical engineering, (12)
   manufacture of data-processing equipment, (13) electrical and electronic engineering, (14) manufacture of transport equipment, (15)
   instrument engineering, (16) food, drink, and tobacco manufacturing
   industries, (17) textile industries, (18) leather tanning, (19) leather
   goods, (20) footwear industries, (21) clothing industries, (22) timber
   and wooden furniture, (23) manufacture of paper and paper products,
   (24) printing and publishing, (25) processing of rubber and plastics,
   (26) jewellery, (27) musical instruments, (28) toys and sports goods,
   (29) miscellaneous manufacturing, (30) construction, (31) wholesale
   distribution, (32) commission agents, (33) retail distribution: food,
   confectioners and tobacconists, (34) retail distribution: dispensing
   chemists, (35) retail distribution: clothing, footwear, and leather
   goods, (36) retail distribution: furnishing fabrics and household

goods, (37) retail distribution: motor vehicles (repair and filling stations), (38) retail distribution: books, stationery, and office supplies, (39) other retail distribution, (40) hotels, (41) catering, (42) repairs of consumer goods, (43) road haulage, (44) transport, (45) financial services, (46) house and estate agents, (47) business services, (48) renting of movables, (49) public administration, (50) professional services, (51) leisure services, (52) personal services, (53) community services.

6. G. Garofoli, 'Le aree-sistema in Italia' *Politica ed Economia* 11, 1983.

7. Rate variables of social characteristics. Population in employment as (1) manager, (2) clerk, (3) employer, (4) manual worker. Population in employment in (5) agriculture, (6) industry, (7) buildings, (8) commerce, (9) services, (10) public administration. Population in employment with (11) degree or diploma, (12) intermediate qualification, (13) elementary qualification, (14) population with no educational qualification, (15) married female in employment. Population in employment (16) aged 14–24, (17) aged 14–24 student, (18) aged 14–24 seeking work, (19) retired from employment, (20) aged 0–5, (21) aged 6–13, (22) aged 14–18, (23) aged 19–24, (24) aged 25–44, (25) aged 45–59, (26) aged 60 or over, (27) Population temporarily present. (28) Population of foreign citizenship. (29) Single-person households. (30) Single-parent households. Households with (31) six or more people, (32) two people both aged 19–59, (33) three or more children, (34) six or more people two of whom aged 60 or more, (35) two people both aged 60 or more, (36) three to five people at least one aged 60 or more. (37) Households sharing private dwelling. (38) Vacant dwellings. (39) Vacant dwellings for sale or rent. (40) Vacant dwellings for second residence. (41) Vacant dwellings for other reasons. (42) Occupied private dwellings owner-occupied. Occupied private dwellings (43) tenanted, (44) in other tenure, (45) with one or two rooms, (46) with six or more rooms, (47) with 1.5 or more persons per room, (48) with 0.5 or less persons per room, (49) with bath and inside WC, (50) with no bath. Dwellings with (51) outside WC, (52) no WC, (53) no flushing toilet, (54) fixed heating system, (55) single-apparatus heating, (56) no heating, (57) outside mains water, (58) outside well, (59) no drinking water, (60) no electricity. (61) Non-permanent household's accommodation.

8. The social pattern is also reproduced with reference to the same area examined previously. Once more the social typologies which describe the mosaic of residential areas give rise to areas where contiguity and extension are determinant features. The upper and middle class is concentrated in central Prato where previously commercial and service activities were located and in the rest of the area the industrial classes, workers, and small entrepreneurs are to be found. A pattern of settlement emerges which, moving from the core outwards in the direction of the countryside, is characterized by the social status of its inhabitants; that is, the upper strata of the service sector followed by industrial workers and agricultural workers.

9. G. Becattini (ed.) *Lo sviluppo economico della Toscana con particolare*

riguardo all'industrializzazione leggera, Florence: IRPET, 1975.
10. G. Becattini, 'The development of light industry in Tuscany', *Economic Notes* 2–3, 1978.
11. See M. Bellandi, Chapter 5 of this book.
12. R. Huggett, *Systems Analysis in Geography*, Oxford: Clarendon Press, 1980.
13. D. Harvey, *Explanation in Geography*, London: Edward Arnold, 1969.
14. F. Sforzi, S. Openshaw, C. Wymer, *La delimitazione di sistemi spaziali sub-regionali: scopi, algoritmi, applicazione*, Florence: IRPET, 1982.
15. The geographical pattern seen here refers to a more extensive part of the area examined before. The purpose is to identify in depth the functional boundaries of the Prato area. Furthermore, we use the municipality as a reference point for evaluating the form and characteristics of spatial organization whilst, before, these were examined at enumeration district level. The geographical system of Prato emerges as a result of the network of interactions generated by the production and residential functions, though what we see here is the resultant and not the representation of the network. In the light of the pattern which the economic and social structure form in this area, we can see that the Prato geographical system includes all the characteristics of an area in the light-industry typology. Even though the boundaries render mutually exclusive the geographical systems, it is clear that they cannot be considered rigorously defined frontiers which do not allow interaction across them. Despite this, in the specific case of Prato, we find a level of self-containment which allows us to define it as a geographical entity.
16. T. Hägerstrand, 'What about people in regional science?' *Paper of the Regional Science Association* 24, 1970.
17. Becattini, *Lo sviluppo*.
18. A. Marshall, *Industry and Trade*, London: Macmillan, 1919.
19. R.W. Gerard, 'Units and concepts in biology', *Science*, 125, 1957.
20. ISTAT–IRPET: *I mercati locali del lavoro in Italia*, Rome, 1986; *Le zone residenziali in Italia*, Rome, 1986; *Le zone produttive in Italia*, Rome, 1986.
21. Hägerstrand, op. cit.
22. F. Sforzi, 'Identificazione degli ambiti sub-regionali di programmazione', in M. Bielli and A. La Bella, (eds) *Problematiche dei livelli sub-regionali di programmazione*, Milan: Franco Angeli.
23. Becattini, *Lo sviluppo*.
24. F. Sforzi and M. Montagnini, *I sistemi produttivi locali in Italia*, Florence: IRPET, 1986.
25. F. Sforzi, 'La geografia dell' Italia marginale', *Politica ed Economia* 3, 1987.
26. L. von Bertalanffy, *Teoria generali dei sistemi*, Milan: ISEDI, 1971.
General note: For statistical sources of population, divisions and classes, see ISTAT industrial census, 1981 and population census, 1981.

Appendix 6

Map 1 Economic patterns. Shaded areas and symbols represent the different economic activites.

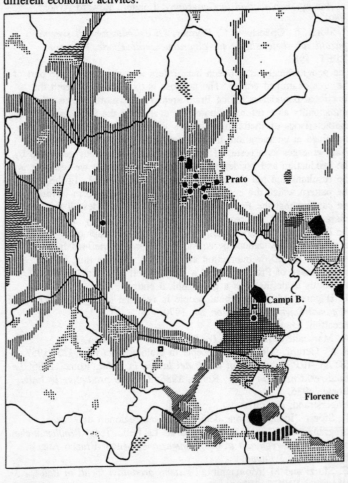

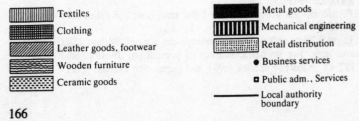

Textiles	Metal goods	
Clothing	Mechanical engineering	
Leather goods, footwear	Retail distribution	
Wooden furniture	• Business services	
Ceramic goods	▫ Public adm., Services	
	— Local authority boundary	

Map 2 Social patterns. Characteristics of the residential areas.

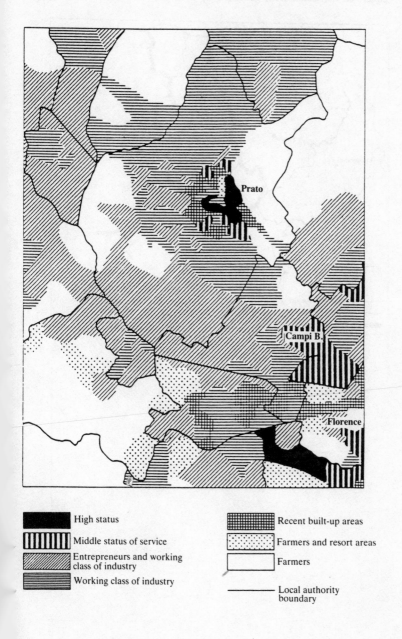

High status

Middle status of service

Entrepreneurs and working class of industry

Working class of industry

Recent built-up areas

Farmers and resort areas

Farmers

Local authority boundary

Map 3 Geographical patterns. Geographical systems corresponding to self-contained functional areas generated by journey to work flows.

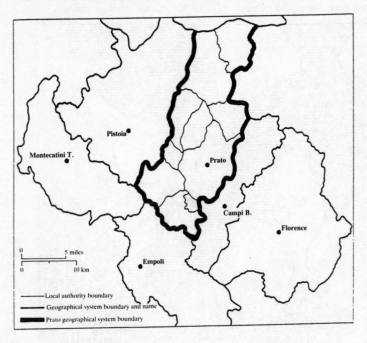

Map 4 Geographical systems in Italy, as identified in 1981. This pattern represents self-contained functional areas obtained by processing journey to work data, fitting the concepts of both daily urban systems and local labour-market areas.

Small firms and industrial districts in Italy

Map 5 Social structures typical of industrial districts. Shaded areas are geographical systems characterized by socio-economic features typical of the Marshallian industrial district.

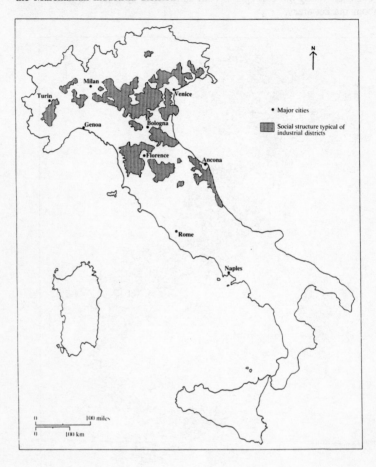

Map 6 Geographical systems corresponding to the Marshallian industrial district.

Map 7 Marshallian industrial districts, according to principal economic activity

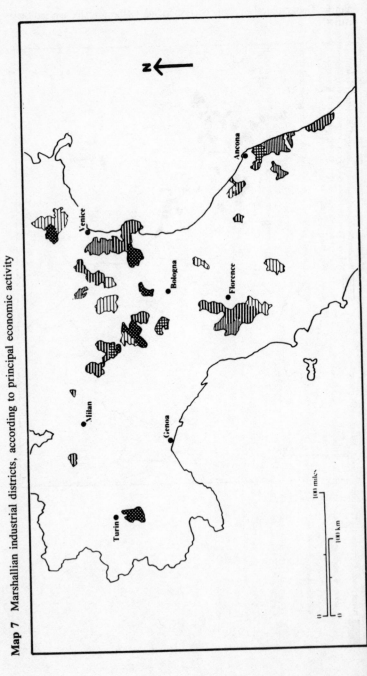

Metal goods: Carmagnola (Piedmont). Rivarolo Mantovano (Lombardy)

Mechanical engineering: Suzzara (Lombardy). Novellara (Emilia-Romagna). Cento (Emilia-Romagna). Copparo (Emilia-Romagna).

Electrical and electronic engineering: Conegliano (Veneto). Guastalla (Emilia-Romagna).

Textiles: Urgnano (Lombardy). Quinzano d'Oglio (Lombardy). Asola (Lombardy). Carpi (Emilia-Romagna). Prato (Tuscany).

Clothing: Oleggio (Piedmont). Manerbio (Lombardy). Pontevico (Lombardy). Verolanuova (Lombardy). Ostiano (Lombardy). Noventa Vicentina (Veneto). Piazzola sul Brenta (Veneto). Adria (Veneto). Porto Tolle (Veneto). Mondolfo (Marche). Urbania (Marche). Corinaldo (Marche). Filottrano (Marche). Roseto degli Abruzzi (Abruzzi). Castelfiorentino (Tuscany). Empoli (Tuscany).

Leather tanning: Arzignano (Veneto). Santa Croce sull'Arno (Tuscany).

Leather goods: Tolentino (Marche).

Footwear: San Giovanni Ilarione (Veneto). Piove di Sacco (Veneto). Civitanova Marche (Marche). Fermo (Marche). Grottazzolina (Marche). Montefiore dell'Aso (Marche). Montegranaro (Marche). Monte San Pietrangeli (Marche). Torre San Patrizio (Marche). Lamporecchio (Tuscany). Montecatini Terme (Tuscany).

Wooden furniture: Viadana (Lombardy). Bovolone (Veneto). Cerea (Veneto). Nogara (Veneto). Motta di Livenza (Veneto). Oderzo (Veneto). Montagnana (Veneto). Sacile (Friuli-Venezia-Giulia). Modigliana (Emilia-Romagna). Saltara (Marche). Poggibonsi (Tuscany). Sinalunga (Tuscany).

Ceramic goods: Sassuolo (Emilia-Romagna). Casalgrande (Emilia-Romagna).

Toys: Canneto sull'Oglio (Lombardy).

Musical instruments: Potenza Picena (Marche). Recanati (Marche).

Chapter 7

Small-firm development and political subcultures in Italy

Carlo Trigilia

The role of particular social factors – extended family, local community, rural–urban interpenetration – in the growth of the Italian small-firm economy has been widely recognized, but this chapter focuses on local political systems. The most typical small-firm regions are characterized by distinctive political subcultures: the Communist one in the central regions of the country and the Catholic/Christian Democratic one in the north-east.

The importance of the development of small firms for the Italian economy in the last ten years is generally accepted. This development can be seen as one of the most significant aspects of the process of adjustment to the economic and social tensions of the 1970s. The term 'adjustment' emphasizes that this process was largely unplanned, though it was influenced by political decisions or, more frequently, non-decisions. In the absence of effective long-term economic policies at the central level, the growth of small firms has, in fact, been based on certain economic, social, and political resources which were widely available in some local areas. These allowed smaller productive units to seize the opportunities for development which were opened up by changes in technology, in the organization of work and in market structures. Furthermore, the strengthening of the unions in large firms, which occurred in the early 1970s, contributed, especially in the initial stages, to the growth of small firms. The study of the political economy of small firms seems, therefore, of particular interest in the Italian context.

The regions in which small firms predominate, Emilia, Tuscany, Umbria, the Marches, Veneto, Trentino, and Friuli, are located principally in the centre and north-east of the country, though the phenomenon is also to be found in the north-west, where, however, large firms undergoing restructuring and the large metropolitan areas are concentrated, and in the south, where the major problems remain those associated with underdevelopment. It is the area of the 'Third Italy' which is most characterized by the predominance of small firms.[1] Indicators such as the rate of growth of value added, investment, productivity and employment show the dynamism of industry in these areas. The 'traditional' sectors of industry – textiles, clothing, shoes, and furniture – predominate, but there is also a significant development of modern sectors, particularly the machine-tool industry. Small firms tend to be found clustered together in industrial districts. They form integrated territorial systems with strong sectorial specialization. These districts usually coincide with small urban areas and consist of one or more communes.

Numerous economic studies of the small-firm economy have been carried out. These clearly indicate that there is a relationship between this form of development and the social context in which it occurs. Less attention has been devoted, however, to the role of the local political context. Yet the regions which are most typical of small-firm development (as well as similar areas in Piedmont and Lombardy) are usually characterized by the existence of specific subcultures. In these areas, one often finds the predominance of a particular political tradition, whose origins usually go back to the beginning of the century, and a complex of institutions (parties, interest groups, cultural and welfare structures) which derive from the same politico-ideological matrix. The central regions, which were originally Socialist in orientation, are now Communist strongholds, while there is a deeply-rooted Catholic subculture in the regions of the north-east (Fig. 7.1)

The purpose of this is to draw attention to the political context of 'diffuse industrialization'. I shall try to show that the Communist and Catholic subcultures fostered a *localist* tradition of the small-firm economy through their influence on industrial relations and on the activity of local governments. On these bases, a social compromise was established which brought about high levels of economic flexibility. Unions and local governments mitigated the social costs of economic adjustment and favoured a local redistribution of the benefits accruing from economic growth. The observations on this theme draw on the results of a research project on the social and political features of small-firm areas. The project consisted of an analysis of central and north-eastern regions, as well as of case studies of two typical areas with differing political subcultures, Bassano in Veneto and Valdelsa in Tuscany.[2]

Dualism or neo-localism

It is not necessary to provide an account of the *problématique* of research on small firms in any detail here. For our purpose it is

Figure 7.1 Small-firm regions and political subcultures, 1971–2

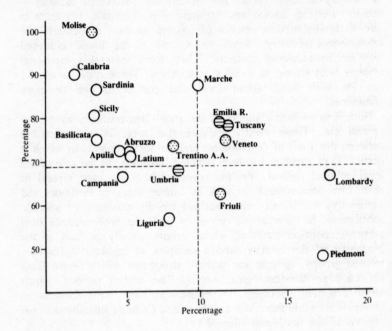

The *vertical axis* shows the percentages of workers employed in manufacturing industries in local units with less than 250 employees in the 1971 census.

The *horizontal axis* measures the level of industrialization by means of the ratio of workers employed in manufacturing industry to the resident population in 1971.

The *political subcultures* are identified by means of the ratio of DC (Christian Democratic Party) and PCI (Communist Party) votes obtained in the elections for the Chamber of Deputies in 1972 to the total DC and PCI vote in each region.

⊜ *PCI dominance* (where the ratio of DC votes to the combined DC–PCI votes in each region is 10 or more points lower than the ratio on a national level, which is 58.7 per cent).

⊙ *DC dominance* (where the ratio of DC votes to the combined DC–PCI vote in each region is 10 or more points higher than the ratio on a national level).

○ *Relative equilibrium between the DC and PCI* where the ratio of DC votes to the combined DC–PCI vote in each region is equal to or higher than the national ratio by less than 10 points).

sufficient to recall some essential points. The interpretations of the origins and characteristics of this form of development have been progressively refined over time. In the early stages, the emphasis was on the idea that the growth of small firms was induced and brought about, principally, by the attempt of larger firms to circumvent the restrictions imposed by the unions, by devolving parts of the productive process to smaller firms. Their aim was to reduce the labour costs and to re-establish the flexibility of the workforce.[3]

This initial conception was later complicated by various developments. Economic research showed that, in some areas, the relationship between firms could not be wholly explained by the phenomenon of productive decentralization introduced for the purpose of cutting labour costs. These relationships often entailed increased specialization and division of labour among small firms, and were rooted in economies of scale, external to the single units of production, but internal to the industrial district in which they were located.[4] The same studies stressed that changes in technology and the growth of demand for non-standardized goods enhanced the chances of autonomy and innovation for small firms.

At the same time, another line of research, this one sociologically oriented, contributed to the clarification of certain essential aspects. It was pointed out that small firms are concentrated, mainly, in the central and north-eastern regions (Bagnasco 1977). In these areas a trend of autonomous development emerged. This was not primarily brought about by the decentralization of existing production, though it was combined with the latter in various ways according to the sectorial specialization of industrial districts. The role of traditional institutions and identities is considered, by this approach, to be an important variable in the development of small firms and in the acceptance of this development by the local communities. In particular, some studies have examined the characteristics of the extended family and its relationship with the small-firm economy from this perspective (Ardigo and Donati 1976; Paci 1980). The research project on which I am drawing here can also be located within this approach. However, the results indicate that diffuse industrialization is supported by a more complex institutional architecture which consists not only of social components like the extended family and the local community, but also of specific political components related to the role of the Communist and Catholic subcultures at the local level.

Within the industrial district market mechanisms and social institutions such as the family, the kinship network and the local community are closely interwoven. These social institutions provide cultural and material resources for the development of entrepreneurship and of flexible productive structures. They motivate people to start new activities and help them in sustaining the costs of setting up and operating small firms. They also mitigate those effects of the market on industrial workers which arise from the higher discontinuity of employment and working time in small firms, and enable labour costs to be lower and incomes to be supplemented at the family level. Furthermore, the persistence of community values which cut across social classes, the low degree of polarization of the class structure and the high rate of social mobility play an integrative role that should not be underestimated in evaluating the success of small-firm areas.

These social aspects of the small-firm economy are already well known. The studies carried out in Valdelsa and Bassano also confirm that they are of great importance. Nevertheless, the insistence on the traditional localism/market duality runs the risk of being misleading, especially when it is applied to those areas where industrialization is more consolidated and where there is a well-established political sub-culture. In these situations, the role played by a specific form of interest intermediation, shaped through the influence of political subcultures on union representation and the activity of local government, must also be taken into consideration.

There is evidence to question a widespread conception (influenced by the early discussions on the decentralization of production) which underestimates the importance of interest representation of workers involved in the small-firm economy. Using a concept recently proposed by Goldthorpe to analyse current trends in some western countries, including Italy, we could define this approach in terms of dualism (Goldthorpe 1984). The concept refers to interest representation. It is used with reference to forms of political economy based on productive and occupational situations in which the representation of workers' interests by trade unions is excluded or strongly discouraged. The use of a migrant workforce, the diffusion of precarious and illegal work relations and the development of productive decentralization and of small firms are considered as indicators of this type of political economy. From this perspective, therefore, a small-firm economy is seen as one pole of a dualism which, unlike the large firms and unionized sectors, is regulated, primarily, by market mechanisms.

In reality, however, things appear to be more complicated, at least as far as Italy is concerned. Dualism, in the sense indicated above, is certainly present and it should not be overlooked. Nevertheless, the development of small firms demands a more articulated interpretative model. Small firms are generally embedded in a particular institutional context which interacts with the market and conditions the effects of the latter on the life chances of people involved. There exists, in short, a process of 'social construction of the market' (Bagnasco 1985) which dualist type models tend to overlook. I propose to use the concept of 'neo-localism' to illustrate the complex interdependence between the various mechanisms of regulation at local level and to draw attention, in particular, to interest intermediation. The division of labour between market, social structures, and to an increasing extent, political structures made the local economy highly flexible and adaptable to rapid market changes in sectors with wide fluctuations in demand.

In the next paragraphs I shall try to clarify the role played by union representation and by local government in the development of neo-localist trends. Of course, caution must be exercised in any attempt to generalize from individual local or regional cases. The different subculture matrices, the period in which economic growth occurs and the sectorial specificity of the various areas all influence the concrete interaction between market and social and political structures.

The historical roots of localism

In looking at the role of interest representation in small-firm areas, one must first of all point out that this representation has a long history which is closely connected to the origins and development of the local Socialist and Catholic subcultures. It is not possible to examine this history in any depth here,[5] but one should emphasize the fact that, in the central and north-eastern regions, the Socialist and Catholic movements were very active from the end of the nineteenth century onwards. Their roots in local society are not only deeper and stronger than in other parts of the country but the traditions themselves have assumed a particular character in that they have produced territorially-based political subcultures. Neither the social influence nor the political representation of these subcultures was confined to specific groups: they tended, rather, to cut across class boundaries and to assume wider community dimensions.

It is possible to identify some of the historical conditions that favoured this phenomenon; for example, the non-polarized class structure of the central and north-eastern parts of the country which was based on agricultural work of a predominantly autonomous variety (sharecropping, peasant and tenant farming); a thick network of small artisan and commercial centres which had enough resources to establish a clear identity and to organize themselves; and a secular (republican, radical, or anarchist) tradition in the central areas and a predominantly Catholic tradition in the north-east. The interaction between these factors, following the development of capitalism and the creation of the nation-state favoured the establishment of socialism in some areas and of the Catholic movement in others.

It is important to emphasize that the differing territorial subcultures that arose from the consolidation of these movements had a particular

179

feature in common; both tried, albeit in different ways, to *defend the local society* from the changes brought about by the market and by the state and tried to halt the process of social disintegration and to contain that of proletarianization by experimenting with localized forms of organization.[6] In the 'red' areas, this process developed through a complex series of relationships, involving unions, labour organizations, friendly societies, co-operatives and communes, which characterized the lively municipal socialism of the beginning of the century. In the 'white' areas, organizations of a specifically union type were less developed, but there was a network of rural savings and other banks, agricultural organizations, co-operatives, friendly societies, and charities, all of which were linked, in one way or another, to the local church. In both the red and white areas, the defence of the local society involved some form of relationship with the 'centre', that is with the national state. This relationship had both conflictive and contractual elements, and the former were often used to improve the terms of political bargains. A typical example of this is the activity of the parliamentary socialists in favour of co-operatives and communes. This type of relationship between centre and periphery is related to the fact that both Socialists and Catholics were excluded, in varying ways and for varying reasons, from the central political power. This exclusion drove them into organizing and strengthening their position at a local level where conditions were more favourable.

There are, of course, differences in the strength of the subcultures and in the periods in which they emerged and were established. As far as the areas under socialist control are concerned, for example, the phenomenon is certainly more widespread and consolidated in Emilia-Romagna and in certain areas of Tuscany than it is in Umbria and the Marches, where Socialist penetration of the countryside occurred, principally, after the First World War and where the social network of associations remained relatively underdeveloped even after that date. In the same way, the Catholic subculture was stronger in some areas of east Lombardy, such as Bergamo and Brescia, and in the inland areas of Veneto, such as Vicenza and Padua, than in other parts of the north-east. Our interest lies, however in emphasizing the emergence of a model of representation which had strongly localist connotations and through which, in the face of the weakness of the central state and of the vertical structures of representation – parties, unions, and interest groups – a decentralized political economy was established. The subculture fostered the emergence of particular local political systems.

It is not possible here to examine the historical evolution of this phenomenon, which involved the establishment, after Fascism and the war, of the Italian Communist Party (PCI) and the Christian Democrat

Figure 7.2 Rate of unionization (CISL and CGIL) in industry, by geographical area

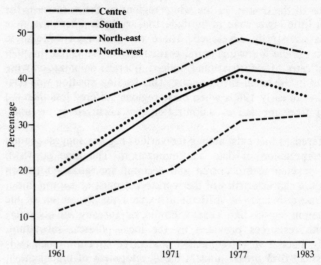

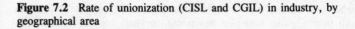

Sources: For the period up to 1977 Romagnoli (1980); for 1983, CESOS (unpublished data). The method used to calculate the rate of unionization in 1983 is the same as that used by Romagnoli (1980, Vol. 3).

Party (DC) in those areas which had originally been under Socialist and Catholic influence.[7]

The context in which these territorial subcultures emerged did, however, have certain consequences for the political economy of small-firm areas. We should like to draw attention to two aspects in particular: the existence of a reservoir of resources for the organization of interests; and the influence of this on a model of representation which was conditioned, to a significant extent, by local and political constraints. We shall try to give an outline description of how these elements combined by examining industrial relations and the activity of local government.

Union representation

As already noted, the idea that areas of small-firm development are characterized by weakness of trade unions and by poorly institutionalized industrial relations is widely held. If we consider the data on unionization (Fig. 7.2), however, the picture appears to be

Small firms and industrial districts in Italy

somewhat less simple and straightforward. In 1961, when the process of small-firm growth was just beginning, or had not yet started, the rate of unionization in industry (CGIL plus CISL) was highest in the red regions of the centre. In the white regions of the north-east, the rate was a little lower than in the industrial triangle, where the large enterprises were fully developed. There was a marked increase in unionization in the following years, particularly in the 1970s. In 1977 the highest rates of industrial (and, indeed, overall) unionization were to be found in the small-firm regions. This leading position was consolidated in the early 1980s when these regions suffered less than the north-west from the fall in unionization that occurred at the same time.[8]

The differences that exist among the various regions suggest caution in the interpretation of data on unionization. The time at which economic development occurred and sectoral specialization (which influences the characteristics of the workforce) must be kept in mind. It would, nevertheless, be difficult to explain the dynamism of the phenomenon in regions like Veneto, Emilia, or Tuscany without reference to the resources provided by the local political subculture, particularly since a very fragmented productive structure, such as is found in small-firm areas, hinders the development of unionization, especially from an organized point of view. It should also be pointed out that the CGIL (the Communist–Socialist union) predominates in the red and the CISL (the Catholic union) in the white areas, even though an area of union monopoly really exists only in the first case (Rossi 1980). In the regions of the north-east, the CISL is stronger than in other parts of the country, but the CGIL is also represented to a significant extent.

The influence of the local context is also confirmed by the studies carried out in the white area of Veneto (Bassano) and the red area of Tuscany (Valdelsa). In the first case, the existence of a long-established Catholic associational network and, especially, the position of influence held by the ACLI (*Associazione Cattolica Lavoratori Italiani*) favoured the consolidation of the CISL. In 1982 the rate of unionization of workers in small firms in this area was 49 per cent, but it fell to 17 per cent for those employed in *artigiani* enterprises with less than ten employees. In Valdelsa, a gradual shift in union representation from the agricultural sector to that of small firms was facilitated by the existence of a very strong sharecropper's organization in the 1950s as well as by the considerable organization and strength of the Communist Party in the area. Unionization of workers in small firms reached a level of 80 per cent, though the rate was considerably lower in the *artigiani* sector.

The two case studies are, of course, very localized, but they

Table 7.1 Indicators of conflict

	1969–73				1974–78				1979–82			
	(a)	(b)	(c)	(d)	(a)	(b)	(c)	(d)	(a)	(b)	(c)	(d)
Piedmont	1,761	28.5	1,481	43.7	1,073	22.2	2,747	18.1	992	14.4	3,452	19.6
Trentino A.A.	889	51.4	458	36.3	643	93.1	660	16.7	503	32.2	1,151	14.2
Friuli	1,552	47.2	1,169	29.3	1,372	36.8	2,856	14.7	1,149	39.8	2,948	9.8
Veneto	1,272	43.8	903	34.2	861	29.8	1,993	14.9	540	14.9	2,766	13.1
Emilia	1,890	37.1	1,815	29.0	1,634	25.5	5,819	11.7	1,191	15.0	6,765	11.8
Tuscany	1,616	45.9	1,337	28.1	1,361	26.7	4,548	12.2	1,195	17.0	5,162	13.8
Umbria	615	35.0	758	25.1	440	14.8	2,113	10.8	410	12.7	2,893	11.1
Marche	780	48.3	571	29.4	902	34.9	1,296	20.8	468	18.2	1,930	13.4
ITALY	1,279	34.1	1,224	32.8	812	24.2	3,436	14.8	674	13.8	3,572	13.7

Source: ISTAT, *Annuario di statistiche di lavoro*, Rome, various years. In order to keep the data homogeneous, strikes for 'motives external to the work relations', that is, political strikes, on which ISTAT provides information from 1975 onwards, have not been included. However, these do not show sufficient differentiation to alter the regional profiles that can be seen from the table.

(a) Hours of strikes per 100,000 employees (in thousands).

(b) Number of strikes per 100,000 employees.

(c) Number of strikers per strike.

(d) Number of work hours lost per striker.

highlight some processes that seem to acquire a more general significance in the light of the data previously analysed. We can maintain that the political subculture provided institutional and identity resources which favoured the organization of workers in small-firm districts, particularly in industrial enterprises with more than fifty employees. This process was more marked in areas with a red subculture, and especially in those with a stronger tradition of association.

Up to now we have described an important, though often underemphasized, aspect of interest representation in areas of small-firm development. The existence of various levels of worker organization cannot, however, in itself provide an adequate explanation of the nature of that representation. In this regard it is necessary to establish the direction taken by union activity and the consequences. If we consider the data on conflict in the period between the late 1960s and the early 1980s, we see that the severity of strikes (hours of work lost per striker) was markedly lower in small-firm regions than in a typical large-firm region like Piedmont (Table 7.1). Though the results are similar in all small-firm areas, these are due to varying factors in the different regions. The regions with the strongest Communist subculture, Emilia and Tuscany, have a very high rate of participation (strikers per strike) but a low rate of severity, while the white regions, Trentino, Veneto, and Friuli, have an appreciably lower participation rate and a relatively higher level of severity, although the latter is still less than that found in Piedmont. The Marches and Umbria have both low participation and low severity rates.[9]

Unionization and conflict would seem, therefore, to have a particular, though differentiated pattern in small-firm areas. A substantial level of unionization is accompanied by a low level of conflict. It would, however, be mistaken to conclude that unionization is to be considered as a consequence of the particular political subculture and that it has a negligible effect on industrial relations in small-firm areas. This view has often been put forward, particularly to explain the situation in the red areas.

There is no doubt that the local subculture did impose constraints on union activity in the initial stages of economic development. It is not difficult to find evidence of this in both the red and the white areas.[10] In the former, the strategies adopted by the PCI certainly did encourage policies which were favourable to small firms, while the growth of the CISL in the white areas, in the initial stages of development, was also largely dependent on the support of the Church, the DC, and the entrepreneurs, and this reduced the autonomy of the unions. Nevertheless, there are indications that this situation has changed.

The labour costs of industrial enterprises increased in the 1970s and, in almost all the small-firm areas, they came close to the national average and to that of Piedmont (Bagnasco and Pini 1981). The available data and studies that have already been carried out lead us to hold that this tendency was influenced by a considerable amount of negotiation at firm level. For example, a regional study in Veneto in the period 1979–80 found that 42 per cent of industrial enterprises with more than twenty employees were involved in negotiations at firm level (Giubilato 1982). This percentage was considerably higher for firms with more than fifty employees. The vast majority of firms above this threshold of size in Emilia and Tuscany also seem to have been involved in firm-level negotiations (Brusco 1982). In the studies on Bassano and Valdelsa, the rates found for industrial enterprises were 45 and 60 per cent, respectively.

Agreements at firm level were concerned, for the most part, with factors like wages and differentials. Other more innovative aspects relating to the processes of restructuring, mobility, and decentralization of production (such as, for example, the right to information and the negotiation of employment levels) are dealt with hardly at all or in a ritual way with limited practical implications. The question of the organization of work, which had, in the past, played an important role in firm negotiations in large factories, appears not to have been an issue at all.[11]

Caution should, obviously, be exercised in generalizing from these tendencies, and the differences between the areas in terms of wage benefits and differentials should not be underestimated. In Valdelsa, for example, we found that the wages negotiated at firm or area level were higher than in Bassano, and in the furniture sector exceeded the wage determined at the national level by 20 per cent. Differences also emerged in the average level of ratings. The degree of local co-ordination and formalization of negotiations is also higher in the red areas. Issues such as working hours and overtime are more frequently the subject of negotiations than in Bassano (in 83 per cent of the cases compared to 40 per cent in Bassano). The fact remains, however, that despite these differences, negotiations at firm level are carried out in an atmosphere where there is little conflict (in both areas about 70 per cent of the entrepreneurs declare themselves to be satisfied with industrial relations while the opinion of entrepreneurs on this subject on a national level is clearly negative). Negotiations at firm level bring economic benefits to industrial workers, especially those in firms with more than fifty employees, and they do not impose rigid constraints on labour mobility and flexibility which are fairly high in both areas. Workers often move from one firm to another (about 60 per cent of the workers changed firm more than once). In addition, substantial proportions of workers – from a third to a quarter – said that they worked more than eight hours a day in busy periods and that they worked on Saturdays and holidays. Interruptions of working activity because of a fall in production are widespread.

In the light of these data it does not seem possible to explain the relationship between high unionization and low conflict in terms of the hypothesis that stresses the subcultural character of unionization and sees it as having little effect on industrial relations. The quantitative data on conflict, to which we have already referred, can be interpreted in another way. These data do not necessarily indicate union weakness or, in the case of the red areas (Emilia and Tuscany), a predominantly political type of conflict which is expressed through high participation and short duration of strikes. They are also consistent with a negotiative and localist model of representation. This is quite different from the combative trade unions of the large factories in the 1970s which have dominated the political debate on the subject.

Further and more detailed research, as well as a thorough examination of the variations in industrial relations are necessary before any satisfactory generalizations can be made. A provisional synthesis can be proposed, however, in the following terms and on the basis of the data to which we have already referred: the existence, in many areas, of deeply rooted, territorial political subcultures favoured the growth of unionization, but at the same time it contributed to directing union activity so that it neither hindered the process of economic development nor weakened the local subculture itself. These original constraints have not prevented trade unions from growing in strength and from increasing their own margin of autonomy over time. This seems to have been achieved (though with specific differences that should not be underestimated) by means of a process of adjustment which involved using available resources to bring advantages to union members either in economic terms through single-firm or single-area negotiations or by means of providing services (consultation, assistance, patronage, etc.).

On the other hand, this tendency has been influenced by the characteristics of the working class in small-firm areas,[12] such as, for example, the low proletarianization of this social group which derives from the predominant forms of the organization of work, from its deep-rooted ties with the traditional institutional and cultural context (family and local community) and from the opportunities for individual family mobility offered by diffuse industrialization. These factors, which were particularly important in the first stage of development, were certainly not very favourable to the militant unionism that prevailed in the large firms and industrial cities at the time, though it is important to remember that this example of militancy did influence union activity even in small-firm areas and that it produced new forms

of conflict as well as internal changes within the political subcultures.[13]

On the whole, however, structural constraints and the characteristics
of the working class directed the unions towards a negotiative and
localist type of representation. This can be seen in negotiations at firm
and area level. Though these were more or less formalized, they
nevertheless reflected the compatibility of local political and economic
systems. There are, of course, likely to be some substantial differences
in the extent and effects of various negotiations. In general, however,
union agreements and activity did not impose rigid constraints on the
mobility and flexibility of the workforce. In exchange, the unions
obtained benefits of a prevalently economic type and a high level of
recognition on the part of the entrepreneurs. In this regard, it is
necessary to bear in mind that the rate of membership of business
associations is probably higher than it is usually thought to be in small-
firm areas. Comparable regional data is not available, but in both
Valdelsa and Bassano more than two-thirds of the craft and industrial
enterprises supported organizations of their category. The majority of
the entrepreneurs, moreover, said that they were in favour of stable
relationships with union organizations, and 60 per cent in Veneto and
45 per cent in Bassano reported that they had frequent contacts with
the union in the firm.

It is within this general context that the role of internal dualism in
the industrial relations of the individual areas is to be considered. This
role is always present, but its importance varies according to the local
economic and political context. Workers' organizations are less likely
to be found in smaller and particularly, craft firms (usually units with
less than fifteen employees) where there are also some legal limitations
on union activity. These firms are often tied to larger enterprises
through the decentralization of production, which is rarely an issue in
union activity or negotiations.

This dualism allows firms in the industrial sector to cushion the costs
of union representation to a certain extent. On the other hand, family
and community ties help to moderate the effects of discontinuity in
employment and of lower pay for workers involved in the sectors not
protected by unions. For example, the wives and children of unionized
workers in industrial firms are often employed in these sectors.

The factors discussed up to now show that there is a complex inter-
relationship, on a local level, between market, traditional social structures, and interest representation. A consideration of local government
activity should further add to our understanding of the small-firm
economy and, indeed, the influence of the subcultural background can
also be established in this context.

The role of local government

We have already referred to the role played in the defence of the local society by the Socialist and Catholic subcultures at the beginning of the century. With the development of small firms, one could say that this role has been revived, though obviously in different forms and contexts, within the processes of interest mediation in the individual areas.

In the climate of marked ideological conflict that characterized the 1950s, the activity of the Communist and Catholic institutional networks was directed, principally, at defending, reproducing and reinforcing their respective subcultures. The Communist Party and the Catholic Church assumed a primary role in this phase and they controlled and co-ordinated local institutions.[14] The communes were among these institutions and, though these did undertake concrete interventions in the social field, they were also used, to a significant extent, to consolidate local political identity. This trend was typical of the red areas in particular. Given the exclusion of the PCI from central power, the activity of the local governments controlled by the party was directed largely at supporting local political mobilization and at channelling demands and pressures towards the central institutions. The choice of a balanced budget in the communes, which was abandoned in the 1960s, is significant from this point of view. This choice certainly arose from the need to avoid central control and often, as far as left-wing administrations were concerned, discrimination; but it also reflected a more general orientation of the Communist subculture which was directed, above all, at defending and consolidating the local political identity.[15] As far as the white administrations were concerned, the choice of a restrictive budgetary policy arose from a tradition of minimal direct intervention on the part of the communes, a policy that was maintained in the following period. In this phase, however, one can note that the degree of autonomy of the DC and the communal administrations from the local church was very limited.

Things changed in the following period. It is possible to discern a shift towards a more concrete and relevant role for local government and unions in the mediation of local interests. This came about within the context of changes on a national political level which opened up greater opportunities for the activity of local agencies, particularly in the 1970s. The development of small firms was, nevertheless, an endogenous and essential condition for this process. The existence of deep-rooted traditional social structures and identities did, as we have emphasized, facilitate the transformation of the economy, and in the process a specific space was opened up for local government activity which began to supplement the role of traditional institutions in the regulation of economic development.

In order to clarify the nature and consequences of this process further, a series of factors must be considered. The parties which controlled local governments, the DC and PCI, enjoyed a high level of ideological consensus. The support was, in fact, an expression of overall cultural identity which, especially in the smaller centres, cut across the class structure and assumed a community character. This generalized support freed the administrators from the necessity of satisfying very specific and sectoral demands.[16] Moreover, even though the DC and the PCI were often part of coalition councils, they enjoyed a dominant role because of their strength in the local subcultures. This factor may have contributed to increasing the stability and decision-making capacity of local governments.[17]

There are, of course, differences in the ways in which the parties held and exercised power and influence. In particular, one can hypothesize that the DC had a more marked inter-class orientation than the PCI. Nevertheless, it is interesting to note that, because of their original characteristics, the social bases of both subcultures included various classes to a greater extent than in other areas. The development of small firms modified this situation over time and the differences between the subcultures were accentuated. But this came about in a gradual and non-traumatic way so that local governments were, for a long time, able to enjoy a reservoir of support that freed them from satisfying particular demands. Another element which increased the chances of success of communal policies in regions of small-firm development compared to large-firm or underdeveloped areas was that diffuse industrialization, particularly in its initial stage, limited the problems that local governments had to face. That the traditional family and the community background were not changed, that there was no great inflow of immigrants, and that employment and consumption were sustained, not only facilitated the task of the communal administrations but also allowed the traditional institutions and local interest groups to be used in the regulation of the industrial districts.

In summary, the policies adopted by the communes were aimed at maximizing the resources available (and these included applying pressure at a regional and central level) in order to favour agreements among the various interests involved in the development of small firms. The activity of local government included both direct policies in support of economic development and, especially, policies in the social field which were directed at mediating the effects of the market as a regulator of the economy and of employment. The creation of industrial estates for small firms, the provision of professional training and of infrastructure and support for the formation of consortia among the firms for the purposes of marketing or export facilities are examples of the first type of policy. Communes also became increasingly involved in attempts to find solutions to crises in those firms which were particularly important to the economy and to employment in the area.[18] This often involved putting pressure on regional and national governments to grant redundancy payments to the workers and even interceding with local banks on questions of credit. It also involved mediating between local unions and entrepreneurs.

The communes, however, have limited powers in the economic field. They were able to contribute to the creation of additional advantages for the firms, but basically, they fostered a process of economic growth which was not politically determined. Their social policies did, however, have a much greater impact. The provision of services in the fields of transport, public housing, schools, day-care centres, and health care often contributed to improving the living conditions of the workers and, in effect, they created a kind of local social wage. These policies also supplemented the resources provided by the traditional institutional fabric, particularly the family, in so far as they promoted a growth in female employment and general flexibility in employment.

There are, however, important differences in the various local policies. Despite the lack of research in this field, we do have some indications, with particular reference to the last ten years. The red administrations tend, on the whole, to be more interventionist than the white councils of the north-east (Ferraresi and Kemeny 1977). This tendency is particularly noticeable in the areas of land use and social policy, while the differences are less marked in the areas of direct economic intervention. Left-wing administrations are, in general, more inclined to adopt urban policies by which they try to control land use in the area and to promote forms of public or co-operative housing. In the area of social services, their tendency towards a higher degree of interventionism can be seen in their attempts to increase the number of services available and to assume direct responsibility for their operation, as, for example, in transport, day care and health care.

The white administrations, by contrast, tend to intervene less and to delegate the provision of services, for the most part, to the Catholic organizations which, however, receive some support from public funds. Data that confirm this picture can be found in various studies on commune expenditure. These show that expenditure and, consequently, the levels of budget deficit and debt, tend to be higher in communes controlled by the left.[19] Expenditure is lower in communes controlled by the DC in the white areas, though this is not true for DC communes in the south (Brosio and Santagata 1978; Aitken and Martinotti 1980). It would, however, be mistaken to conclude from these data that the white communes operate on a purely *laissez-faire* basis. It can, in fact, be shown that they do intervene to maintain the equilibrium between the dynamics of the market and the traditional local institutions (Cacciari 1975). There are two principal aspects to be considered in this respect. Land use and urban policies have aimed at promoting the interpenetration of factory and residence, even though this involves considerable costs, in order to minimize community uprooting and to make use of the integrative role of the family. Moreover, these policies are, in general, accompanied by support, including financial support, for the Catholic network of assistance. In this way, a series of services with important cultural and material effects is provided, albeit indirectly.

Strength and weakness of neo-localism

In conclusion, communes have contributed to the localist mediation of interests. This has been achieved by means of political resources which, directly or indirectly, have facilitated the integration of, and agreement between, the various actors involved in the development of small firms. One should emphasize here that this model of activity does not imply direct intervention in negotiations between unions and entrepreneurs and their associations but does promote the chances of agreement between them. On the other hand, the development of concerted action by local government and interest groups like unions and business associations is discouraged by the restricted powers of the communes in the economic field and by the limited autonomy of interest organizations. The characteristics of this form of representation are therefore different from those of local corporatism.[20] Unions and entrepreneurs operate, rather, along the lines of traditional pressure-group politics, directed at the parties with a view to obtaining particular advantages. In evaluating this phenomenon, we must obviously bear in mind the fact that the local political market is influenced by the specific subcultural context which determines differences in the presence and influence of the various interest groups. In both respects, the organizations which are closest to the local subculture are in a privileged position.

Another characteristic of this model of relations between interest groups and local government is that the former may forego the use of vertical organizational structures – for example, of the unions or the business associations – for the transmission of the political demands towards the outside. The horizontal representation which is provided by the dominant party/local government circuit is, in fact, often preferred. Examples of this can be found in the recourse by the unions to the communes in the case of crises in local firms, or in attempts by entrepreneurs to influence the way in which regional-level benefits are allocated. Territorial representation is considered in these cases to be more effective than the functional representation provided by the various interest organizations at regional or central level, because the latter could entail a greater loss of control over the outcome of the issues involved and can be less satisfactory from the point of view of local interests.[21]

On the whole, representation plays an important role in the localist regulation of the small-firm economy. Representation operates through a network of functional structures (unions, business associations, and other interest groups), which interact among themselves and with the local government in the individual areas, and through structures of territorial representation (parties, communes), which promote localist regulation by means of their intervention and their activity at regional and central level. The entire process is influenced by the local subculture, which provides for the organization of interests but also conditions the forms of interaction among the various actors in the local political arena.

In the small-firm areas, a social compromise has thus been established, based, on the one hand, on the high flexibility of the economy and, on the other, on the control of the costs and the redistribution of the benefits of development. In this way small firms could compensate for the shortcomings of the central political economy in Italy, and mitigate disruptive effects on employment and income. It is appropriate to emphasize the local dimension of this performance: not only is the individual area the primary unit of reference but the economic, social, and political resources that facilitate adjustment are predominantly endogenous. This perspective is also important because it offers a key to the problems of modernization which are likely to affect the small-firm areas in the future.

The ability to confront international competition and, particularly, the challenge posed by countries with lower labour costs, depends on technological innovation, the promotion of entrepreneurial skills, and the training of the workforce. What is required, therefore, is the development of resources and services which are not always in adequate supply at the local level. The economic literature on small firms deals extensively with these questions and shows that it is not easy for the smaller units of production to internalize functions, such as managerial training, marketing, and export activities, which become increasingly important under the new conditions of the international market. At the same time, one has also to take into account that the process of diffuse industrialization involves the consumption of local resources and brings about new costs – in terms of land use, energy supplies, pollution, waste disposal, and traffic congestion – that cannot be dealt with adequately at the local level and only with local resources.

In the context of the small-firm economy, therefore, economic innovation poses a problem of scale. This raises, in turn, the question of the relationship between small-firm areas and the cities as centres of service provision. Constraints of scale imply that the local economy becomes more dependent on the efficient operation of the regional political system. The need to experiment with forms of co-operation and organization among firms, to ensure that the necessary credit facilities are available and to stimulate relationships conducive to innovation among industrial districts and towns, makes the role of the regional political system more important.

In the Italian situation, the regional level could provide favourable opportunities for attacking problems of scale of the small-firm economy, which seem to require an intermediate level of government between the centre and the individual communes. These opportunities, however, have not so far been effectively exploited. In evaluating this issue, the emphasis is usually placed on the limited powers of regions in the industrial field and on the institutional and organisational constraints posed by central government. Less attention has been devoted to the shortcomings of a regional system of representation. Even though this aspect should be more carefully investigated, it is likely that the strength of localist networks has hindered the emergence of adequate structures of representation at the regional level. These, however, tend to become increasingly necessary for tackling the constraints of scale which will affect the small-firm areas in the future.

Acknowledgement

From Carlo Trigilia, 'Small firm development and political subcultures in Italy', *European Sociological Review* (1986) 2(3). Reprinted by permission of Oxford University Press.

Notes

1. It is well known that definitions of small firms are historically variable and can only be relative and conventional. In this chapter firms with less than 250 employees are defined as small. In the central and north-eastern regions of Italy, about 80 per cent of those employed in industry are concentrated in small firms. The average size is less than ten employees per unit, and this average decreased during the 1970s.
2. For a comprehensive picture of the research project which was co-ordinated by Arnaldo Bagnasco and Carlo Trigilia, see Bagnasco and Pini (1981), Trigilia (1981), and Bagnasco and Trigilia (1984, 1985).
3. For an analysis of the initial debate on the labour market see Paci (1973); for the following discussion on the decentralization of production, see Bagnasco (1977)
4. Among the numerous contributions, see: Becattini (1978, 1979),

Varaldo (1979), Garofoli (1981), Rullani (1982), Brusco (1982), Sabel (1982), Sabel and Piore (1984).

5. For a more thorough discussion of this aspect, see Trigilia (1981). On the concept of political subculture, see Pizzorno (1966), and for an application to the Italian regions, Sivini (1971) and Farneti (1971).

6. The expression 'defence of the local society' recalls that used by Polanyi in *The Great Transformation* (1944). Polanyi is influenced by the English case and primarily refers to the national response to the challenges posed by the market, which entails an expansion of the state. The Italian experience shows the relevance of local responses which can also precede the full penetration of market mechanisms through the social fabric and can anticipate state responses.

7. For an analysis of these developments from an electoral point of view, see Galli (1968).

8. On the dynamic of unionization up to 1977, see Romagnoli (1980), and for a review of more recent trends, Romagnoli (1985).

9. On the development of conflict in Italy, in terms of strikes, see Bordogna and Provasi (1979), and for a review of more recent tendencies, Bordogna (1985).

10. For the former, see Hellman's discussion of the PCI, *Politica delle alleanze* (alliance strategy) at local level. On the relationship between unions and the white subculture, see Fasol (1980).

11. On the development of collective bargaining in Italy, and on firm-level negotiations, see Cella and Treu (1982).

12. For a more thorough examination of this aspect, see Bagnasco (1985).

13. These changes are probably more noticeable in the white areas, where there were greater tensions between unions and the dominant Christian Democrat Party.

14. For an ideal-typical construction of the characteristics of both subcultures in this phase, see Alberoni (1967).

15. On the evolution of the activity of the 'red' communes, see Cammelli (1978) and Galli (1981).

16. On the relationship between ideological support and political demand, see Pizzorno (1969).

17. Some empirical evidence of the greater stability of local governments in the subcultural areas can be found in Parisi (1984).

18. A study which documented this process well was carried out in Veneto (Fondazione Carazzin 1984).

19. Since 1977–8, institutional measures which limit increases in deficit expenditure have been enacted. On the effects of these policies, see Dente (1985).

20. This concept was used with reference to the Norwegian case by Hernes and Selvik (1981); see also Cawson (1984).

21. Tarrow (1978) has pointed out the possibility of territorial representation being revived because of the shortcomings of functional representation.

Bibliography

Aitken, N. and Martinotti, G. (1980) *Left Politics, the Urban System and Public Policy: An Analysis of Municipal Expenditure among the Largest Cities in Italy*, mimeo.

Alberoni, F. (1967) 'Il PCI e la DC nel sistema politico italiano', in F. Alberoni (ed.) *L'attivista di partito*, Bologna: Il Mulino.

Ardigo, A. and Donati, P. (1976) *Famiglia e industrializzazione*, Milan: Franco Angeli.

Bagnasco, A. (1977) *Tre Italie. La problematica territoriale dello sviluppo italiano*, Bologna: Il Mulino.

Bagnasco, A. and Pini, R. (1981) 'Economia e struttura sociale', *Quaderni della Fondazione Feltrinelli* 14.

—— (1985), 'La costruzione sociale del mercato', *Stato e Mercato* 13.

Bagnasco, A. and Trigilia, C. (eds) (1984) *Società e politica nelle aree di piccola impresa. Il caso di Bassano*, Venice: Arsenale.

—— (eds) (1985) *Società e politica nelle aree di piccola impresa. Il caso della Valdelsa*, Milan: Franco Angeli.

Becattini, G. (1978) 'The development of light industry in Tuscany: an interpretation', *Economic Notes* 2–3.

—— (1979) 'Dal "settore industriale" al "distretto industriale". Alcune considerazioni sull'unità d'indagine dell'economia industriale', *Rivista di Economia e Politica Industriale*, 1.

Bordogna, L. (1985) '*Conflittualità*', in CESOS. *Le relazioni sindacali in Italia, 1983–1984*, Rome: Edizioni Lavoro.

Bordogna, L. and Provasi, G. (1972) 'Il movimento degli scioperi in Italia (1881–1971), in G.P. Cella (ed.) *Il movimento degli scioperi nel XX secolo*, Bologna: Il Mulino.

Brosio, G. and Santagata, W. (1978) 'Il ciclo dell'autonomia nei comuni capoluogo', *Archivio di studi urbani e regionali*, 8.

Brusco, S. (1982) 'The Emilian model: productive decentralisation and social integration', *Cambridge Journal of Economics*, 6.

Cacciari, M. (1975) 'Struttura e crisi del modello sociale veneto', *Classe* II.

Cammelli, M. (1978) 'Politica istituzionale e modello emiliano', *Il Mulino* 259.

Cawson, A. (1984) 'Corporatism and local politics', in W. Grant (ed.) *The Political Economy of Corporatism*, London: Macmillan.

Cella, G.P. and Treu, T. (eds) (1982) *Relazioni Industriali*, Bologna: Il Mulino.

Dente, B. (1985) *Governare la frammentazione*, Bologna: Il Mulino.

Farneti, P. (1971) *Sistema Politico e società civile*, Turin: Giappichelli.

Fasol, R. (1980) 'Una provincia del nord a prevalenze CISL', in G. Romagnoli (ed.) *La sindacalizzazione tra ideologia e pratica*, Rome: Edizioni Lavoro.

Ferraresi, F. and Kemeny, P. (1977) *Classi sociali e politica urbana*, Rome: Officina.

Fondazione Corazzin (1984) *L'intervento della regione nei conflitti di lavoro. L'esperienza veneta*, Rapport di ricerca/5.

195

Galli, G. (ed.) (1968) *Il comportamento elettorale in Italia*, Bologna: Il Mulino.
―――― (1981) 'Il partito e le amministrazioni locali. Il caso dell'Umbria (1944–1979)', *Annali della Fondazione Feltrinelli* 21.
Garofoli, G. (1981) 'Lo sviluppo delle aree periferiche nell'economia italiana degli anni '70', *L'industria* 3.
Giubilato, M. (1982) *La contrattazione industriale in Veneto*, Fondazione Corazzin.
Goldthorpe, J. (1984) 'The end of convergence: corporatism and dualist tendencies in modern western societies', in J. Goldthorpe (ed.) *Order and Conflict in Contemporary Capitalism*, Oxford: Oxford University Press.
Hellman, S. (1976) 'La strategia delle alleanze del PCI e il questione dei ceti medi', in D. Blackmer and S. Tarrow (eds) *Il comunismo in Italia e Francia*, Milan: Etas.
Hernes, G. and Selvik, A. (1981) 'Local corporatism', in S. Berger (ed.) *Organising Interests in Western Europe*, Cambridge: Cambridge University Press.
Paci, M. (1973) *Mercato del lavoro e classi sociali in Italia*, Bologna: Il Mulino.
―――― (ed.) (1980) *Famiglia e mercato del lavoro in un'economia periferica*, Milan: Franco Angeli.
Parisi, A. (ed.) (1984) *Luoghi e misure della politica*, Bologna: Il Mulino.
Pizzorno, A. (1966) 'Introduzione allo studio della partecipazione politica', *Quaderni di Sociologia* 3–4.
―――― (1969) 'Uno schema teorico per l'analisi dei partiti politici', in G. Sivini (ed.) *Partiti e partecipazione politica in Italia*, Milan: Giuffre.
Polanyi, K. (1944) *The Great Transformation*, New York: Rinehart & Winston.
Romagnoli, G. (ed.) (1980) *La sindacalizzazione tra ideologia e pratica*, Rome: Edizioni Lavoro.
―――― (1985) 'Sindacalizzazione e rappresentanza', in CESOS (ed.) *Le relazioni sindacali in Italia 1983–1984*, Rome: Edizioni Lavoro.
Rossi, M. (1980) 'Sindacalizzazione e sistema politico: la consistenza delle aree di monopolio sindacale', in G. Romagnoli (ed.), op. cit.
Rullani, E. (1982) 'L'economia delle differenze: il capitalismo industriale delle periferie', in S. Goglio (ed.) *Italia: centri e periferie*, Milan: Franco Angeli.
Sabel, C. (1982) *Work and Politics*, Cambridge: Cambridge University Press.
Sabel, C. and Piore, M.J. (1984) *The Second Industrial Divide*, New York: Basic Books.
Sivini, G. (1971) 'Socialisti e cattolici in Italia dalla società allo stato', G. Sivini (ed.) *Sociologia dei partiti politici*, Bologna: Il Mulino.
Tarrow, S. (1978) 'Introduction'; S. Tarrow, P. Katzenstein, and L. Graziona (eds) *Territorial Politics in Industrial Nations*, New York: Praeger.

Trigilia, C. (1981) 'Le subculture politiche territoriali', *Quaderni della Fondazione Feltrinelli*, 16.
Varaldo, R. (ed.) (1979) *Ristrutturazioni industriali e rapporti tra imprese*, Milan: Franco Angeli.

Chapter 8   198 – 222

Technical change and the industrial district: the role of inter-firm relations in the growth and transformation of ceramic tile production in Italy

Italy
6315
9412
6212

Margherita Russo

This chapter reports the results of a study of technical change in the ceramic tile history of Italy. Two hypotheses are developed. First, the process of invention, adoption, and diffusion of new techniques throughout the ceramic tile firms can be better understood in the light of the interrelationships between firms operating in the ceramic tile industrial districts. Second, the impact of forces of a technical nature in shaping the structure of the ceramic tile industry is characterized by a pattern of vertical disintegration which finds its most important explanation not so much in the economies of scale as in the product and process specialization of the production units operating in the industrial district.

The next section presents background material on the Italian production of ceramic tiles. The third section details the definition of an industrial district and illustrates the process of technical change in the ceramic tile industrial district. The fourth section focuses on the link between particular technical developments and the texture of interrelationships between firms in the industrial district in question.

Ceramic tile production in Italy

Until the Second World War the Italian production of ceramic tiles was insignificant, and the few ceramic tiles for decorative purposes were produced by small artisan firms. Emerging at the end of the 1940s, large-scale production thereafter increased rapidly, especially in the period 1960–80, which witnessed the most consistent growth rate (11.3 per cent per year). Output expanded from nearly 38 million square metres of tiles in 1960 to over 355 million in 1980. In the same period the proportion of exports went from 3.5 per cent in 1960 to 45 per cent in 1980, giving Italy a clear lead in the world market. In 1984 world sales were 1×10^{12} square metres of ceramic tiles, of which 30 per cent were produced in Italy.

The 1960s and 1970s witnessed the entry by many new firms into the ceramic tile industry; entry was made easier both because the initial investment required – at that time – for a factory of minimum efficient size was almost insignificant and because the know-how was not difficult to acquire.

A crucial factor in the development of production has been the increase in both domestic and internal demand for tiles. In particular, the sharp increase in domestic demand was induced partly by changes in the housing legislation[1] of the early 1960s, and partly by changes in the technical and aesthetic characteristics of the ceramic tiles that enabled this product to enter into competition with the flooring and wall-covering materials traditionally used in Italy, such as graniglia-tiles, marble, and linoleum.

The greater part of the increase in ceramic tile production has been provided by the building of new factories or the expansion of existing ones in a very limited area in the provinces of Modena and Reggio Emilia. In 1981 the two provinces were responsible for more than 70 per cent of the national production of ceramic tiles. In the same year, 250 out of 433 Italian ceramic tile firms were located in the two provinces, but – what is more relevant to our analysis – four out of ten tile factories were in the six *comuni* that constitute the core of the *comprensorio delle ceramiche*. (The *comune* is the smallest unit of local government in Italy. The *comprensorio* is an intermediate unit between *comune* and *regione*. It groups contiguous *comuni* with similar economic and environmental conditions. This unit, proposed by the early 1970s reform of the *regioni*, has limited planning power and has been established only in a very few regions of Italy.)

This *comprensorio*, at least in territorial terms, delimits the industrial district under consideration. The main factors in the development of ceramic tile production in the *comprensorio* have been the following: (1) easy access to raw materials (different kinds of clays) in the mountains in that area; (2) an abundant labour force owing to the depressed conditions in that area during the 1950s; (3) tax reliefs lasting till the middle of the 1970s.

In examining technical change in the production of tiles, I shall focus on this district since it is here that the technical change has come about.

Notes on the process of ceramic tile production

The first stage in the production process is the preparation of the mixture by grinding the clay into a fine powder, which is then moistened and pressed into tile shape. Tiles are then fired to produce 'biscuit'. The biscuit is then glazed and fired again to give the final

Small firms and industrial districts in Italy

Figure 8.1 The production process of ceramic tiles

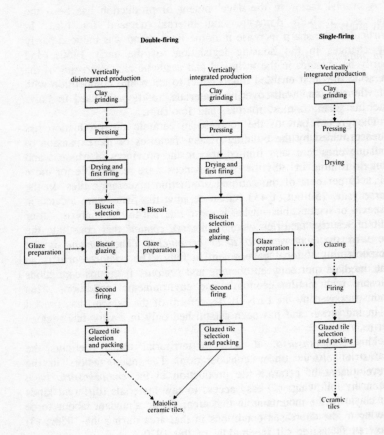

200

product. This process of production is called double firing as opposed to an alternative process in which tiles are glazed directly after the pressing operation and then fired only once. Figure 8.1 represents a more detailed schema of the two methods of production.

An analysis of the process of technical change

The industrial district

A necessary step in the analysis of technical change is the definition of who are the progenitors in this process. Two strands emerge in the literature: one attributes the main role to the entrepreneur-innovator (McLansin 1949, 1955; Schumpeter 1939), the other stresses the importance of the large corporation carrying on research and development activities (Mansfield 1972; Schmookler 1966). Since the practical application of scientific discoveries, the process of accumulation of small improvements, experience and learning activity, as well as the creation of new products, are all related aspects of technical change (Pasinetti 1981; Rosenberg 1978; Salter 1960; Schumpeter 1939), such a complex phenomenon cannot easily be understood if we attribute to one particular source complete responsibility for that process, whether it be the innovative firm or the large corporation. I propose, instead, to focus on a group of closely related firms – in particular, the firms' operation in an industrial district.

In industrial economics, when an analysis deals with a group of firms, reference is usually made to the industry to which those firms belong. Industry is a concept capable of various definitions: firms can belong to the same industry on the basis of the raw materials they utilize, the products they produce, or the techniques they use. In analysing technical change these definitions of industry are all unsatisfactory since technical change itself shifts the boundaries between industries: new techniques, together with the creation of new products, give rise to new production processes and hence to the splitting-up of an industry, or to the birth of a new one, or to the decay of some existing industries. What we need is a unit of analysis that will remain distinct and stable through time.[2] And – as Becattini has suggested – we can find it if we shift the focus of analysis from the industry to the industrial district (Becattini 1979). Becattini defines the industrial district as 'a localised thickening (in this spatial definition lies its strength and its weakness) of inter-industrial relations', whose 'composite nature, generally over different industries, lends the industrial district, even during the process of most thorough-going change, a stability which a unit such as industry in the strict sense does not possess'.[3]

In the study of industrial economics, the use of this unit of analysis is not new. Especially in analyses of vertical disintegration of the production process we can find several references to the industrial district. One of the first studies in which this type of analysis can be encountered is that of Chapman (1904) on which Marshall based many of his remarks on industrial districts in *Industry and Trade* (Marshall 1972). Chapman describes in great detail the forces that operated in the development of the Lancashire cotton industry during the nineteenth century; he also explains how the vertical disintegration of the production process finds its maximum functionality when there is a spatial clustering of firms. This enables maximum specialization of the production unit in a particular stage of the production process, and at the same time guarantees each producer a sure market for his particular product.

Although analysis of vertical disintegration apparently finds in the industrial district a fertile area for interpreting that phenomenon, in the analysis that follows I shall, instead, adopt an extension of the concept of industrial district. The phenomenon of interrelations between firms will be examined, a phenomenon that extends beyond the cases of vertically disintegrated production. As will be seen in the following paragraphs, it is precisely this broader definition which makes the concept of industrial district useful in understanding the process whereby new techniques arise and are adopted.

The innovators in the process of technical change

With a few exceptions, the ceramic tile firms have not been the ones to invent new machines or new methods of production. Certainly the demand for improvements and modifications to existing techniques of production may spring from them, but (at least through the 1960s) these demands took the form of vague suggestions. In fact, given the lack of technicians, firms could hardly have acted differently. Moreover, even with the increase in size of firms during the 1970s, R & D activities did not flourish within the individual firms themselves because of the high costs involved.

Instead, research developed largely outside the ceramic tile firms. It is enough to remember the technical evolution of presses, where the monopoly on research has always been held by the technical staff of the biggest Italian producer of presses for ceramic firms (SACMI); the specialized technical and designing centres that have made possible the development of new firing techniques and the development of the integrated system kiln-factory; and the more recent development put forward by some engineering firms for a whole ceramic tile factory as an integrated production line. These projects have drastically reduced the problems of internal transport by eliminating the loading and unloading of trucks and by introducing small 'deposits' of tiles on the production lines themselves, the so-called 'compensators'. But in addition to this group of producers and researchers, credit must be given to the engineering artisans and the small engineering firms that build machines for tile factories. And last but not least, a not insignificant role has been played by the factories that produce glazes and have invented new colours and products.

For a long time now the machine producers have had daily contact with the tile producers so that they constitute a sort of external technical staff of the tile firms. This allows the latter to avoid the cost of an internal technical staff. On the other hand, the engineering firms, instead of having laboratories for testing prototypes, *use* the ceramic firms to test how the new machinery actually works. This is a very important step in the process of technical improvement of machinery that Rosenberg (1982) has christened 'learning by using'.

It is only within this overall picture that the impetus for technical change in individual tile firms can be explained. It is worth noting that the rate of growth of employment in the engineering firms producing machines for the ceramic firms has been, in the last twenty years, similar to the rate of growth of employment in the ceramic firms themselves.

It is important to observe that among the machine producers there are only a few innovators; others imitate. However, the role of imitation itself should not be underestimated. Indeed, though a great number of machine producers are not involved in original research but copy the work of others, this mostly has a positive effect, because of what imitation means in terms of overall improvement in the results of basic research. Moreover, the capacity for imitating-modifying of this group of firms has given a new impetus to the technical development of tile production.[4] The individual tile firm is not constrained to adopt a single kind of serigraphic machine or compensator, but can choose, according to its particular needs, from among ten or twenty different models of the same machine.

But the process does not stop there. The tile firms reveal needs and particular technical problems of their own and demand specific devices that will enable them to be more competitive in their own markets. Then, apparently unexpectedly, the machine producers come up with just the device that will satisfy those needs, and once the solution has been found, it is offered to other ceramic firms too.

In other words, the chain relationship linking insight, set-up, imitation, and the improvement and diffusion of technical innovations, which can be described as the process of technical change, takes place not only within each of the two groups of firms (those producing machines on the one hand, and those producing tiles on the other), but also between the two groups as a whole. It is this bond that creates an industrial district from the set of firms belonging to the two groups. The choice of this unit of analysis does not hinder the study of the process of development of each particular portion of the industrial district. On the contrary, it helps in interpreting it.

Technical change in the ceramic tile industrial district

In illustrating the process of technical change in ceramic tile production since the Second World War one may distinguish three sub-periods, each of which is characterized by particular technical conditions.

1945–63: initial industrialization

The first period, 1945–63, saw the setting up of large-scale production. This was done by introducing electricity to work the presses and by their technical modification so that greater pressure could be applied to produce larger sizes of tiles and to increase the output of each press; also by using natural gas as fuel in the firing, and by the adoption of tunnel kilns; and lastly, by starting the glazing operations on line. Research performed in this period was mainly devoted to improving the grinding operation by adapting techniques already in use in the making of other granulated products, such as milk powder. In the following years, this research led to the wide acceptance of a type of grinding machine that produced a better quality biscuitware. In the period 1945–63, all the equipment in the ceramic tile factories, except for the grinding machine and the presses, was built and installed by engineering artisans, and was elementary in its mechanical structure, or (as in the case of the kilns) was made simply of brick-work. Few firms had technical staff capable of projecting modifications to the machinery, and the organization of production, at factory level, was usually entrusted to the oldest workers. Their main task was the control of the workers' pace of work and, in general, the control of the labour force. Even in the first half of the 1970s (and today in very small factories) the organization of production was directed by a foreman assisted only by a couple of workers who were, usually but not necessarily, competent in mechanics, hydraulics, and chemistry and who were responsible for ordinary maintenance and small repairs. The modification of machinery and equipment, the solution of technical problems, and the more complex maintenance tasks – these were the domain of the locally based engineering artisans or the small engineering firms.

1964–73: a decade of growth

The next period, 1964–73, is characterized by the continuous growth of demand. Up to the early 1960s the greater part of output consisted of monochromatic tiles. The very few tiles produced with polychrome decorations were hand-painted. Research in this period was aimed at mechanizing the process of polychrome decoration in order to increase the production of polychrome tiles at low cost. And this, in turn, created a new source of demand for ceramic tiles. These developments depended on research both into different kinds of glazes and biscuit, and into new techniques for the application of glaze to the tiles (the latter resulting in an adaptation of techniques in use in the printing industry).

The outcome of this research brought about the first important transformations of the product's characteristics and initiated major changes in the glazing department. These, together with the mechanization of transport and the storage of materials prior to each firing, are the only substantial changes in this period. The increased output in the second half of the 1960s – matched by an almost proportional increase in employment – was achieved not only by the opening of new factories but also by various technical changes over and above those already mentioned: the use of grinding machines for longer periods, the installation of a second press, the lengthening of the kilns and of the glazing line, the enlargement of the hangar in which the manual selection of the product was made. At factory level, the transformations that occurred in the various departments led to chaos in the layout of equipment. In the surrounding district, the growth of new industrial settings and the expansion of existing firms showed the lack of any co-ordinated development plan. Thus, in this period, ceramic tile production developed by means of extensive investment that repeated on a larger scale the organizational structure of the small firm.

1974–80: radical transformation

The last period began with a drastic reduction of demand, in 1974, and lasted until the end of the 1970s. The crisis of 1974 marked the end of an era of easy growth. Declining demand, which lasted from the middle of 1974 to the middle of 1975, particularly affected the worst-equipped and worst-organized factories with a poor quality product. But the crisis became an important opportunity for creative thinking about the future developments in the industry. Aware that the market was almost saturated and that the opening of new markets would require very big efforts, many firms responded to the crisis by reducing labour costs, increasing labour productivity, and rationalizing the whole process of production. At factory level this was done by reducing the dead loss time and the time of firing, and by introducing new machines so as to allow for greater flexibility in running production and a decrease in unit costs.

Here we see for the first time the use of machines for the automatic piling of pressed material; automatic cleaning of the die of the press and of the serigraphic machines; the semi-automatic and later completely automated loading and unloading of the production lines (both for selection and glazing), and the mechanized transport of materials through the various stages of the production process. The increased productivity was impressive. Many of these devices were available, though in a very experimental form, in the previous period and the stimulus to adopt them came both from the crisis of falling demand and in response to the trade unions' attempt to control the pace of work and the organization of labour at factory level. At the end of the period, this rationalization of the process of production was to lead to a situation in which the pace of work was no longer determined by the worker but programmed in the machine. And, later on, the use of microprocessors, both for selecting and firing the product, would eliminate that final touch of worker's intervention that consisted in registering and changing the pattern of actions performed by the machine.

Another important form of reorganization took place at inter-factory and inter-firm level: the product and process specialization between factories and firms which resulted from the creation of new holding and new marketing agreements between firms. This led the ceramic tile industry to take on a structure more suited to dealing with the changed market conditions and, incidentally, speeded up the diffusion of certain of the new techniques. This aspect of technical change will be discussed in more detail in the next section.

A last observation on this period concerns the stimulus to technical change provided by institutions. In this period attempts were made to control the increase in the level of output within the *comprensorio*. In 1974 the mayors of the *comuni* within the *comprensorio* decided to forbid the establishment of new factories in the area because of pollution and the increasing difficulty of providing an adequate infrastructure. (Since that decision new factories have been set up outside the *comprensorio*, but they still create problems for it because they are very close to its borders, and make use of the services within the *comprensorio*.) Moreover, the trade unions proposed that a limit be set on the expansion of production throughout the Emilia-Romagna region in order to send new investment to the south of Italy.[5] Each factory was compelled not to increase its output, and the constraint was imposed by controlling the increase of those pieces of equipment that constituted bottlenecks in the production process – the kilns. If made of brickwork, these could and still can be installed only if a building licence is provided by the *comune* in which the factory stands. But kilns may also be made of metal, as modern one-layer kilns are, and the regional tribune has argued that the installation of this kind of kiln does not require a licence. As a result, this kiln, firing only one layer of tiles at a time, came to be used not only for the original purpose for which it was designed (the single-firing process), but for other processes as well. Once this happened the leverage of the unions on this issue disappeared.

The analysis so far has highlighted two major points. First of all, the historical development of new techniques is more easily interpretable, as Rosenberg has pointed out, in terms of the reaction of the firms to whatever appears as the major constraint on their established position at a particular time (Rosenberg 1969). The second point is that the protagonists in the process of technical change in the industrial district include not only the firms belonging to it but also those institutions, like trade unions and local government, that have an impact on the firms.

Technical change, economies of scale, vertical integration and specialization of firms

Economies of scale and vertical disintegration

Technical change gives rise to modifications in the industrial structure through a multiplicity of channels. One of these is the level at which economies of scale are realized. Changes at this level can determine modifications in the interrelationships between firms, or variations of the level of vertical integration in the production process within the individual firms. The analysis of economies of scale thus offers a means of identifying at what stages of the production process, and with what significance, such modifications appear. The following analysis will deal only with economies of scale of a technical nature at factory level.[6]

In the study of economies of scale we must first define what scale of production means. Here, I adopt Silbertson's distinction between the three 'dimensions of scale': unit of analysis (factory); period of time whose specification concerns both the life of the machines and the life of each product; product mix and degree of standardization of each product.[7] A second point to discuss is the definition of optimum scale. The smallest scale of production beyond which average costs stop decreasing is defined by Bain as the optimum size (Bain 1956). This definition should be extended to take into account two factors. First whether an increase in the level of output is realized by increasing the number of machines of the same type, or by adopting an alternative technique. Second, it is necessary to specify on what items of cost economies of scale are realized: whether on labour or depreciation costs.[8] In relation to these two points, Pratten's definition of minimum efficient size (m.e.s.) is particularly useful (Pratten 1971).

The study of economies of scale is closely related to the level of vertical integration. The phenomenon of the splitting of the production process – *vertical disintegration* as Robinson calls it – is linked partly to the past history of the industry, and partly to technical and economic conditions. Moreover, the relationship between the level of vertical integration and the scale of production needs to be investigated.[9] In order to study the scale effects caused by the technical characteristics of individual phases of the production process, it is necessary to consider the relation between costs and the scale of production at the same level of vertical integration as the scale increases. The various steps in the analysis of economies of scale are the following: first I examine the role of technical change in varying the m.e.s. at department level; the study then turns to the analysis of economies of scale at factory level, considering both the same level of vertical integration as the scale increases, and alternative levels of vertical integration (see Robinson 1958).

The results

Technical change and minimum efficient size in the vertically integrated double-firing factory is the first consideration. The empirical investigations undertaken in this study showed that the m.e.s. of all but the grinding and firing departments is greater with the most up-to-date technique than with the oldest technique. But since the m.e.s. of the grinding and firing departments largely determines the m.e.s. of the factory, it follows that, despite the many changes produced by the new techniques over the last twenty years, the m.e.s. of the production unit has not changed (at least as far as engineering data are concerned).[10]

The significance of economies of scale in shaping the structure of the ceramic tile factory

Study of the technical opportunities for vertical disintegration in the production of ceramic tiles shows that the double-firing production process can in principle easily be split up after the grinding operation, the first firing, the biscuit selection, and the second firing; but problems of transport make it impossible to separate pressing from the first firing and glazing from the second firing. The single-firing process is, by contrast, conceived as an integrated production line from the pressing to the firing operation, and thus the only possible breaks in the whole production process are after the grinding operation and after firing.

These technical opportunities for separating off the various operations in both processes have indeed been partially exploited. The stimulus to vertical disintegration in these cases has come both from cost advantages gained in terms of product and process specialization. Before discussing the economic reasons for vertical disintegration it is useful to discuss the significance of economies of scale in the two methods of production in shaping the structure of the ceramic tile industry.

Vertical disintegration in the single-firing process is rare. In those few cases where the process is split into separate production units, one produces the ground clay and the other performs the rest of the operations. For this reason, for single-firing tiles, I shall consider only the case of vertically integrated production. For double-firing production, economies of scale can be discussed with regard both to the integrated factory and for each of the two stages into which the process is usually split (biscuit production and the production of glazed tiles).

For each of the cases in question, Table 8.1 provides an estimate of the m.e.s., the percentage of increase both in the total cost per unit of output and of the sum of labour costs plus fixed costs when output is half that of the m.e.s. These data, which refer to the minimum cost curve calculated on the basis of engineering data, are used in estimating the relative and absolute significance of the m.e.s.[11]

Concerning the minimum cost curve, there are several observations to be made. Whereas in the vertically integrated production process of both types of tile there is a small increase in total costs per unit of output at half the m.e.s., in the biscuit production and glazing there are more relevant economies of scale. Second, in each of the processes considered, economies of scale realized on labour plus fixed costs (Table 8.1, column 5) are stronger than on total costs. What diminishes the economies of scale on total unit costs is

Table 8.1 Minimum efficient size (m.e.s.), investment, costs, and economies of scale in the production of double-firing tiles (size 200 × 200 × 10 mm) in biscuit, glazing, and vertically integrated factories; and in the production of single-firing tiles (size 200 × 300 × 11 mm) in a vertically integrated factory

	(1) Minimum efficient size sq. m/d of final product	(2) Investment (millions of Italian lire at 1979 prices) in a factory of m.e.s.	(3) Total cost per unit of output* at the m.e.s. (1979 prices)	(4) % increase in total cost per unit of output* at 50% m.e.s.	(5) % increase in labour plus fixed costs of 50% m.e.s.
Two firings					
Biscuit	7,680	5,016.7	901	14.4	22
Glazing	3,840	2,772.9	3,252.5	13	36
Vertically integrated	7,680	9,709.5	2,989	6	11
Single firing	3,900	6,779.2	2,649.5	7.5	15.2

Source: Engineering data taken from my interviews with engineers in the ceramic and machine producer firms.
* A unit of output is a square metre of final product.

the constant trend in the cost of raw materials, energy, and fuel, which constitute a substantial part of the total unit cost. Finally, I have estimated the relative significance of economies of scale by expressing the m.e.s. as a percentage of the size of the market. Using 1980 data on sales by Italian firms in the home market, the m.e.s. of a vertically integrated factory producing double-fired tiles represents 1.6 per cent of the size of this market and those producing single-fired tiles 2.5 per cent. If the world market for tiles (which is the market of the Italian firms) is considered, it follows that these values are much smaller. The conclusion is that economies of scale do not constitute a barrier to entry into this industry. The conclusion will seem quite obvious if we note that in the late 1970s there were almost 400 firms in the ceramic tile industry in Italy and most of them were exporters.

Vertical disintegration in the double-firing production process

It is important to ask, however, how relevant are questions of cost to the pattern of vertical disintegration that we find in practice in the production of double-fired tiles in the late 1970s.

Cost data for vertically integrated and non-integrated production units at m.e.s. are found in Table 8.1 (column 3). The tile production of a vertically integrated factory enables a reduction of about 9 per cent in cost per unit produced. Although this cannot be considered an irrelevant incentive towards vertical integration (i.e. production in factories with a complete cycle) other considerations seem to have weighed more heavily on the side of vertical disintegration.

Investment costs are one of these. The m.e.s. of a glazing factory was, in the 1970s, half that of a vertically integrated factory, and the investment required to build a glazing factory of m.e.s. was almost one-third of that of a vertically integrated factory of m.e.s. If we are also to explain the desire to build biscuit-only factories, it is important to understand that some firms preferred to avoid trading on the final market, which in this case was and is both national and international, with the risks this entails.

Investment decisions are, however, inseparable from product decisions in the three kinds of factories (vertically integrated, biscuit, and glazing). The production of long runs of tiles of standard size found, and finds, its most efficient productive structure in the vertically integrated factory, while separate production units for biscuit and glazing were and are better suited to specialization in small batches of special sizes of tiles.

This pattern of product specialization – which, although not the only one, was the most widespread in the 1970s – was clearly dependent on the techniques adopted up to the early 1970s. Since then, technical change and the changed market conditions have given rise to new opportunities for diversification of output and new types of product and process specialization.

The effects of technical change on product and process specialization between the ceramic tile firms

Product differentiation as a weapon of competition

In the last twenty years technical developments in the production of ceramic tiles have given rise to the creation of new products that have served to widen the range of existing ones rather than to replace them. This is true of a new kind of clay mixture, called *pasta bianca*, that, in the early 1960s, first made it possible to mechanize the glazing process and thus to increase the market for glazed tiles. It is also true of single firing tiles, which, in the 1970s, opened up a new market for glazed tiles for use on external walls, and of the larger and larger sizes of tiles (up to 60 × 100 cm) produced with the modern presses.

Here, I want to discuss the role played by changes in the product

211

mix in modifying the product and process specialization of the ceramic tile firms.

The image of a firm, or of the trade-mark used to sell its products, is stronger the wider is the range of types of tiles it is able to offer, and product differentiation is thus an important weapon in competition between firms. But very often it is difficult for the individual firm to produce a wide range of tiles. The vertical disintegration of the double-firing process is particularly valuable in this context in that it allows for greater diversity in the product mix.

The vertically integrated double-firing firms

It was only in the second half of the 1970s that the single-firing process became widespread. The patterns of vertical disintegration typical of the techniques in use until the middle of the 1970s consisted of four types of firms producing double-fired tiles: mono-factory vertically integrated firms; multi-factory firms producing biscuit and glazed tiles separately; biscuit firms (mono- or multi-factory). In order to understand this typology it is useful to observe that double-fired tiles can vary in two ways: in size and in the decoration of the glazed surface.

The size of the tile is obtained in the pressing operation, and the production of a range of sizes can easily be realized by changing the die of the press. But a different size also implies a different arrangement of the pressed material on the trucks, and when the difference in the size produced is very big, the time and the cycle of firing must also be changed. The decoration of the tile's surface is obtained by changing the colour of the glazes, the method of applying the glaze (pouring, spraying, brushing), and lastly, by changing the screen of the serigraphic machine. These changes, too, are easily managed on the glazing line, but problems occur with the need to combine changes in size and decoration. The production of different sizes on the same glazing line means, in fact, that as the sizes of the tiles in the batch to be glazed changes, the distance between the two conveyor belts that support the tiles must be changed, and with it the running speed. Finally, the size of the saggars used to store the glazed tiles for the next process (firing) must also be changed.

When manual (non-automated) techniques were used for loading, unloading, and moving material between the various operations, it was possible for a mono-factory vertically integrated firm to produce a wide range of sizes and decorations. But, already at that time, product specialization was quite common, and these firms participated in the purchase and sale of biscuit in order to widen the range of sizes of the final product. It is important to note that the standardization of tile sizes is a source of economies of scale in biscuit production, whereas the minimum efficient size of a glazing factory is mainly affected by kiln capacity.

A similar strategy was followed by the multi-factory firms producing biscuit and glazed tiles separately. In this picture, the role of the biscuit and glazing firms is not simply that of satellites of the vertically integrated firms. At that time the glazing firms, in general of a very small size, either produced a very wide range of decorations and bizarre sizes in very small batches or produced particular kinds of glazed tiles.

The group

When the more automated techniques came to be adopted in the second half of the 1970s the typology of firms changed in a consistent way.

First of all, the automated selection of biscuit made it possible to introduce an integrated production line for selecting and glazing. This encouraged the reorganization of the vertically integrated factory in order to fully exploit the advantages of that technique. But the automation of the loading and moving of materials introduced a new barrier to frequent changes in the size of the tiles. In the case of mono-factory vertically integrated firms, where the size of the factory was large enough, an efficient solution was found by organizing the factory into sub-processes, one for each size of tile. (This applied mainly to the press and the glazing departments, and – for very big factories – also to the firing departments.) On the other hand, the multi-factory vertically integrated firms chose instead to reorganize the productive structure of the various factories so as to allow each factory to specialize in one size of tile.

But, in the late 1970s, two important events changed this pattern of product and process of specialization: the financial crisis that hit many ceramic tile firms and the technical developments of the late 1970s (see below). There is no space here to discuss the nature of the financial crisis that changed the ownership of many firms. The result of that crisis was a concentration of firms within 'groups'. (There is no exact English equivalent of the Italian *gruppi*; British groups of companies may have larger components and more centralized management.) These were based either on reciprocal shareholdings or trading bonds.

The existence of groups in this industry was not a completely new phenomenon. But, whereas in 1973 no more than 15 per cent of the ceramic tile firms in the provinces of Modena and Reggio Emilia were operating in five groups, in 1979 almost 50 per cent of the firms were linked to twelve groups.[12] The formation of new groups and the expansion of existing ones gave new impetus in the late

213

1970s to the reorganization of the productive structure of the industry. None the less, this can be completely understood only if interpreted in the light of the technical developments of that time.

Among the factors of a technical nature that encouraged product and process specialization, three stand out. First, there was the diffusion of the single-firing production process that resulted both from the building of new factories and the transformation of existing double-firing factories (mainly the vertically integrated and the biscuit factories).

The second important technical development was the process of 'quick-firing'. This involved firing one layer of glazed tiles at a time and allows for an extraordinarily short firing time: 30 minutes as against the 16 hours required with the traditional kilns. The one-layer kiln was first introduced in single-firing production but was soon viewed as an important means of transforming the second firing into the double-firing process. The adoption of this kiln frees both the glazing and firing processes from the constraint imposed by the size of the tile because the saggars of different sizes (used for different sizes of tiles) are replaced by standard-sized trays. It also allows for the production of tiles of very large size. In addition, the short time of firing permits faster feedback on the glazing process. This is important because quality control in the glazing operation is possible only after the glazed tiles are fired. As a result, fewer tiles are wasted. Since its first use, the quick-firing process has been adopted both by single-firing vertically integrated factories and by those glazing factories that were switching from double-firing to single-firing production.

The third technical development is the 'third fire'. It was noted above that the decoration of the biscuit surface is a crucial factor in differentiating the product, but it is very costly to hold in stock tiles with a wide range of decorations. A brilliant solution to this problem was devised as a result of the fashion for using large numbers of plain glazed tiles mixed with a few decorated tiles. The ceramic firms were able to offer the clients the particular decoration they liked by decorating the plain glazed tiles from the same batch the client had ordered and by producing the decorated tiles in a separate department. The decoration is done either by hand or, more often, by applying transfers to the tiles. The decorated tiles are then fired to vitrify the decoration on the already glazed surface, and this is done in a small kiln. It is a very short step from having a separate department for this process to decentralizing it. And, indeed, in the *comprensorio delle ceramiche* there are now sixty-seven firms producing a third fire on order from other ceramic tile firms. These are mainly family-based production units or artisans.

214

When a typology of firms is attempted for the present decade we find a productive structure in which the groups play the most important role. The old pattern of specialization, characterized by the vertically integrated firm that purchases and sells biscuit to differentiate its output and has trading relationships with the glazing factories, has been almost completely replaced by the mulit-factory multi-firm group that develops its organizational structure to achieve the image of the multi-product firm so important for marketing purposes.

Conclusions

One main theme runs throughout this whole chapter: the role played by the interrelationships between firms and their proximity to each other. Together these provide the basis for the process of generation and adoption of new techniques, and, moreover, it is within the network of interrelationships between the ceramic tile firms of the industrial district that the effects of technical change on the structure of the industry are felt.

The first point to emerge from this analysis is that the historical development of new techniques is more easily interpretable – as Rosenberg suggests – in terms of the reactions of firms to whatever appears as the major constraint to their established position at a particular time. The discussion on the case study has particularly focused on the role played by four kinds of constraints. First, there are the competitive pressures, including those on the ceramic firms to expand their output, or to face new market conditions; and those on the engineering firms to invent new techniques in an effort to diversify their own output and expand the market for their inventions. Second, there are the constraints of a technical nature that inhibit the process of modification of the various stages of the production process. Third, there are the constraints imposed by labour resistance as expressed in the desire of the trade unions to control the pace of work. Finally, there are the constraints imposed by decision-making bodies outside the firms: the state, as in the case of the housing legislation that gave impetus to the production of tiles on a large scale; and local government authorities and trade unions that impose planning decisions on the firms.

The second point to emerge follows from this: that the actual working of those constraints in stimulating the process of technical change in the ceramic tile industry is better understood where the unit of analysis is the industrial district. Indeed, the definition I give of the industrial district simultaneously involves all the basic elements of the analytical framework that I need to understand

215

technical change: the sense of belonging to a group which is defined on the basis of relationships that go beyond the boundary of the industry defined on a product basis to include those firms producing machines, providing services, and supplying intermediate goods; and lastly, interrelationships representing that particular texture of economic, social, and institutional features which must be considered if the process of technical change is to be fully understood.

Attention then turns to the industry level, and to the effects of technical change on the structure of the industry within the industrial district. The analysis of the engineering data on m.e.s. has shown that economies of scale have had a minor role in shaping the industrial structure. The strong pattern we observe of vertical disintegration finds, instead, its most important explanation in the product and process specialization of the production units. This is clearly shown by tracing the relation between the changing typology of firms and the technical developments in the industry. In the 1970s, product and process specialization was pursued through a close network of interrelationships between vertically integrated double-firing firms and biscuit and glazing firms. This industrial structure has now been largely replaced by the articulated structure of the groups, which achieve the same degree of specialization within their extended production units, alongside a texture of small and medium-size firms.

This transformation has only partly changed the process of generation and adoption of new techniques in the industry. The engineering firms remain separate from the ceramic tile firms and the interrelationships between them still remain a crucial aspect of that process. Indeed, the more and more sophisticated techniques that require an ever larger financial outlay can now more easily be attempted by the engineering firms because they have in the groups a ready market which they could not have in the individual firms. The modalities of the process of technical change are themselves changed without in any way altering its character: that of a cumulative process stimulated by the need to respond to shifting constraints.

Note on methodology

Certain methodological aspects arising from the analysis performed in the section on technical change, economies of scale, vertical integration and specialization of firms, must be noted here.

The analysis has been made by comparing two techniques for the production of ceramic tiles. These are, first, the one which was most widely used in the early 1960s in the factories of the *comprensorio delle ceramiche* and, second, the most up-to-date technique in use in the late 1970s in the same area. Choice of this type of comparison derives from awareness that a crucial problem in the comparison of techniques over time is that relative prices change, and other conditions – like infrastructures or institutions – change too. The comparison of these two techniques in terms of degree of flexibility in producing different kinds of tiles, minimum efficient size, level of vertical integration, is made possible only by the fact that the main technique in use in the early 1960s was still available and in use at the end of the 1970s, and as a result, not only every piece of technical information but also all the relevant cost data were easily available at the time data were collected. This allows the comparison of these two techniques in the same economic environment, and though this kind of comparison is an unusual analytical device, I consider it a valid approach in this kind of study.

Data were collected in 1980 by interviewing engineers and technicians in the ceramic tile industry and machine-producer firms. The methodology I have adopted in collecting and computing the relevant data is typical of the so-called engineering studies (see Chenery 1949, 1953; Ferguson 1950).

The units I use in the analysis of data are the operation, the task, the department, and the factory. Operation is the most elementary unit into which the production process can be split up. Task is the set of operations performed by the worker. Department is the physical place where groups of operations are performed; it corresponds to the unit Chenery calls 'processing' (Chenery 1953). Factory is here synonymous with production unit. (On the specification of the unit of analysis, see Chenery 1949 and Georgescu-Roegen 1965, 1967, 1971).)

The specification of the various operations, tasks, and departments for each of the two production processes considered is entirely conventional. However, the delimitation of each unit of analysis is by no means arbitrary. In the case of the department, which is the unit of calculation of cost data, the definition of the limits of each department was checked with the technicians designing the plant. Case by case they explained at which points the manufacturing process might reasonably be split up by separating one group of operations from another, even if only with an imaginary partition.

For each department, and each of the two techniques in question, I have collected data on raw material inputs, intermediate goods, labour, and machinery, as well as on the other inputs – such as fuel, electric power, and so on – required in the production process. The basic assumption in the calculation of cost data is that it is possible to specify for each type of machine and each type of task performed the largest average level of output corresponding to the use of this particular type of machine in a given industrial district at a given point of time. I call such a productive capacity a *module*, defined in terms of quantity of output per unit of time. It is important to observe that I am not referring to data taken from a book of blueprints but rather to those values which would be considered the most frequent in the factories of the *comprensorio*. An additional simplifying assumption contained in the analysis is that the quantities of labour and machinery needed are at least those necessary to produce the quantity of output corresponding to the module. Greater quantities of output cannot be realized by a more intensive or longer use of given labour and machines, but only by adding more labour and machinery modules.

Once I had collected data for the two techniques related to the cost of a unit of labour and to the initial investment cost of machines and their life, I set up – for each department – the curve of cost per unit of output for each of the techniques considered. Such a curve consists of a series of traits, of different hyperbolas, that can be interpreted as the decreasing parts of the usual short-run curves.[13] This is calculated by adding the unit cost curve for raw material and other inputs to the unit-cost curve for labour and machinery.

Finally, I have calculated the curve of the minimum total cost per unit of output in each department. This curve consists of the lowest parts of the cost curve for each technique.[14]

Acknowledgement

This chapter is based on an article which first appeared in *Research Policy* (6), December 1985, Amsterdam: North Holland Publishing. It is published by permission of North Holland Publishing.

Notes

1. There was an allowance for building non-luxury houses, and one criterion used in the classification of houses was the amount of ceramic tiles used. The abolition of this rule led to an increase in the demand for ceramic tiles in every type of house.
2. On the definition of boundaries in the analysis of partial processes, see Georgescu-Roegen (1964, 1971).
3. Marshall (1919) is a key reference in the conceptualization of the industrial district. He based his observations largely on the empirical work of Chapman (1904) and Lloyd (1913).
4. In my approach, invention, innovation, and imitation are understood as important steps in the process of cumulative synthesis (see Usher 1929) but are not ranked in priority as they are in most of the

literature on technical change.

5. The analysis of this proposal constitutes in itself a very interesting topic. The basic ideas involved were those viewing growth as a repeatable phenomenon.

6. Robinson (1931) distinguishes forces of technical nature from other forces favouring the economies of scale. On this point see also Bain (1956). Economies of scale are reductions in the costs of production realized as the capacity of the factory or firm increases. Following Bain (1956), one should note the case where reductions in cost arise not merely from more intensive use of labour or a longer use of machines – given the size of the production unit – but from an increase in the size of the production unit.

7. See Silbertson (1972). Ferguson (1950) expressed a view analogous to that of Silbertson. For the first detailed formalization of the problem of scale of production, see Alchian (1959).

8. In the analysis of economies of scale in the ceramic tile production process, I assume that the prices of other inputs are constant irrespective of the quantity bought in, and that the quantity of other inputs per unit of output does not vary as the scale of production increases.

9. See Lavington (1927), Marshall (1919), and Young (1928) on vertical disintegration.

10. If, for each department, we had compared the most up-to-date technique with the technique widely used in the late 1950s, we would have observed a lower m.e.s. for the firing departments and consequently a lower m.e.s. at factory level. This is because at that time the kilns were built according to the desired level of output, and the kiln capacity – which is almost proportional to its length – had a very low minimum. During the 1960s, the size of the kilns became more and more standardized, till it reached the present modules of 4,000 and 2,000 square metres of daily production, respectively for the first and second firing.

11. In studying the influence of technical economies of scale in shaping industrial structure, I adopt the following indicators of the significance of economies of scale. One indicator is found by estimating whether the costs per unit of output are significantly higher at a quarter or half the m.e.s. than at the m.e.s. itself. *Ceteris paribus*, we can assume that for a size which is half the m.e.s., an increase of the total costs per unit of output greater than 10 per cent will indicate the presence of considerable economies of scale in absolute terms. Another indicator of the absolute significance of economies of scale is the amount of initial investment required to set up a factory of minimum efficient size. In this way, it is possible to have an idea as to whether economies of scale constitute a barrier to entry for new firms into the industry in question. It is important to observe that even if considerable economies of scale are realized in absolute terms, this is not in itself sufficient to evaluate the importance of scale in determining the structure of the industry. Then some measure of relative significance is necessary, and

for this purpose it is useful to estimate whether a factory of m.e.s. supplies a considerable share of output of the market in which it operates. (On the determination of absolute and relative significance of economies of scale see Bain 1956 and Silberston 1972.)

12. There are no official data on groups. The above information on groups has been taken from Bernardi's thesis (Bernardi 1974) and from trade-union surveys (FULC 1976, 1980) on the ceramic tile industry.
13. See Salter (1960).
14. See Chamberlin (1969).

Bibliography

Alchian, A. (1959) 'Costs and output', in M. Abramovitz *et al.* (eds) *The Allocation of Economic Resources, Essays in Honor of B.F. Haley*, Stanford: Stanford University Press.

Bain, J.S. (1956) *Barriers to New Competition*, Cambridge, Mass.: Harvard University Press.

—— (1959) 'Survival-ability as a test of efficiency', *American Economic Review* 59 (May): 99–104.

Becattini, G. (1962) *Il concetto di industria e la teoria del valore*, Turin: Boringhieri.

—— (1979) 'Dal "settore industriale" al "distretto industriale". Alcune considerazione sulla unità di indagine della economia industriale', *Revista di Economia e Politica Industrial* 4(2): 7–21.

Bellandi, M. (1982) 'Il distretto industriale in Alfred Marshall', *L'industria* 3(3) (1982): 355–75.

Bernardi, U. (1974) 'Aspetti giuridici delle imprese ceramiche. Le forme giuridiche delle imprese, prassi statutaria, fenomeni di concentrazione', Modena.

Chamberlin, E.H. (1948) 'Proportionality, divisibility and economies of scale', *Quarterly Journal of Economics* 62: 229–62.

Chamberlin, E.H. (1969) *The Theory of Monopolistic Competition*, Cambridge, Mass.: Harvard University Press.

Chapman, S.J. (1904) *The Lancashire Cotton Industry: A Study in Economic Development* Manchester: Manchester University Press.

Chenery, H.B. (1949) 'Engineering production function', *Quarterly Journal of Economics* 63: 507–31.

—— (1953) 'Process and production functions from engineering data', in W.W. Leontief *et al.* (eds) *Studies in the Structure of the American Economy*, New York: Oxford University Press.

Ferguson, A.R. (1950) 'Empirical determination of a multidimensional marginal cost function', *Econometrica* 18: 217–35.

Georgescu-Roegen, N. (1964) 'Measure, quality and output', in C.R. Rao (ed.) *Essays on Econometrics and Planning Presented to Professor P.C. Mahalanobis on his 70th Birthday*, Oxford: Pergamon Press.

—— (1965) 'Process in farming versus process in manufacturing: a problem of balanced development', reprinted in N. Georgescu-Roegen, *Energy and Economic Myths*, New York: Pergamon Press, 1976.

—— (1967) 'Chamberlin's new economics and the unit of production', in R.E. Kuenne (ed.) *Monopolistic Competition Theory: Studies and Impact*, New York: Wiley.

—— (1971) *The Entropy Law and the Economic Process*, Cambridge Mass.: Harvard University Press.

Grosse Carter, A.P. (1953) 'The technological structure in the cotton industry', in W.W. Leontief *et al.* (eds) *Studies in the Structure of the American Economy*, New York: Oxford University Press.

Lavington, F. (1927) 'Technical influences on vertical integration', *Economica*, March:

Levi, T. (1979) *L'industria metalmeccanica in provincia di Modena*, Modena: FLM.

Lloyd, G.I.G. (1913) *The Cutlery Trades: An Historical Essay in the Economics of Small-Scale Production*, London: Longmans, Green & Co.

Maclaurin, W.R. (1949) *Invention and Innovation in the Radio Industry*, New York: Macmillan.

—— (1955) 'Innovation and capital formation in some American industries', in M. Abramowitz *et al.* (eds) *The Allocation of Economic Resources: Essays in Honor of B.F. Haley*, Stanford: Stanford University Press.

Mansfield, E. (1972) 'The contribution of research and development to economic growth in the US', *Science* 175: 477–86.

Marshall, A. (1919) *Industry and Trade: A Study of Industrial and Business Organisation; and their Influences on the Conditions of Various Classes and Nations*, London: Macmillan.

Pasinetti, L.L. (1981) *Structural Change and Economic Growth, A Theoretical Essay on the Dynamics of the Wealth of Nations*, Cambridge: Cambridge University Press.

Pratten, C.F. (1971) *Economics of Scale in Manufacturing Industry* , Cambridge: Cambridge University Press, Occasional Paper 28.

Robinson, E.A.G. (1931) *The Structure of the Competitive Industry*, Cambridge: Cambridge University Press. (Revised edition 1958.)

Rosenberg, N. (1969) 'The direction of technological change: inducement mechanism and focusing devices', *Economic Development and Cultural Change*, Chicago: University of Chicago Press: reprinted in Rosenberg, *Perspectives on Technology*, Cambridge: Cambridge University Press, 1976.

—— (1976) *Perspectives on Technology*, Cambridge: Cambridge University.

—— (1978) 'Progresso tecnico: l'analisi storica', in *Il Mondo Contemporaneo*, Vol. 7, *Economia e Storia*; reprinted in Rosenberg, *Inside the Black Box: Technology and Economics*, Cambridge: Cambridge University Press, 1982.

—— (1982) *Inside the Black Box: Technology and Economics*, Cambridge: Cambridge University Press.

Salter, W.E.G. (1960) *Productivity and Technical Change*, Cambridge: Cambridge University Press.

Schmookler, J. (1966) *Invention and Economic Growth*, Cambridge, Mass.:

Harvard University Press.
Schumpeter, J. (1939) *Business Cycles*, New York: McGraw-Hill.
Silberston, A. (1972) 'Economies of scale in theory and practice', *Economics Journal Supplement*, March: 369–91.
Usher, A.P. (1929) *A History of Mechanical Inventions*, Cambridge, Mass.: Harvard University Press. (Revised edition, 1954.)
Young, A. (1928) 'Increasing returns and economic progress', *Economics Journal* 528–42.
FULC (1976) 'Indagine sulla ristrutturazione del settore ceramico nella provincia di Modena', Modena.
——— (1980) 'Aggiornamento dei dati sull'occupazione nel settore ceramico in provincia di Modena', Modena.

Chapter 9

The small-firm economy's odd man out: the case of Ravenna

Mario Pezzini

(Translated by Julia Bamford)

Italy
9412
6110

2 23 – 38

The industrial structure of the Emilian provinces of Bologna, Modena, and Reggio-Emilia is fairly homogeneous, with highly competitive small firms, high levels of technology, and innovation in both methods of production and products.[1] The province of Ravenna borders on this area, its more recent political history is the same, the fertility of its agricultural land is similar, yet its industrial structure is both less extensive and less intensive.

The research upon which this chapter is based compares the industrial structure of Ravenna with that of the neighbouring provinces of Emilia with particular attention to artisan manufacturing. It tries to explain why Ravenna has experienced such a different type of development. This sort of analysis implies that those features which are common to the most advanced areas of small-firm development must be singled out. A glance at some common historical elements of this area rather than rigid historical preconditions of small-firm industrialization might help to illustrate the problem.

The differences between Ravenna and the Emilian provinces

The province of Ravenna differs from the Emilian provinces both in its industrial and employment characteristics. The level of employment in manufacturing industry is the lowest in the region: 33 per cent against a regional average of 41 per cent. Moreover, unlike the rest of the region it lacks the widespread industrial fabric of small locally owned manufacturing firms. The sectoral distribution is also different; building and construction are important as are also the oil and energy sector, chemicals, rubber, plastics, and food processing. Those sectors which are important in the other Emilian provinces and are characteristic of small-firm areas in general – such as textiles, clothing, and above all metal and mechanical engineering – are weakly represented in Ravenna.

Linked to this is the difference in size of firms, the average size of firm being much larger in Ravenna. Petrochemical firms are often held up as examples of high levels of vertical integration. Firms which process agricultural produce also tend to be medium to large. Furthermore, there are important differences in firm ownership from the Emilian provinces. Ravenna has high numbers of firms partially owned by the state, in addition to branches of firms belonging to industrial groups and co-operatives, whilst in the Emilian provinces these are very few. The larger firms have ownership structures which are for the most part extra-regional and a sizeable number have head offices outside the region.

The industrial structure of diffused small-firm growth in Ravenna is not only rather weak but decidedly less developed than in other parts of the region where there has been intense development of a diffused small-firm economy.[2] The majority of artisan manufacturing firms work on commission for clients; these are very small, rather backward firms working almost exclusively for the local market. They are particularly important in the Ravenna province accounting for 51 per cent of the artisan manufacturers, whilst even ten years ago as little as 40 per cent of total artisan manufacturing was done on this basis in Modena. Even among the more strictly industrial firms very few have their products sold directly by a sales network; those that work on commission for other firms are more common. The ratio of the first type of firm to the second is one to five whilst recent studies have shown it to be much higher in small firm areas; that is, one firm in every four and in some cases one in two.[3] This ratio can be seen as a gauge of the quality of an area's small firms and as we have seen, puts the Ravenna area in an unfavourable light.

On the other hand, the situation of artisan firms producing on commission for other firms in the manufacturing sector is less critical. These are larger firms with networks of production relationships outside the province and large numbers of clients, so that it would be reasonable to suppose that they work within competitive markets. Favaretto's research on the Emilian metal-worker shows that in both Modena and Ravenna, more than 70 per cent of firms work on commission to other firms and have more than ten clients, while the regional average is 65 per cent and in other areas much lower.[4] The same research shows, however, that Ravenna has relatively low numbers of firms working on commission to other firms: 43 per cent compared to 65 per cent in the Emilia-Romagna region as a whole.

The characteristics of the structure of production which we have described so far do not apply to the whole area: differences can be found between the various parts of the province.

The Ravenna area is where most of the province's petroleum and chemical industries are located. They account respectively for more than half and around a quarter of the regional employment in these sectors. The area employs a number of people in electrical energy production, and metal manufacturing. The large firms are either partly owned by the state or by large companies from outside the province.

The Lugo area is where most of the province's food and agricultural products processing is situated, and this accounts for more than a quarter of all industrial employment in the area. The footwear industry is the nearest to an industrial district to be found in the province, having generated small firms producing rubber and plastics. It is not, however, a very advanced industrial district, its products being of low quality, its firms all very small, and its industrial atmosphere as yet undeveloped.

The Faenza area is the main producer of ceramics. Despite the fame of Faenza pottery the industrial development of this sector has occurred mainly in the post-war period. Previously production was of artistic ceramics and only more recently has a ceramic tile industry developed. Mechanical engineering firms and instrument makers are fairly flourishing and a clothing and textile industry producing high-quality women's clothing has been developed by the ex-workers of two firms making hosiery and tents.

In short, there are fewer small *artigiani* firms in the province of Ravenna than in the Emilian provinces, and their degree of integration in networks is less developed, though within the province the areas of Lugo and Faenza are less dissimilar to the Emilian provinces than the Ravenna area.

Some hypotheses on what makes Ravenna different from her neighbours

What lies behind these fundamental differences in the industrial structure of two contiguous areas? Research on the specific conditions which have led to the concentration of small-firm development in the *Terza Italia* in general and Emilia-Romagna in particular, has shown a possible correlation between this kind of development and the past social structure of the area. This backward glance has picked out a combination of rural and urban factors which recent studies indicate as being a crucial element in the development of small firms (Bagnasco and Pini 1981). In addition, the relationship between small-firm development and the past organization and specialization of agriculture is important.

On the other hand, recent studies have attributed little relevance to stages of industrialization preceding the present one. They underline, for example, how Emilia-Romagna, which can be considered Italy's foremost small-firm economy region, had a very low economic profile until the post-war years and the growth of small-firms. However, a closer look at particular cases of development rather than aggregates shows that behind present small-firm success there are or have been large or medium-size firms producing the same or related products to those of the present-day small firms (Brusco 1985).[5]

It has been shown that those areas included in the 'Third Italy' are characterized by family-run firms. In addition, the development of the small firm seems to be strongest where *mezzadria* (sharecropping), small holding, and renting of land was widespread.[6] There are several reasons why this should be the case. In the first place there is a labour supply which, although not the prime mover of development, has been a crucial factor in the areas with this type of agricultural organization. A former peasant, or *mezzadro*, family often continues to work a piece of land in order to maintain a subsistence base but using only part of the workforce of the family. Furthermore, the family puts its experience to use in the internal organization of the members, enabling them to work either full time or part time or seasonally or at home, making use of its past skill in flexible labour organization. In this way, total family income can be quite considerable despite the fact that individual wages may be low. Finally, the culture of work which is deeply ingrained in such families leads them to accept working conditions which others might refuse, and for longer periods.

In the second place the presence of family-run farms has also had important *indirect* effects on the emergence of entrepreneurs. In areas with widespread traditions of self-employment it is reasonable to think that there should be less resistance to someone who became an entrepreneur. The decision to set up a new firm is influenced by the social climate present in various societies, and the existence of social costs which can dissuade a would-be entrepreneur has also been noted (Shapero 1983; Barth 1963). These costs are of little relevance here, particularly in the case of *mezzadria*, where social mobility has been to some extent written into the contract. When the family moved from one farm to another it could change its status from one year to another whilst remaining within the *mezzadria* system. If the landowner was an agrarian capitalist interested in running the farms himself, then the *mezzadro* was little more than an employee, whereas an absentee landlord engaged in one of the professions in an urban context would be anxious to avoid involvement, and thus the *mezzadro* would be more independent.

Finally, the *mezzadro* or peasant agricultural structure is at the origin of those local political subcultures in north-eastern and central Italy which have influenced the process of small firm industrialization. They have provided the resources for the organization of interest groups, contributed to the conservation of a traditional society in which easily regulated relationships exist, and influenced the social legitimation of self-employment (Trigilia 1986).

Forms of agricultural organization and family structures have not, on the contrary, influenced the formation of entrepreneurs *directly*. Several empirical studies show that industrial entrepreneurs are mainly of urban origin (Capecchi 1982). The rural influence seems to be stronger in the formation of *artisan* entrepreneurs although it is not a determining factor (Bagnasco and Trigilia 1984, 1985). The chances of setting up in business are not particularly high for ex-peasants compared with other social groups. Similar results emerge from the research undertaken in Ravenna. Here the rural origin of artisans is striking. Of all those presently employed as artisans, 72.5 per cent have a grandfather employed in agriculture and 44 per cent a father. However, the influence of smallholding, sharecropping, or tenant farming on the formation of artisans is less; only 42 per cent of them had a grandfather in this category and 21 per cent a father. Moreover, if we compare this data with the number of males who in 1951 were self-employed in agriculture (37 per cent), we can see that this category did not tend to become artisan entrepreneurs.[7] An urban background seems to be much more formative of artisan entrepreneurs and in particular the presence of a father employed in industry – this is the case for a third of entrepreneurs in the study.

In comparing Ravenna with the rest of Emilia-Romagna with reference to agricultural organization, we find that at the beginning of the century family-run farms, mostly smallholdings, are more frequently to be found in mountain areas, whilst sharecropping was more common in the hill farms. As we approach the plains larger farms with wage-earning workers or less frequently tenant farmers become more common (Bellettini 1953), This layout of the agricultural landscape is the result of important changes in the past which consisted mainly in land-reclamation works. These changes have influenced the characteristics of the relationships of production in agriculture.[8] Land reclamation schemes, to a minor degree in the Modena and Bologna areas and more widely in the Ravenna and Ferrara areas, have created a greater density of wage-earning farm workers and fewer sharecroppers, smallholders, and tenant farmers. Neither Ravenna nor Ferrara have on the whole developed a network of small firms comparable to that of the other Emilian provinces. Moreover, since land reclamation they have always been at the bottom of the regional classification of employees in manufacturing industry (Bellettini 1953; Bergonzini 1986).

In comparing the areas within the province of Ravenna we again find that for most of this century family-run farms have been numerous in the hills, while in the plains they are considerably less common. The province of Ravenna can be divided into the Faenza area, where there were few wage earners on the farms; Ravenna, where there were large farms worked by wage earners; and Lugo, where there were equal numbers of both family-run farms and others with a wage-earning labour force (Pagani 1928). Today these differences are reflected in the industrial structure. Ravenna has principally large firms whose ownership and management is elsewhere, whereas Lugo and Faenza have more small, locally owned firms.

All the 'Third Italy' regions, including Emilia-Romagna, are characterized by a network of towns interspersed with rural settlements. Their role has been that of activating the process of growth at the moment of expansion of demand (Bagnasco and Pini 1981).

The towns which have been favoured by good communication links have also been centres for commercial activities dealing with foreign countries and have helped in the founding and development of small firms in the area. Becattini has given an example of this in his discussion on the industrialization of Tuscany. In Florence even before the Second World War a nucleus of buyers, mainly for British and American stores, existed. The buying offices married foreign demand to local Tuscan production, exploiting their knowledge of both worlds (Beccattini, Bellandi, and Falorni 1983).

Towns have also long been centres of local artisan activity which was usually of the traditional type, relying on local markets and responding in a non-specialized way to fixed local demand, regulated by reciprocal trust and knowledge. Sometimes other types of industry existed, based on products characteristic of a particular town with a wider market. In Carpi, for example, from the sixteenth-century onwards, straw products were made in small workshops or through the putting out system. Initially the market was national, but from the middle of the eighteenth century straw hats were exported, to England initially and later to France, Germany, the East, and the Americas. At the beginning of the nineteenth century, the *Società Anonima del Truciolo* was founded (alongside the small entrepreneurs who continued to function) and set up a commercial network abroad, with branches in Paris, New York, London, Manila, and Tien Tsin; it controlled the quality of the raw materials imported from Canada and organized the work of the women who did piece-work at home with the help of machinery (Capello and Prandi 1973).

In these cases the entrepreneur/merchant jobber was the centre of a set of economic relationships helping to expand 'know-how'. Naturally this knowledge was very limited – to gaining access to markets, to quality standards for products, to the use of the division of labour and of machinery. However, it served to create an industrial tradition and culture useful for future development, and produced a labour force capable of responding to market requirements. Gradually the labour force could change from unskilled work in the home or traditional craft work (pottery, glass, etc.) to skilled work of craftsmanship.

Finally, the towns have provided the technical institutes that transmitted the technical knowledge which is by now widespread but which at one time could not have been generated spontaneously by the artisan firms. The most famous of these schools are the Aldini-Valeriani of Bologna, the Corni in Modena, the Alberghetti in Imola, the Taddia in Cento, and the school of apprentices in the Reggiane factory. They have been responsible for the diffusion of high levels of mechanical knowledge, further strengthened by their continuing to perform as advice and consultation services for ex-pupils (Capecchi 1982; Brusco 1985).

The province of Ravenna differs from the rest of the Emilian provinces in these respects also. There are no comparable technical schools to create a skilled workforce. Nor are there cases of cottage industry to speak of. Within the province of Ravenna there are some differences. The town of Ravenna itself has an exceptionally poor artisan tradition and it is at some distance from the main road of the region (Porisini 1966; Annali di Statistica 1888, 1898). On the other hand Faenza which is situated on an important crossroads, has developed differently, with markets and manufacturing activities of some importance and a ceramics school which gives technical competence to would-be artisans in this field. At the beginning of this century a domestic textile industry producing flannel flourished. There was also a silk industry with drying and spinning sheds which reached factory size. In 1888 there were over 4,000 looms located in the homes of the female workers organized by merchant jobbers. The thread was bought from the principal national producers, dyed and spun, and given to the homeworkers to weave, then pressed in a hydraulic mangle and sold.

Artisan manufacturing was, however, the most relevant manufacturing activity. Carriages, carts, and furniture were exported to Tuscany and the Marche besides being sold in the immediate region. Ceramics and pottery had been produced here since the twelfth century and were very flourishing in the sixteenth when artisan shops sold not only in Italy but also to the rest of Europe. After a long period of decline the industry began to expand once more at the beginning of this century using new techniques and new raw materials (Albonetti 1977; Berselli 1977; Cellini 1978; Ghelardoni 1971).

The central areas of Emilia and in general the areas with the most interesting forms of small-firm development have had in the past small and medium-sized firms which have contributed to their present structure (Brusco 1985). The process which leads to the diffusion of firms can take on many forms. In some cases it was the result of the dismantling of a pre-existing large firm as happened in the Marche at Serra de' Conti (Bronzini and Grassini 1981) or in Emilia in the food-processing and mechanical-engineering industries. Some of the skilled workers who were made redundant set up on their own, occasionally in co-operatives. The early years were often difficult but, with the help of general economic expansion, success was consolidated (Daneo 1971).

Large or medium-sized firms can decentralize production to surrounding small plants, which can either be traditional artisans, or firms set up with the encouragement of the large firm. This is the case when a suitable supplier cannot be found and workers are pressed to set up on their own. These situations can also occur when large firms have parts made by the ex-workers they have fired in the past (Brusco and Sabel 1981). Once an initial network of firms has been established, a complex system evolves leading to the development of industrial districts with their highly articulated systems of production. Processes of imitation by people coming from smaller firms lead to the birth of new firms. Progressive specialization can take place, using the division of labour between firms, instead of vertical integration, and creating further expansion (Capecchi 1982).

A high number of entrepreneurs has previously had a career as either worker or white-collar worker in medium or large firms or at the very least has grown up in their industrial atmosphere. Foremen and maintenance workers know how to control and organize the production process, and office workers have learnt how to co-ordinate supplies, orders, and subcontracting or have come to know the market for a given product; very little encouragement is needed for them to start up in business. Artisans find it a logical step to move into subcontracting work modifying thus not only their product and their market but also their technology and technical skills.

The most important industrial complex in the Ravenna area produces chemicals and petrol derivatives and arrived there in the second half of the 1950s. It has a highly integrated production system as most plants of this type, with few possibilities for decentralization. Whilst the location of this plant in the area has influenced the local economy, increasing income, the volume of local taxes and population, it has had little effect in creating secondary firms or firms producing other unrelated goods.

While the plant was being installed, the economy of the area which was originally agricultural was mobilized to provide manual labour, cleaning services, and the building of parts of the plant. Most of the actual construction and setting up of the plant was done by specialized firms from outside the area. In the years that followed, workers in charge of controlling complex automatic machinery or of maintenance have acquired experience. Local sub-contracting firms have also sprung up to deal with maintenance and plant overhaul which is particularly important in the petrochemical industry. Some of these now operate at a national and international level, having expanded into areas beyond that of maintenance in the petrochemical industry or offshore oil-rig maintenance. However, whilst there was a considerable demand for specialized plant-construction workers in the initial stages, this is now reduced and does not encourage the formation of small firms catering for this particular demand.

The forward linkages have also been weak. The development of the shoe-making industry has stimulated rubber manufacturing, and plastic bag manufacturing and packaging of fruit and vegetables has developed, but the links of both of these to the petrochemical firm are weak. These activities have not been started up by ex-workers of the Ravenna plant.[9] Moreover, there have been no real advantages for the entrepreneurs using its products in locating their firms near the Ravenna petrochemical plant. In the rubber and plastics industries the proximity of sources of raw materials is less important from the point of view of costs than the delivery of the finished product, so that being near customers is more important than being near sources of raw material.

Apart from this large manufacturer, the industrial structure of Ravenna after the Second World War has been rather weak. There have been a few attempts to set up mechanical-engineering firms. Fascist policy had not helped the market gardening and wine-producing sector, which had begun to expand in the 1920s. The cutting-off from foreign markets which were becoming increasingly important, and the low levels of domestic consumption, meant that this sector could come into its own only after the war. Similarly, industrialization was also slow to develop in other sectors. The shoe-making district of Fusignano and the industrial production of ceramic tiles in Faenza are less well developed than their equivalents in other areas, and this is related to their relatively recent development. If we look only at those areas in Emilia which specialize in footwear, we can see that while in Fusignano development on the industrial scale appears after the Second World War and production is concentrated on cheap products for local markets, in the province of Forli by the 1930s there was a large shoe-making firm (Battistini) with a network of small artisan firms working around it, and in Bologna the Montanari footwear factory employed 750 workers during the Second World War (D'Attorre 1980). A similar phenomenon can be seen in the Faenza ceramic tile industry. By the 1930s, technology and production methods were becoming industrialized in Sassuolo; and in the post-war period the Modena/Reggio area produced almost all the ceramic tiles manufactured in Italy. Faenza, on the other hand, did not develop industrial production of ceramic tiles until the 1960s. This is particularly interesting because the Sassuolo industry was started using in its initial stages skilled workers from Faenza, whose experience in craft pottery was invaluable. Later these workers returned to Faenza to start industrial production of ceramic tiles with the knowledge of technical and marketing skills acquired in Sassuolo.

There has been so far little investigation of the role of agricultural production as one of the factors leading to the development of small firms. Different types of *crop* tend to include manufacturing production and both influence the local economy. It is not possible here to compare the Emilian provinces with Ravenna; we can only venture some tentative hypotheses about the differences of industrial development within the provinces of Ravenna. In the Ravenna area the reclaimed land belonged to large landowners and was worked by wage earners or large-scale agricultural co-operatives. The Ravenna area was one of the most productive in the country because of changes in the type of cultivation, the use of chemical fertilizers and mechanization (Porisini 1966). Large-scale cultivation, like that of beet, induced a processing industry to set up in the area. The creation of sugar-processing plant further stimulated beet cultivation. For a long period the sugar factory of Mezzano was the only large firm in the area. However, its presence did not stimulate industrialization. The sugar processing plants have grown up around the areas of beet cultivation because beet has to be processed rapidly and transport costs are high. Choice of location was made for technical reasons rather than planned autonomously by local growers. Due to lack of local technical knowledge when the plant was being set up, control was taken by non-agricultural interests from outside the area.

In the central part of the province, around Lugo and Faenza, agriculture and connected industries have developed slightly differently. Small farms have become involved in the development of livestock, wine production and above all market gardening. The development of fruit growing has brought about the growth of industrial and commercial initiatives, including the selection and packing of fruit for European markets. Commercial organization initially was undertaken by single growers who were the first to specialize in one type of fruit; subsequently, growers' associations took this over. Producing for export meant that the product had to be of standard size and good quality, and therefore growers established packaging stations on the farm and refrigeration to keep the fruit and sell it gradually. Fruit processing has also developed in the area as a by-product of the rejection of non-standard fruit. Several local firms have sprung up, some already existing in the 1920s, such as Massolombarda, which was started by local producers, exporters, and agricultural co-operatives. Some firms have emerged which produce goods and services for fruit processing, such as wood and cardboard for packing, labels, refrigerating systems, machinery for fruit processing, lifting, and transporting. The technology for processing fruit and vegetables is less complex than that needed for sugar refining and thus more easily accessible to local entrepreneurs. The preparation of the product for sale could thus be carried out by the producers themselves who encouraged the production locally of machinery and packaging materials. Market gardening was usually carried out on family-run farms, and this type of organization was not suitable for intensive agriculture. Thus there is a particular mix of industrial culture and family-run agriculture where the family is involved in economic activities which require a great deal of work but even greater organization capacities.

Conclusion

The province of Ravenna is characterized, as we have seen, by fewer manufacturing firms, few and underdeveloped industrial districts and an artisan framework which on the whole is not industrial. From this point of view Ravenna bears little resemblance to the areas of small-firm economy, and this points to differences in structural elements at the heart of small firm industrialization.

These differences do not lie so much in agriculture itself as in its social relationships. Whether or not the family-run farms of the past have helped to structure the later labour market and bring about a social atmosphere conducive to entrepreneurial activity or the formation of artisan entrepreneurs, it is certain that these are a good forecaster of future small-firm development. Ravenna has been subjected to large reclamation schemes which have transformed the agricultural landscape, resulting in large capitalist farms and wage-earning workers while the areas around Lugo and Faenza have not been involved in this way. However, the agricultural past is not the crucial factor in the explanation of the differences between more or less advanced forms of industrial development.

Those factors which have helped to activate the growth process are a more apt explanation of qualitative differences. The towns of the Third Italy which have grown up around crossroads and have often been places of commercial and financial activity, market-places, centres of specific artisan production, and occasionally of technical schools, have played an essential role in this. While Faenza is similar to other classic small-firm towns in having had a wealth of manufacturing activities which have facilitated later growth, the other areas of the province do not seem to have had such artisan and industrial traditions. The differences in development between Ravenna and the more highly evolved small-firm areas clearly point to the diffusion of technical know-how as a crucial factor. There has been a lack, for a critical period, of large or medium-sized firms which could have contributed to the spread of industrial skills among the local population, or stimulated production of supplies or by-products. The local artisans have managed to develop local craft goods but have rarely had the initiative to organize an industrial district. Finally, with the exception of the Faenza art school, which has made a contribution to the ceramics industry, there are no instances of technical schools comparable to those in other areas.

It would seem reasonable, therefore, to expect that only in cases in which the production process is relatively simple and access to sales outlets easy, will local entrepreneurs wish to set up in business. In this case the simple notions of cost–benefit analysis and work organization picked up in the peasant family farm will suffice to run small manufacturing firms. However, when it comes to industrial activities which require specific technical skills, knowledge of markets, and networks of relationships with other producers, experiences within the peasant family are no longer sufficient.

Notes

1. For a description and analysis of the development of small firms in the provinces of Modena, Bologna, and Reggio-Emilia, see S. Brusco, 'The Emilian model: productive decentralisation and social integration', *Cambridge Journal of Economics* 6, 1982.
2. In order to describe the qualitative characteristics of artisan production in a specific area, we have used the indicators recently proposed by Brusco:

(a) The geographical range of the market in which the firms operate; through this we can identify those working within local markets.
(b) Whether or not the firm works in a market of finished goods: the greater the number of firms having access to this type of market the more developed is the industrial structure.
(c) The number of clients which the subcontracting firms have: when the number is large, the smaller the possibility for a single commission to determine the price and the greater the distance from the condition of dependent decentralization; moreover, the firm which produces in short runs tends to have a high level of technology and skills.
(d) The presence in a given area of firms making machinery for the production of goods in that area: where this happens, skills are sharpened and perfected and the division of labour between firms more developed.

Following Brusco's suggestions some qualification must be made. In the first place traditional small firms are identified as operating in local markets and it is reasonable to assume that they do not operate much outside this. However, some types of non-traditional firm have local clients; for example, those which produce goods which have high transportation costs.

In the second place it is important to underline that the market I am referring to in connection with the traditional firm, is that of finished goods. In other words, when we find a high percentage of firms which operate in local markets it is important to distinguish between those which produce finished goods for other local firms and those which produce parts on commission. Firms which produce directly for the market may work indirectly for wider markets, thus making an analysis of the degree of 'openness' of the local economy more problematic. In the case of direct production for the local market of finished goods, it is more likely that the artisans are in a weak position and working in restricted markets.

Brusco underlines another consideration. An analysis of the type of market within which firms operate – that is, direct or indirect – can only be made when we have isolated the traditional type of firm. Firms which work directly for the market are more lively than those which work indirectly, so that the higher the percentage of the former, the more developed is the artisan structure. However, most of the traditional firms (e.g. carpenters, blacksmiths, tinsmiths) work by themselves for private clients on the basis of acquaintance and mutual trust. Thus artisan areas with strong traditional crafts can be confused with areas with developed artisan industrial manufacturing.

In the Ravenna research a sample of artisan firms has been used. This was drawn from the statistical archive of the artisan association recently updated. A one-in-four sample was used, choosing the firms on the basis of two parameters: the category of economic activity and geographical location. The total of firms in the sample was 929.

3. This is a research project undertaken in 1982 comparing two areas of the Third Italy. Bassano del Grappa and Colle Valdelsa are typical of areas of small-firm development. In each area around 100 firms were studied, half of which fell into the artisan category. The firms studied produced the sorts of goods for which the area was renowned (Bagnasco and Trigilia 1986).

4. This research on the metal-working firms of Emilia-Romagna was undertaken on behalf of the National Confederation of Artisans. Some 982 artisan firms were interviewed, and chosen on the basis of their speciality and the area in which they worked (Favaretto 1985).

5. Before the Second World War industrial development in central and north-eastern regions of Italy was very limited. This is to be taken as a picture of the Third Italy as a whole. In some areas, however, past industrialization was quite important. Reggio-Emilia province was one of the least industrialized in the region, yet the *Officine Reggiane* in the town of Reggio itself created very important nuclei of skilled workers. The aggregate data does not do justice to single cases such as this, which has helped to make Reggio one of the most lively areas of small-firm mechanical engineering. Examples can be cited in Bologna, Modena, and other areas. There seems to be little doubt that medium and large firms have contributed in large measure to the diffusion of skills.

6. Massimo Paci has pointed out the relation between forms of agricultural organization and small-firm development. His research in the Marche region has shown a close link between small firm development and the sharecropping form of agricultural organization previously dominant in the region. This in turn favoured the development of entrepreneurial qualities and the habit of hard work. The interest this interpretation has awakened is due to its being applicable to all the areas of small-firm development. However, the relationship between these areas and pre-existing forms of agricultural organization cannot be limited to sharecropping alone. Although sharecropping has characterized the agriculture of most of central Italy, regions such as the Veneto, which is an important part of small-firm Italy, have had large numbers of small tenant farmers or owner-worked smallholdings (Bagnasco and Pini 1981).

7. Once we have demonstrated the rural background of present-day artisans and in particular a sharecropping, smallholding, or tenant-farming one, we have to see if this has been the determining factor in the decision to start up a small firm. We have followed the methods used in the research co-ordinated by Bagnasco and Trigilia to verify this. This consists in comparing the percentage of present-day entrepreneurs, who are sons of agricultural workers with that of self-employed agricultural workers in 1951 out of the total employed male population, using the latter as an indicator of the importance of peasants in the social and employment structure of the previous generation.

8. The wage-earning farm worker, however differentiated this social category may be, is very different from the sharecropper. Their families

tend to be smaller, often nuclear, and they live in poor rural villages or towns with relationships of social solidarity outside the family. Their working life is also very different; they tend to work in an unskilled context within a team. In the areas of land reclamation agricultural work can be supplemented with work in industry processing agricultural products or maintenance. This is often seasonal and periods of unemployment are also frequent (Evangelisti 1982).

9. It is certainly possible that in these sectors small businesses may have been started by ex-foremen of corresponding types of production in large firms in the Ravenna area, but it does not seem to have happened in any significant way. If we ignore those who declared that they had never worked before (almost 35 per cent) only 22 per cent of the remaining artisans at present operating in the rubber or plastics sector have been employed in either the chemical industry or in the extraction and transformation of minerals. Also, none of the entrepreneurs of the relatively larger more industrial firms were ex-workers of the large petrochemical concern.

Bibliography

Albonetti, A. (1977) 'Caratteri della produzione economica, classi sociali, ideologia (1875–1945)', in A. Monetvecchi, B. Nediani, and M.G. Tavoni (eds) *Politica e società' a Faenza tra '800 e '900*, Galati Imola.

Bagnasco, A. and Pini, R. (1981) *Sviluppo Economico e Trasformazioni Sociopolitiche dei Sistemi Territoriali a Economia Diffusa. Economia e Struttura Sociale*, Feltrinelli, Milan.

Bagnasco, A, and Trigilia, G. (1984) *Società e Politica nelle Aree di Piccola Impresa. Il Caso di Bassano Del Grappa*, Arsenale Venice.

—— (1985) *Societa e Politica nelle Aree di Piccola Impresa. Il Caso della Valdelsa*, Angeli, Milan.

Barth, F. (1963) *Introduction to the Role of Entrepreneurs in Social Change in Northern Norway*, Scandinavian University Books, Oslo.

Becattini, G., Bellandi, M., and Falorni, A. (1983) 'L'industrializzazione diffusa in Toscana: aspetti economici', in G. Fuà and C. Zacchia (eds) *L'industrializzazione senza fratture*, Il Mulino, Bologna.

Bellettini (1953) 'Il mercato del lavoro nell'industria emiliana' in *Commissione Parlamentare d'inchiesta sulla disoccupazione*, Camera dei deputati, Rome.

Bergonzini (1985) 'Alcuni aspetti dei cambiamenti in lungo periodo della struttura economica e socio-professionale della regione Emilia-Romagna', in *Rapporto sul mercato del lavoro in Emilia Romagna nel 1984*, Regione Emilia Romagna, Bologna.

Berselli, B. (1977) 'Momenti dell'evoluzione sociale tra '800 e'900 in A. Montevecchi, B. Nediani and M.G. Tavone (eds) *Politica e società a Faenza*, Galati, Imola.

Brusco, S. (1985) 'Small firms and industrial districts: the experience in Italy', in D. Keeble and E. Wever (eds) *New Firms and Regional Development in Europe*, Croom Helm, London

Capecchi, V. (1982) 'Classe Operaia e Cultura Borghese', in *Famiglia Operaia Mutamenti Culturali, 150 ore*, Il Mulino, Bologna.

Cappello, S. and Prandi, A. (1973) *Carpi: tradizione e sviluppo*, Il Mulino, Bologna.

Cellini, G. (1977) 'Lo sviluppo industriale nel comune di Faenza dopo la seconda guerra mondiale', *Torcelliana* 28.

Daneo, C. (1972) 'Struttura Economica e strategia politica nell'Emilia del dopo guerra', *Note e Rassegna*.

D'Attorre, P. (1978) *Una dimensione periferica. Piccola industria, classe oeraia e mercato del lavoro in Emilia Romagna 1920/1940*, Feltrinelli, Milan.

Evangelisti, V. (1982) *Il Galletto Rosso*, Arsenale, Venice.

Faveretto, I. (1985) *Il comparto artigiano metalmeccanico manufatturiero dell'Emilia Romagna nella trasformazione industriale*, Il Mulino, Bologna.

Ghelardoni, P. (1977) 'Faenza', *Bollettino della società', Geografica Italiana* 4/6.

Paci, M. (1980) 'Struttura e funzioni della famiglia nello sviluppo industriale periferico', in M. Paci (ed.) *Famiglia e mercata del lavoro in un'economia periferica*, Angeli, Milan.

Pagani, A. (1928) *Monografia economica agraria della provincia di Ravenna*, Osservatorio di Economia Agraria di Bologna, Bologna.

Porisini, G. (1966) 'Aspetti e problemi dell'agricoltura ravennate dal 1883 at 1922', in L. Dal Pane (ed.) *Nello Baldini nella storia della cooperazione*, Giuffrè, Milan.

Shapero, A. (1983) *New Business Formation*, Euchede.

Trigilia, C. (1986) *Grandi Partiti e Piccole Imprese*, Il Mulino, Bologna.

Chapter 10

Specialization without growth: small footwear firms in Naples

Ash Amin

Within the advanced economies, the experience of a small number of areas whose economies have been modernized and developed rapidly through the growth of small firms, has unleashed a fervour of excitement among academics and policy-makers who had run out of ideas for resolving the intransigent problems faced by the depressed areas in their respective countries. There is now a feverish search for the common elements which have underpinned the success of areas such as Silicon Valley, Boston, Cambridge (UK), and Montpellier around the high-tech industries, as well as that of other areas such as the Swiss Jura and towns in central or north-eastern Italy, around the traditional consumer goods industries. The role of small, innovative, flexible, and specialist firms, the presence of local business networks, and the supremacy of community-based consensus over divisive class norms in the cultural and political sphere, appear to be some of the basic factors underpinning their success. If the development of such structures could somehow be encouraged, this would, so the argument goes, lay down the foundations for self-reliant growth among the areas dominated by crisis-ridden mature industries, abandoned by larger foot-loose corporations, and unable to modernize their manufacturing base.

This chapter explores some of these issues in the context of an area called Stella, in Naples, that is dominated by small firms in the footwear and leather goods industry. This *quartiere* (quarter) stands out as a distinctive and closely-knit community in the *centro storico* (historic centre) of the city, where high levels of poverty and unemployment co-exist with a bustling, and often illegal, small-firm economy (Collida 1984). Stella possesses an old artisan class, whose activities extend beyond the petty commerce of goods and services, into the manufacture of shoes, belts, bags, wallets, and to a lesser extent, pasta, pastry, shirts, furniture, and metallic luxury items such as brass lamps. The firms employ up to thirty workers in some cases; they often draw upon a high level of skilled craftsmanship;

and their products are not sold merely to local customers but also in the national and, sometimes, international market-place. This is particularly true in the case of the footwear industry, in which the *quartiere* specializes and for which it has built up a certain reputation. However, notwithstanding its accumulated skills, its product specialization, its entrepreneurship, and its small flexible firms, the *quartiere*'s economy remains underdeveloped and shows few signs of encouraging growth. Indeed, its experience illustrates the dangers of deriving growth strategies of the type illustrated above, from a superficial and partial scan of the characteristics of areas in which growth *has* occurred around small firms. Stella, too, possesses some of these characteristics, but has failed to develop.

The chapter begins with a critical assessment of an increasingly popular assertion that small local entrepreneurship has come to play an important role in the economy of southern Italy since the early 1970s. It then draws upon material (documents and interviews) gathered in Naples during Spring 1984, to describe the anatomy and growth problems of different types of small firms in the footwear industry of Stella. This is followed by a discussion of the supports and obstacles to growth erected by the local *milieu* in which the firms operate. The conclusion outlines some of the key differences between Stella and the successful areas in central and north-eastern Italy, and suggests that the absence of an extensive and articulated inter-firm division of labour is a major reason for the lack of growth in the Neapolitan example.

The resurgence of the small-firm economy in southern Italy

In recent years, there has been an important debate on the role of small firms and local entrepreneurship in the growth of the southern Italian economy since the early 1970s. One school of thought, utilizing the 1981 industrial census data, has argued that during the 1970s the region witnessed a reversal of its long-term decline of small firms in manufacturing industry (Censis 1981; De Rita 1979; Lizzeri 1983; Pontarollo 1982 and 1983). Offering few explanations and showing little concern for empirical detail, this school maintains that the south appears to be slowly shaking off its age-long lethargy, by giving rise, in a number of different places, to thousands of small enterprises in the traditional consumer goods industries in which competition is fierce. It is held that though this 'growth from below' is still relatively weak, encountering difficulties associated with the region's backward social, institutional, and political environment, it nevertheless promises, for the first time since the war, to unleash a process of self-sustaining development along the lines of the central and north-eastern regions (the Third Italy).

The optimism of the above school has been severely criticized by economists who for long have studied the 'Southern Question' (Giannola 1979, 1982; Del Monte and Giannola 1984, 1986; Graziani 1985). They argue that only until the mid-1970s was there a slight reduction in the north–south gap (measured in terms of per capita income), and this was due to emigration, the provision of state welfare subsidies (Sylos Labini 1985), and intensive industrialization by the state and large private corporations in the years between 1969 and 1974 (Giannola 1982). In more recent years, however, as is belatedly recognized even by certain official organizations (SVIMEZ 1987), the gap has actually increased, owing to a slower growth in output, employment, and investment in the south. One important cause that is singled out is the decline of inward investment in manufacturing, notably since the early 1980s (Graziani 1985), and the progressive disengagement of the large-firm sector from the region (Graziani 1987), whose effects have outweighed the compensatory effects on income deriving from welfare subsidies and small firm development.

The view of the pessimists, therefore, is that the recent successes and failures of the southern manufacturing economy have had more to do with the activities of inward investors than with the spontaneous growth of local entrepreneurship during the 1970s. The role of small firms in the region has been analysed by Del Monte and Giannola (1984, 1986) through a rigorous study of the size, sectoral, and ownership characteristics of manufacturing establishments based upon the census data as well as the fuller IASM-CESAN data bank on southern industry (which the optimists have tended to ignore). Their analysis shows that while the number of establishments at the national level rose by 20 per cent in the inter-census period, with 60 per cent of the growth in employment occurring in firms with less than twenty employees, the number of establishments in the south actually *dropped* by about 8 per cent, largely due to a massive decline in the number of firms with less than ten employees. In fact, over 35 per cent of the increase in manufacturing employment in the south occurred in establishments with more than 500 employees, nearly all which belong to the state or to large national and international private enterprises (Martinelli 1985).

Employment in the south, however, also rose among certain smaller establishments, especially those in the 10–50 and the 200–500 employee category, which respectively were responsible for 39 per cent and 19 per cent of the increase in manufacturing employment between 1971 and 1981. Though the growth rates among these two size bands have not been too dissimilar from those for the rest of the country, there is strong evidence to suggest that the developments in the south have not been representative of a spontaneous burst in local entrepreneurship as is the case in the Third Italy. As far as the medium-sized establishments are concerned, studies of their ownership have shown that only about a quarter are owned locally (Martinelli 1985; Martinelli and Mercurio 1985). Hence their growth has resulted from the activities of inward investors utilizing regional incentives to decentralize production away from the north during the 1970s.

The establishments employing between ten and fifty employees, in contrast, are owned by local entrepreneurs, but even their growth appears to have been associated with externally-led industrialization. The greatest growth in employment appears to have occurred in the metal products, vehicle, mechanical, electrical, and instrument engineering industries. These are sectors with no historical presence in the region, but are the outcome of heavy inward investment by large private and public corporations during the 1960s and early 1970s. According to Del Monte and Giannola, many of the small firms have grown as part of the supply or subcontracting network of the inward investors (Del Monte and Giannola 1986). Another study which lends weight to this argument is that of Pennacchi (1981); he shows that employment in small establishments (21–100 employees) rose twice as much in the period of intensive inward investment (1971–5) than it did in the 1976–80 period, when investment by the external corporations was substantially reduced. The argument of the second school of thought, therefore, is that small-firm development in the region during recent years has involved above all local and external firms operating in sectors which have no historical presence in the region, and which are associated directly or indirectly, with the activities of the inward investors.

In numerical terms, however, locally owned small firms in the traditional low value-added consumer industries continue to play a major role in the south. The food, textile, clothing, footwear and leather goods, wood and furniture, and paper and printing industries accounted in 1981 for 53 per cent of the region's manufacturing establishments and 33 per cent of its manufacturing employment. Locally owned firms accounted for an average of 93 per cent of the establishments and 71 per cent of the employment in these industries (Giannola 1986). Furthermore, the vast majority of the locally owned firms were very small: 12 per cent had less than nine employees; 48 per cent had between ten and nineteen employees; 31 per cent had between twenty and forty-nine employees; 9 per cent had between fifty and 199 employees; and only 1 per cent employed more than 200 workers.

Despite the persisting numerical importance of small-scale local entrepreneurship within the traditional industries of the south, a key question which needs to be raised is whether this sector represents a dynamic and growing force in the region's economy. Though it is virtually impossible to measure this sector's contribution to the region's manufacturing output or revenue, there are other indicators which suggest that the development of these industries, which are dominated by small local firms, has not been particularly healthy. The census data contained in Marco Bellandi's chapter in this volume shows that their share of the region's manufacturing employment dropped from 45 per cent in 1961 to 30 per cent in 1981. This has occurred not only because of the higher rate of employment growth among the modern industries but also because of their own very poor level of growth, especially in comparison with the level of employment in the traditional industries within the Third Italy regions, which rose by 25 per cent during the 1960s and by 19 per cent during the 1970s. Furthermore, Giannola's study of local entrepreneurship demonstrates that the average efficiency of these industries in the south, measured in terms of output per capita, has actually *declined* relative to the performance of these industries elsewhere in the country, falling from 12 per cent to 26 per cent below the national average between 1970 and 1981 (Giannola 1986).

It is for these reasons that the pessimists have reached the conclusion that those local firms whose growth has not been tied to the modern industries, to the inward investors or to the public sector, continue to be relatively inefficient, uncompetitive, and unable to grow. This is a conclusion which has been drawn from an analysis of macroeconomic variables referring to the south as a whole, which of course, does not rule out the existence of more encouraging signs of independent and self-standing local entrepreneurship in particular localities (Amendola 1986; Bagnasco 1985). Several direct survey-based case studies have begun to acknowledge the existence of some small firm growth within certain provincial towns of the south. A certain buoyancy in the light engineering, construction, food, timber, and furniture industries has been noted to have occurred during the 1970s in Caserta (Cotugno, Del Monte, Di Luccio, and Zollo 1981), Bari (Pirro 1980), and Catania (Catanzaro 1979; Pontarollo 1982). Other studies have noted the growing consolidation of particular industries, involving local firms, around some of the smaller urban centres, such as, for example, leather tanning near Avellino (Biondi 1984; Pontarollo 1982), food canning near Salerno (Stampacchia 1974), and consumer goods such as musical instruments, leather goods and clothing in the Abruzzi (D'Antonio and ITER 1985).

With the exception of Pontarollo, most of the above-mentioned authors and others (Falcone 1983; Messori 1986) tend to agree that the experience of even the product specialist areas are quite different from those of areas in the Third Italy. In general, the firms are inefficient and uncompetitive; the growth is not of a 'systematic' nature, involving linkages between firms in the same or related sectors, and with firms supplying producer services or local institutions supporting business activity; and the firms are too few in number or too weak in the market to constitute a 'growth pole' for the area (although the resurgence of hand-made ceramics, inlaid wood products, and knitwear along the Sorrento-Amalfi coast is an exception). In other words, the studies tend to be sceptical about the view that the new local entrepreneurship of the 1970s has the capacity to initiate a process of self-sustaining growth, even within the localities where it has burgeoned, not to mention the region as a whole. The experiences of the area considered in this chapter do not differ greatly, as is described below, from this description of small-firm growth areas in the south.

The anatomy and problems of the footwear industry in Stella

As mentioned earlier, the footwear and leather goods industry dominates the economy of this small *quartiere* in the heart of Naples. It is virtually impossible to put a precise figure to the number of firms there are in this industry, since official statistics are not disaggregated at the level of the single *quartiere*, and since many of the firms are not registered with the Naples Chamber of Commerce and therefore do not appear in the official figures. However, according to our own calculations based upon a head count of all firms in an area covering less than one square kilometre of the *quartiere*, there were, in early 1984, no less than sixty-five footwear or leather goods firms (belts, wallets, and bags) which accounted for about 60 per cent of all manufacturing firms in the survey area. These were all small 'factories' and not workshops manned by one or two artisans. The footwear sector alone consisted of about forty small family firms employing between five and fifteen workers each. A figure which was commonly cited at the time of the survey was that the sector employed at least 1,000 workers, if part-time employees and domestic outworkers were to be included.

Many of the firms are not registered with the Chamber of Commerce, because this allows them to avoid tax payments. Those firms which are registered, nevertheless manage to avoid paying welfare contributions by utilizing a large corpus of undeclared (illegal) workers who, as a result, possess very few rights enforced in the unionized sections of the Italian footwear industry. Owners and workers tend to have always lived in the *quartiere*, and their working relationship is often overlaid or mediated by kinship, family, or community ties. The firms are tucked away in narrow alley-ways and in the courtyards of crumbling eighteenth-century buildings. The workshops are small, cramped, and lacking in even the most rudimentary services, but they pulsate with the sound of busy hands and machines at work and of scurrying feet bringing materials and goods in and out of the shop. Superficially, at least, the firms in Stella are an echo of the Dickensian sweatshop, which can still be found today, for instance, in the East London clothing industry, which exploits the cheap labour of migrant women, or in many of the towns and cities of the Third World. And yet the firms are also different in so far as they do not rely simply on producing standardized and low-quality goods through the intensive exploitation of generally the weakest and least skilled sections of the labour market. They also combine the qualities and skills of the craft worker, much eulogized by Harry Braverman (1974), with the established state-of-the-art technologies for batch production, to produce shoes of varying quality and style, for the more discerning and flexible niches of the national and international market. There are, as is described below, three types of footwear firm in the *quartiere*, the general characteristics of which can be gleaned from the examples cited in two Tables in Appendix 7 (pp. 257–8).

The modern small factory

The first type, numerically the least representative (fewer than five firms), but probably the most significant in terms of profitability, is composed of firms which make medium-quality shoes for the national market. They are legally registered, they employ up to twenty-five workers, they respect the wage standards and working conditions stipulated by the national contract drawn up between the employers and the union in the industry, they are not subcontractors but rely upon experienced sales representatives to procure commissions for fairly large batches from a number of clients, they utilize modern production and organizational techniques, and they have an adequate return on profits or sufficient collateral to procure bank loans, in order to meet running costs and for new investment.

The organizational structure of these firms is no different from that of any other firms utilizing well-established factory production methods. Their success derives initially from the ability of the family or the partners to attract funding, and later, from their ability to use their accumulated knowledge of the market to build up a good portfolio of clients and orders. By gradually building up a reputation for reliability, quality, and flexibility (in response to new market signals), the firms manage not only to obtain a sufficiently large volume of work which enables them to plan production schedules over several months, but also to select the largest orders. Large batch production and access to finance, in turn, allows the firms to minimize unit costs and maximize productivity through mechanization, the exploitation of scale economies, the division of tasks among specialized workers, and the imposition of a formal control mechanism (supervisors and fixed output norms) to intensify the pace and flow of work. The efficiency of these firms does not derive, therefore, from low wage costs or long working hours, but from scale economies and the 'Taylorization' of the labour process, even though it is certainly true that the offer of an abundant and underemployed labour market in the *quartiere* has helped the firms to maximize on labour productivity.

The sweatshop

At the other end of the spectrum, there are a handful of firms which have appeared since the late 1970s, whose survival is almost entirely based on the use of sweated labour. Founded by entrepreneurs who possess few craft skills, but perhaps some knowledge of the industry as well as a sufficient amount of start-up capital, these firms produce low-quality leather or plastic shoes, sandals, belts, and bags. Their status as independent firms is questionable, as they are often simply the assemblers of materials belonging to one or two large Neapolitan distributors or manufacturers who supply low-income-group retailers and market stalls not only in the region but as far as North Africa and the Middle East. The prices which are offered to the workshops are minimal since they have little bargaining power, and since the sizeable informal economy of Naples offers a vast number of 'jobbers' eking out a meagre living and therefore willing to accept poorly paid subcontracts.

The sweatshops have poor profit margins and face an uncertain future because payments are often either reduced in the middle of an order or delayed, thus provoking a liquidity crisis. This is compounded by the fact that orders are short-lived and often broken, while new ones are difficult to find. For these firms, then, staying in the market is a question of survival and securing an adequate family income, rather than one of growth, which is achieved by keeping costs down to a minimum through the following means: the evasion, though illegal, of tax on revenue as well as social-security contributions for employees, the minimization of expenditure on land, rates, rents, and other overheads, by locating in small, run-

Specialization without growth

down, and barely furbished premises; and most importantly, the employment of very young or women workers, who, because of their abundance, lack of skills, and absence of both trade-union protection and bargaining power in the labour market, can be paid paltry wages on a daily or weekly basis, made to work long and hard hours, and laid off when orders run out. The market circumstances and the basis for survival for these deskilled firms which produce cheap goods are quite different, therefore, from those which characterize the first type of firm.

The craft firm

The majority of footwear manufacturers in the *quartiere*, however, belong to a third category which bears some resemblance to the craft-based, specialist, and flexible firm of the classical and modern industrial district. There are few areas in southern Italy which still possess a concentration of such firms. Stella has a long-standing artisan tradition in the footwear industry that can be traced back to skills developed in the eighteenth and nineteenth centuries when the area specialized in the production of quality hand-made gloves for the Neapolitan and European aristocracy or bourgeoisie. Though this craft tradition came under serious attack from cheaper mass-produced footwear in the post-war period, it has managed to persist and even enjoy some revitalization in recent years. In Stella there are many small firms (fewer than fifteen workers) in which the employer and his offspring, together with a handful of multi-skilled, middle-aged artisans and a small number of apprentices, produce medium- to high-quality footwear for specific market niches (e.g. ballet, 'top-notch' casuals, evening wear, etc.), which command a healthy price and growing demand among Italian and European middle-class consumers.

The owners are master craftsmen or ex-employees with technical or white-collar skills. Some have returned to the *quartiere* after having built up sufficient experience and savings from years of work with footwear manufacturers in Italy or overseas. Most, however, have always lived in the *quartiere*, having worked in the past for local small firms such as their own, or for the few quality shoe manufacturers of recent origin in Naples, among whom the most famous is Mario Valentino, situated on the outskirts of Stella. Not all of the entrepreneurs, however, are ex-workers who have skimped, saved, and borrowed to start up their own firm. The owner (almost always a man) plays a pivotal and heavily burdened role in the running of the business. He is the master craftsman, the overseer of the work process, the paymaster, the designer, the financier, the bookkeeper, and the salesman. Sometimes his burden is shared by family members, notably sons and daughters possessing some higher educational training in business management, marketing, accountancy, or law.

Before undertaking the survey, it had been assumed that the majority of the craft firms would have been working as subcontractors for Mario Valentino, who is known to use several scores of small firms in Naples, to produce over two-thirds of his top-quality designer fashion-wear sold in Rome, Paris, London, and New York. The survey results, however, proved this hypothesis to be incorrect. Only about 10 per cent of the craft firms in Stella work for Valentino. Instead, the majority are independent producers who buy their own materials from local retailers, own their tools and machinery, use designs copied or adapted from fashion magazines and trade fairs, and who sell their goods to retailers, wholesalers, or buying agents. In contrast to the putting-out system in some areas of the *Terza Italia*, where each firm produces for a number of clients and succeeds in obtaining sufficient work throughout the year, Naples offers a very small number of firms who put out work. Consequently, subcontracting usually implies becoming dependent on one client, who then has the power to squeeze on prices and productivity, as well as threaten closure for the small firm by dropping a contract. It is therefore actively avoided by the craft firms in Stella and tends to be practised only during periods of slack demand, or in the early years of a firm's life, when it lacks the marketing experience, the design knowledge, and the finance to purchase materials in order to stand on its own two feet.

However, the number of firms with a healthy list of clients and a widely reaching sales network is quite small. Few firms have the finances to hire a good sales representative, or the time, expertise, and personnel to travel around the country in search of new or better market outlets. Market access is one of the major problems faced by the firms, and their plight is made worse by the fact that the *quartiere* as well as the city lack the private and public business services and infrastructure to help them resolve their marketing difficulties. The firms do not possess their own marketing facilities, nor do they sell under their own brand name. Instead, the most common practice is to settle for small and often short-lived commissions for shops or wholesalers situated either in Naples or in other Italian cities. It is in this sense that they are not fully independent actors in the marketplace.

Though working for pre-established commissions has the positive effect of providing some protection from the cold winds of the market in the highly competitive footwear industry, it nevertheless carries a number of penalties which prevent the firm from growing. First, goods are sold at a much lower price than their quality could command on the open market. Second, similar problems to the putting-out system, such as dependence on one or two clients, lack of continuity, and so on, continue to be encountered. Third, liquidity problems are seriously aggravated because payments are made on or long after delivery, thus leaving the firms to rely on their own resources to buy the materials and shoulder the production costs. The wait between expenditure and payment is long, and savings are used up very quickly, thus forcing the entrepreneur towards taking on work as a subcontractor (which allows savings on materials which are provided by the client), reducing the workload, or borrowing cripplingly high interest rate loans from local usurers (illegality or lack of collateral rule out bank loans). Finally, the commission indirectly traps the firm in a vicious circle, because in the middle of a contract, all its resources are fully utilized and therefore there are few possibilities for finding other market outlets, while during slack periods, the entrepreneur is frustrated in his search for new outlets by his lack of marketing experience. The craft firm in Stella, therefore, is neither a subcontractor for another manufacturer nor a fully independent operator in the market-place with its own brand-name and a healthy portfolio of clients. Instead, it uses its own resources and ideas to create the product but has virtually no contact with the final customer owing to its dependence upon a small number of intermediaries who commission its work.

The *economic status* of the craft firm is almost as contradictory as is its relationship with the market. On the one hand, it possesses or has access to certain advantages which in terms of profitability and market potential set it apart from the struggling, deskilled firm that produces low-quality footwear. One of the most significant advantages is the accumulated artisanal skill of the owner and the craft workers, which enables the firm not only to produce designer quality shoes but also to respond easily to new market signals. The latter is also greatly facilitated by a certain flexibility that comes from being in a community in which workers and bosses are either acquainted or related to each other. Workers are recruited almost exclusively from the *quartiere* not only because it offers the appropriate skills but also because of the belief that someone who is known is more likely to accept the erratic output norms and fluctuating market conditions which the craft firm faces. Furthermore, the craft tradition itself encourages flexibility, and on a least-cost basis. The 'composite' worker, displaying a wide array of skills, produces, with the help of apprentices and rudimentary tools, the whole or a large part of the entire product, and is paid on a piece-work basis. There is no technical pressure, therefore, as there is in modern industry, to maintain constant and high levels of output, or even the continuous flow of parts from one production phase to the next. Instead, each self-contained work group regulates its own output, is forced to maximize productivity when work is plentiful (since wages are tied to the volume of output), and is constrained to lay down its tools without further remuneration when there is no work (since there is no formal employment contract).

Another advantage which the craft firms can draw upon is the *quartiere*'s long-standing specialization in shoe manufacture, which attracts a small number of local buyers and sales representatives, on the look-out for better-quality footwear. It should be emphasized, however, that the 'marketing potential' of the area is rudimentary and informal. There are none of the trade fairs, sales co-operatives, independent buyers, marketing consultants, or export agents which have come into existence in some of the areas of the *Terza Italia*. The producers in Stella, in general, are forced to rely on their own resources to market their product.

Market uncertainty, together with other factors, have a neutralizing effect on the above-mentioned advantages, and constrain the growth of the craft firm in Stella. Unlike the larger and more modern firm, there is no division of management tasks, first because the owner lacks knowledge of the techniques, and second because he cannot afford to employ specialized management staff. The owner performs a multitude of functions and is overworked. The net effect of this is a reduction not only in day-to-day efficiency but also in the entrepreneur's ability to anticipate the future by looking for better organizational and market alternatives. Consequently, the firm is locked into meeting immediate needs, which in a situation of market uncertainty and erratic demand, implies that short-term budgeting, small-scale production, limited product renewal, and poor profit margins become a more or less permanent condition. The firm's precariousness is exacerbated by its poor financial situation as well as its semi-illegality (evasion of social security contributions), which rule out the possibility of obtaining bank loans or incentives from the special funds for artisan (*Artigian cassa*) or non-artisan firms located in the south (*Casmez*). The lack of funds, in turn, prevents the firm from buying in professional advice which could help it to improve its standing in the market-place. Thus, to conclude this section, although the craft firm in Stella possesses the professional skills to produce good quality shoes for which there is a growing demand, its potential for growth is ultimately frustrated by its inability to develop or purchase expertise in other areas such as marketing.

The economic role of the *quartiere*

The question which concerns the craft firm and the sweatshop is how to survive from one day to the next. The *quartiere* plays an important role in the process of survival, notably in terms of providing certain labour market conditions. Through its poverty, Stella provides an abundant supply of the cheap and unskilled labour that is vital for the survival of the sweatshops. However, its long-standing artisan tradition in the footwear industry has meant that the area is also a training ground for the learning of the craft, a seed-bed for new product ideas, and a source of the skilled workers who keep the craft firms afloat. The *quartiere* also provides an ample supply of women domestic out-workers who live in the vicinity of the factory and whose role is to machine stitch the finished shoes onto the soles. They are not used by firms which use glue to assemble the final product, or by the firms which still produce hand-sewn shoes. Their use is therefore relatively contained. The women are known to the entrepreneur and they are paid piece-work rates. Homeworking enables the firm to utilize women who are tied to their homes and children and also helps it to avoid the cost of sewing machines and overheads which would be incurred if the women worked within the firm. The initiative does not appear to offer savings on wages of any significance.

The *quartiere* also plays an important role in underwriting the flexible working practices which prevail within the firm. Stella is a community in which workers and owners have always lived and interacted through family or kinship ties, as a result of which the entrepreneur is able to choose his workers carefully, anticipate a certain degree of trust, and avoid a rigid formalization of labour practices within the factory. The lack of job opportunities, the absence of notable class divisions, together with a widespread resignation to the reality of economic uncertainty within this poverty-ridden community, also plays a part in preparing workers to accept the ephemeral rewards offered by the employers. This is facilitated also by the negligible cultural and economic distance between workers and employers: workers aspire towards owning their own small firm, and employers are only too often forced to rejoin the labour market when their businesses collapse.

Stella's network of personalized relations also temporarily shore-up workers and employers when revenue is short. For instance, the purchase of basic consumer goods on credit is an accepted practice in the *quartiere*, without which the principal of job insecurity and discontinuous production could not be sustained. A similar buffer is provided by the use of personal contacts to acquire loans from friends and, at worst, from avaricious money-lenders, in order to cover for temporary shortfalls in revenue. Finally, face-to-face contact and informal contractual agreements between the producers and their local suppliers of materials and machinery, or their local buyers and sales representatives, provide a minimum of negotiability over payment and delivery schedules.

The positive support of the local milieu, however, does not extend much beyond its provision of the labour-market conditions and social flexibilities described above. Despite the long-standing specialization of the *quartiere* in footwear manufacture, it does not possess a well-developed market for specialist and general services or for material inputs which can be purchased easily and at cost-saving prices by the producers. Though there is a small market for second-hand machinery, as well as for boxes and packing materials, which are produced locally, most other means of production, including the leather, are purchased in small quantities from retailers in Naples; there are no cost advantages in this form of purchase.

Similarly, although the area's reputation attracts some sales representatives and retailers, which goes some way towards helping the producers to find a market outlet, this practice is not extensive, nor is it particularly profitable, as the buyers and intermediaries exercise a considerable downward pressure on the prices of the firms who depend on them for their sales. There are no collective or independent agencies providing services which help the producers to find their own market outlets, and on the best possible terms. There is also an absence of sales intermediaries who have a sufficiently large volume of work to be able to offer the individual producer only a small rake-off price for selling their goods.

The problem of adequate or low-cost provision of business services within the community extends to other services ranging from legal advice to fiscal, financial, organizational, and technical matters. The need for these services does exist because the firms are too small to provide them internally. Alternatively, when they have to be bought in, the firm either lacks the resources to buy them or it cannot afford them because the price for professional services in Naples is high. An added problem is that the services are rarely designed to meet the particular needs of the footwear firms. Consequently, the firm is forced to rely on either its own stretched resources or the limited and often unqualified help it can find through its network of informal contacts.

The isolation of the manufacturers is reinforced further by the absence of a division of labour among the firms in Stella. The *quartiere* is not composed of a corpus of firms who produce for each other, for the purpose of sharing surplus work or performing different production tasks. Stella does not have a good enough reputation to attract volumes of work which are too large for the individual firm, and therefore a tradition of sharing work loads with other firms in the *quartiere* has failed to develop. Furthermore, an individualism based upon the law of self-interest, which often governs communities in which resources are scarce, prevents producers from linking up even when a firm is offered more work than it can cope with. Firms are suspicious of one another and regard co-operation as an opportunity for territorial encroachment rather than as an exercise of mutual benefit.

Co-operation between firms is also hindered by the lack of task-related ties. There is no flexible specialization in Stella: the labour process in footwear is not divided among firms performing individual tasks such as cutting, stitching, moulding, finishing, and so on. Instead, the division of labour is retained within the firm, as a result of which opportunities for the development of new, task-based initiatives in the locality are reduced. In other words, the functional self-containment of each firm limits its multiplier effects and its contribution to the development of the *quartiere*. In turn, the lack of an inter-firm division of labour penalizes the individual firm since the latter's already stretched resources have to be devoted to a large number of different tasks. This, especially in the case of small-batch production, tends to raise unit costs as it prevents the firm from deriving the time and scale economies which task specialist production would allow.

There is, however, one important exception to the above rule. In the past the production of soles for shoes was an in-house function, but in more recent years an independent industry has grown to supply the shoe manufacturers with finished soles of different sizes, shapes, and quality. In Stella, at the time of this survey, there were two firms producing only soles and selling exclusively to a number of local shoe manufacturers. Specialization, mechanization, and a high volume of demand have allowed the two firms to offer soles at a much lower price than it would cost the shoe manufacturers to produce them in-house. There are, however, no other examples of this kind of inter-firm division of labour, which has been clearly advantageous to both parties involved in the exchange of the product.

Thus local milieu, on the one hand, acts as a buffer without which many firms would not survive. On the other hand, it does not ease the burden of the producers in terms of the supply of machinery, services, and goods, and therefore, does little in the way of helping the individual firms or the footwear industry as a whole within Stella, to grow.

253

Conclusion: an industrial district?

There can be no doubt that Stella exhibits a certain economic vitality associated with its specialization in a particular industry, the inventiveness and experience of its artisan class, and the flexibilities and resources provided by key social institutions such as the extended family and the close-knit community. These are characteristics which are common to the areas of small-firm-led industrialization in the *Terza Italia*, and could be interpreted as evidence in support of the optimists' argument concerning the economic revitalization of the south by small-scale local entrepreneurship. Such an interpretation, however, would be grossly superficial and biased.

Two of the distinctive and unique features of the classical and the contemporary industrial districts are first their prosperity and ability to increase output, employment, and revenue, and second their constitution as self-contained industrial systems in which each small firm is a component of and is supported by a complex and interconnected division of labour between firms and institutions (Becattini 1979; Bellandi 1982; Brusco 1986; Garofoli 1982; Marshall and Marshall 1879). Stella is neither a prosperous *quartiere*, nor are its footwear firms strong enough to act as a 'growth-pole' for the area. Furthermore, as has been demonstrated above, the firms are not networked into a wider division of labour but are left to their own devices to face the market. As small and isolated operators, they face a number of difficulties ranging from the lack of finance to their inability to explore the best market opportunities, and the management inefficiencies deriving from the entrepreneur having to perform too many duties. In contrast to areas in the *Terza Italia*, Stella is not a source of business services or goods, with individual firms playing a particular role in the production and sale of the final commodity, and with the locality acting as an intermediate market for firms exchanging goods and services among themselves.

The future of the *quartiere* and its dominant industry remains uncertain, since, as things stand, the responsibility for further growth rests almost entirely upon the not too robust shoulders of isolated entrepreneurs. The *quartiere* (and Naples in general) lacks the corporatist political subculture and the institutional mechanisms which, as Carlo Trigilia's chapter in this volume (Ch. 7) demonstrates, have played a vital role in supporting small-firm-led growth in areas such as Valdelsa and Bassano in the *Terza Italia*. Furthermore, the prospects for public sector, political, or institutional support for the small firms in Stella remain bleak, not only because of the in-built corruption and inefficiency of such institutions in the south (Graziani 1987) but also because few would wish to openly champion the cause of the so-called underground economy. The latter is an understandable reticence, but it runs the risk of sacrificing the hard-won specialization and skill base of the area's footwear industry, since the small firms will not grow if left to their own devices.

Acknowledgement

I am very grateful to Edward Goodman and Julia Bamford for their helpful comments.

Bibliography

Amendola, A. (1986) 'Mezzogiorno: Il dibattito sull' industrializzazione', *Nord E Sud* 3(2).

Bagnasco, A. (1985) 'La costruzione sociale del mercato: strategie di impresa e esperimenti di scala in Italia', *Strato e Mercato* 13.

Becattini, G. (1979) 'Dal settore industriale al distretto industriale. Alcune considerazioni sull'unità d'indagine dell'economia industriale', *Rivista di Economia e Politica Industriale*, No. 1.

Bellandi, M. (1982) 'Il distretto industriale in Alfred Marshall', *L'Industria: Rivista di Economia e Politica Industriale* 3(3): 355–75.

Biondi, G. (1984) *Mezzogiorno Produttivo: Il Modello Solofrano*, Naples: Edizioni Scientifiche Italiane.

Braverman, H. (1974) *Labour and Monopoly Capital*, New York: Monthly Review Press.

Brusco, S. (1986) 'Small firms and industrial districts: the experience of Italy', D. Keeble and E. Wever (eds) *New Firms and Regional Development in Europe*, London: Croom Helm.

Catanzaro, R. (1979) *L'Imprenditore Assistito*, Bologna: Il Mulino.

Censis (1981) *La Nuova geografia socio-economica del Mezzogiorno*, Censis: Rome.

Collida, A. (ed.) (1984) *Napoli 'Miliardaria': Economia e Lavoro dopo il Terremoto*, Milan: Franco Angeli.

Cotugno, P., Del Monte, A., di Luccio, L., and Zollo, G. (1981) *Mezzogiorno e Terza Italia: Il Modello Casertano*, Naples: IRES-OGIL.

D'Antonio, M. and ITER (1985) *Il Mezzogiorno degli Anni Ottanta: dallo Sviluppo Imitativo allo Sviluppo Autocentrato*, Milan: Franco Angeli.

Del Monte, A. and Giannola, A. (1984) 'Imprenditoria locale e sviluppo del terziario nel Mezzogiorno d'Italia: una nuova politica per il sud?', *Rivista di Politica Economica* 74(10).

———— (1986) 'The relevance and nature of small and medium-sized firms in southern Italy', D. Keeble and E. Weaver (eds) *New Firms and Regional Development in Europe*, London: Croom Helm.

De Rita, G. (1979) 'Nuovi termini della questione meridionale' *Sviluppo* 21.

Falcone, F. (1983) 'Industrializzazione diffusa e Mezzogiorno: una rassegna

Small firms and industrial districts in Italy

della letteratura sull'argomento', *Rassegna Economica* 47(6).

Garofoli, G. (1982) 'Sviluppo periferico e sistemi produttivi locali', *Economia Marche* 1.

Giannola, A. (1979) 'Lo sviluppo del Mezzogiorno secondo Lizzeri', *Inchiesta*, September.

—— (1982) 'Industrializzazione, dualismo e dipendenza economica del Mezzogiorno negli anni '70', *Economia Italiana* 1.

—— (1986) *Industria Manufatturiera e Imprenditori del Mezzogiorno*, Naples: Guida.

Graziani, A. (1985) 'Il Mezzogiorno e l'economia italiana di oggi', mimeo, Department of Economics, Naples University.

—— (1987) 'Mezzogiorno Oggi', *Meridiana* 1.

Lizzeri, G. (ed.) (1983) *Mezzogiorno Possibile: Dati per un altro Sviluppo*, Milan: Franco Angeli.

Marshall, A. and Marshall, M.P. (1879) *The Economics of Industry*, London: Macmillan.

Martinelli, F. (1985) 'Public policy and industrial development in Southern Italy: anatomy of a dependent industry', *International Journal of Urban and Regional Research* 9(1).

Martinelli, F. and Mercurio, R. (1985) 'Investimenti esogeni, grande impresa e sviluppo dei rapporti internazionali del Mezzogiorno', A. Salghetti-Drioli (ed.) *I Potenziali di Sviluppo Industriale Endogeno nel Mezzogiorno d'Italia*, Venice: Marsilio.

Messori, M. (1986) 'Sistemi di imprese e sviluppo meridionale. Un confronto fra due aree industriali', *Stato e Mercato* 18.

Pennacchi, L. (1981) 'Mezzogiorno: un'industrializzazione sopravvalutata', *Politica ed Economia* 9.

Pirro, F. (1980) 'Lo sviluppo dell'industria manufatturiera in provincia di Bari negli anni '70', *Rassegna Economica* 6.

Pontarollo, E. (1982) *Tendenze della Nuova Imprenditoria nel Mezzogiorno degli anni '70*, Milan: Franco Angeli.

Pontarollo, E. (1983) 'Una politica industriale per il Mezzogiorno', G. Lizzeri (ed.) *Mezzogiorno Possibile: Dati per un altro Sviluppo*, Milan: Franco Angeli.

Stampacchia, P. (1974) 'L'industria nella provincia di Salerno', mimeo, Instituto Superiore per la Formazione Aziendale, Salerno.

SVIMEZ (1987) *Rapporto 1987 Sull'Economia del Mezzogiorno*, Rome: SVIMEZ.

Sylos Labini, P. (1985) 'L'evoluzione economica del Mezzogiorno negli ultimi trent'anni', *Studi SVIMEZ* 1.

Appendix 7

Table A7.1 General characteristics of the leather goods firms in Stella

No.	Product (quality)	General characteristics			Production				The market		
		Date of opening	Officially registered	Size of premises (m²)	No. of workers Total	Illegal	Use of domestic outworkers	Subcontractors for another firm?	Destination of product	Method of selling product	State of the market
1	Shoes (medium)	1980	Yes	200	24	7	No	No	Italy	Directly to shops	Stable
2	Shoes (medium)	1972	Yes	200	10	0	Yes	No	Italy	Own sales rep.	Stable
3	Shoes (medium)	1983	Yes	50	10	10	n.a.	No	Naples	Directly to shopes	Growing
4	Shoes (medium-high)	1980	Yes	150	9	7	No	Yes & No	Italy & overseas	Via subcontracting firm and directly	Stable
5	Shoes (medium)	1978	Yes	120	11	8	Yes	No	Naples	Independent sales rep.	Declining
6	Sandals (low)	1978	n.a.	100	6	6	n.a.	No	Naples	Directly to shops	n.a.
7	Handbags (low)	1979	n.a.	35	9	9	No	Yes	Italy	Via subcontracting firm	Stable
8	Soles (varied)	1972	n.a.	50	6	6	No	No	Local	Directly to local shoe firms	Growing
9	Shoes (high)	1970	Yes	75	4	2	No	No	Italy	Directly to shops	Growing
10	Wallets (low)	1977	n.a.	70	11	10	Yes	No	Naples	Directly to shops	Stable
11	Belts (low)	1981	n.a.	70	6	6	No	Yes	Italy	Directly to shops	Declining

Source: Interview survey, Naples, March 1984.

Table A7.2 Some economic characteristics of the leather goods firms in Stella

Firm (from Table A7.1)	No. of waged workers (manual)	The wage relation		Total weekly salaries £	Daily output/ worker	Market value of each product £	Weekly output	Weekly sales £	Weekly sales income minus labour costs £	Level of technology
		Industrial earnings (weekly) £	Mode of wage payment							
1	20	87	Monthly (T. Union rate)	1,740	10	17	1,000	17,000	15,260	70% mechanized
2	9	87	Monthly (T. Union rate)	783	9	n.a.	375	–	–	50% mechanized
3	9	65	Weekly	585	5	11	200	2,200	1,615	Manual
4	8	33	Weekly	264	3	28	625	17,500	17,236	Manual
5	10	87	Piece-work	870	5	7	250	1,750	880	Manual
6	5	n.a.	Weekly	n.a.	n.a.	n.a.	n.a.	–	–	Manual
7	8	33	Weekly	264	12	2	450	900	636	Mechanized
8	5	43	Weekly	215	200	1	5,000	5,000	4,785	Manual
9	3	n.a.	Fixed daily rate	n.a.	15	5	230	1,150	–	Manual
10	10	21–30	Fixed daily rate	250	20	2	1,000	2,000	1,750	Manual
11	5	n.a.	Weekly	n.a.	200	n.a.	4,000	–	–	Manual

Source: Interview Survey, Naples, March 1984.
a Monetary values are at 1984 prices.

Chapter 11

A policy for industrial districts

Sebastiano Brusco

(Translated by Julia Bamford)

259-69   Italy
9412
6160

In Emilia-Romagna and elsewhere there has been a long debate on the nature and characteristics of industrial districts. This has taken into account the advanced technological level which the most forward-looking districts have reached. However, their capacity to survive in a world in which a continuous high level of innovation is a fundamental feature is less clear.

One of the first points to be clarified concerns the conditions under which an industrial district is capable of producing at competitive prices using the most efficient and technologically advanced machinery currently available. To be able to answer this we must go back to the factors which are behind the growth and development of industrial districts. In the past the role played by the decentralization policies of large firms in developing the productive flexibility of industrial districts has often been reiterated. It is certainly correct to emphasize that from the end of the 1960s onwards many small firms were born as a result of decentralizing by large firms trying to get round restrictions imposed by trades unions. However, another phenomenon underlying the development of industrial districts may be a better explanation: the progressive specialization of all the firms working in the same sector in the same area. The model to which this refers no longer has industrial relations as a main variable, but the growth of the size of the markets. The references in economic literature are to Stigler's 1952 model or, to go back to the original, Adam Smith's principle according to which 'the division of labour is limited by the size of the market'.

Progressive specialization is easily verifiable in many industrial districts. One of the most interesting examples is to be found in the agricultural machinery sector of Modena and Reggio-Emilia. Here the story begins in the years between the two wars when there were very few large firms (such as Fiat, Ruggerini, and Lombardi) which produced tractors, most of the components being made internally. In the years that followed, as the market for smaller agricultural machinery grew, some firms specialized in the production of motors, others in carpentry and trucks, others in differentials and yet others in the assembly of motors and the various components of motor cultivators and diggers. Specialization has taken the place of vertical integration, thus enabling the industrial district to have at its disposal high-level skills such as those needed to produce oil-filled circuit mechanisms or gears.

One of the characteristics peculiar to industrial districts, once they reach a certain level of development, is the numerous markets for different components and different processes. These are highly competitive, with a large number of both buyers and sellers. From this competition derives the stimulus and the capacity to innovate: the stimulus because the subcontractor who does not innovate finds himself rapidly excluded from the market and because the variegated flexibility of the productive system encourages the buying of specialized machinery; the capacity because competition does not allow buyers to impose prices on sellers and reduce their profits, thus enabling them to make necessary investments.

The surest index of the intensity of competition – not only between buyers but also between sellers – is that of the number of clients the small subcontractors each have. In Modena in 1982, 65 per cent of the mechanical engineering artisans working on a subcontracting basis had more than twenty regular clients. This state of affairs does not apply in all industrial districts. Even in the Veneto, recent research shows that the proportion of *artigiani* with twenty clients does not exceed 35 per cent, and in Naples subcontracting means using antiquated machinery and accepting low wages.

We have seen how the industrial structure described above is capable of using relatively sophisticated machinery. But to what extent are they capable of evolving new techniques of production or new products? Our point of reference here is Sabel's well-known model in which he shows that the relationship between clients and subcontractors is original and different from that of the research and development office and the production department of a large firm. In large firms research and development departments have high levels of technical competence and knowledge of the market. Projects are worked out down to the last detail. However, those who work on the production side do not collaborate with R & D even at the highest levels. The production manager's job is to organize the production of a series of parts laid out in the R & D department in the most efficient way. In small firms, on the other hand, technical competence and the capacity to plan are less refined. A single idea goes through all the phases of its development in a continuous confrontation between clients and subcontractors, that is designer-draughtsmen and producers. The relationship between clients who want to make a certain product and subcontractors is extraordinarily rich and complex, full of reciprocal stimulation. The producer is not asked to design the part but very often to help in the solution of a problem. This collaboration between small producers of finished goods and subcontractors is a collaboration between someone who has an idea to be transformed into a product and someone who has to produce parts for this product. It reduces production costs to a minimum and enables a series of modifications or later adjustments to be made to the product which differentiate it from the others on the market and thus make it able to compete both at national and international level.

Examples abound of how creative the process of collaboration between producers of finished products and their subcontractors, or even between producers and users of machinery, can be. We have only to look at what has happened in Bologna in some of the more advanced mechanical-engineering sectors such as the packaging machinery or food-processing machinery sectors; or in the field of machinery for manufacturing ceramic tiles, where small firms have been able to make drastic reductions in costs.

Furthermore, recent research shows that the phenomenon is not limited to Emilia. The development of a sector which specializes in the making of machinery for the shoe manufacturing industry has developed in the shoe-making area of Vigevano. This very particular type of collaboration which ties small entrepreneurs who sell finished goods on the market to both subcontractors and skilled workers, kindles a capacity to produce innovation and to use innovation.

However, two observations are pertinent at this point. The first is that the vision of technical progress implicit in Sabel's model is not the more widespread traditional one. Technical progress is not seen in Schumpeterian terms as a flow of important innovations brought about by a particularly daring and far-seeing entrepreneur which radically change the production process or open new markets or introduce new products. The hypothesis from which we set out is that of technical progress as put forward by Rosenberg: advance by means of tiny successive steps, with strong links between sectors, which in the end manages to achieve success in terms of production process and product. The second observation, while more banal, has several implications. Progress made by small steps takes place less visibly within one sector or branch of manufacturing. In this case, innovation is not characterized by the identification of whole new sectors of activity such as has happened in the past for chemical dyes and the petrochemical industry and more recently in electronics. Innovation of this kind occurs within traditional sectors, unnoticed by official statistics. However, this innovation brings about further changes, differentiating segments of the market with different degrees of prestige, capacity for growth and profit. Thus those sectors which have been considered homogeneous, and 'mature' or 'backward', are in reality composed of non-communicating heterogeneous compartments. They are so heterogeneous as to consider themselves producers of different products altogether. As Salvatore Biasco has said, 'are we sure when we compare the aggregate Italian textile sector to that of Hong Kong that we are referring to something comparable as far as technology, organization, type of product and market are concerned?'. The history of Emilia in recent years has been the history of how in different sectors Emilian industry has gradually passed to higher segments of the market acquiring international competitiveness and escaping from the competition of newly industrialized and Third World countries.

It is on this basis that we must elaborate the measures of an industrial policy to create the conditions for future developments. Before we proceed to analyse possible measures, two preliminary questions must be examined. Should these policies aim to change substantially the characteristics of the Emilian industry or should they respect its present fragmentary structure? Can this system of disintegrated and complementary firms survive the introduction of new electronic technologies?

The end of the overflow of Emilian industry towards nearby regions has caused many observers to think that this type of structure of production had its magic moment at the end of the 1970s but that now, with different market conditions, it runs the risk of being overcome. It has also been alleged that industrial districts are finished, meaning that they would not be capable of dealing with different competitive conditions. If by this we mean that the system of firms must make a qualitative change and that they have to organize to get to know the market better, learn to use new technologies creatively, then this is certainly true. It is also true that market forces alone are not enough to provide the firms of a district with the essential services they need. If, however, we mean that these services can only be utilized by larger, more integrated firms, then the statement above is probably untrue.

What has happened in the years of crisis in fact seems to demonstrate that a system of small firms survives better than large firms, and to confirm this we can look at the rates of employment and unemployment in small-firm Emilia and the predominantly large-firm Piedmont or Liguria regions. In the last years of the 1970s Emilia remained unscathed, the intensity of the depression having been felt much less here than elsewhere; and above all in the last few years the movement up-market has continued to guarantee competitiveness in international markets.

Elsewhere in the industrialized world, West Germany, Great Britain, France, and the United States, there is a tendency towards a reduction in the average size of the firm. The principle cause of this is to be found both in the realm of industrial relations and in the personalization of demand. Everything leads us to think that systems of small firms are particularly suited to operate in this context. As far as the introduction of electronic technology into these systems is concerned, the answer is not easy or obvious. However, it can be seen that this sort of technology can make the production of non-standard goods in large firms possible, but this does not mean they cannot be produced in small firms also. Thus the evidence of their good performance in the most recent economic crises and the characteristics of the market lead us to think that systems of small firms can compete successfully. It is, however, essential that they are given capacities that the market does not provide spontaneously.

The second question stems directly from an analysis of the discussions which have recently involved both industrial economists and the government. We must bear in mind that after the miserable failure of sectoral plans – which were the backbone of industrial policy in Italy during the 1970s – a consensus seems to have emerged in favour of measures of other kinds, mainly horizontal policies directed towards factors of production and not only to sectors or branches. The importance of introducing new technologies into the apparatus of production has changed the attitude of the experts and those responsible for industrial policy. Unlike the situation in the relatively recent past, the new technologies are now universally considered as being one of the factors of production.

In this change of attitude there are both acceptable and unacceptable elements. In general there is a feeling of disillusionment with plans, especially sectoral plans which had no operating powers and which left all the important choices to the market. There is also a realization that all national information structures must be urgently updated because of their vital importance for firms. The need for an adequate market policy co-ordinated between the various ministries is recognized. However, the problems raised by the introduction of new technologies, the use of means to get to know markets, and the availability of sophisticated technical services are undervalued. They raise problems of translation from the general to the specific for sectors of production, problems which are often difficult to solve. If we take, for example, skilled training, this certainly involves the need for a general policy, but at the same time we need to define the type of training necessary for specific production processes.

Small firms and industrial districts in Italy

Monitoring of markets differs considerably between sectors connected with fashion goods and those producing investment goods, as does promotion and marketing.

It seems that the passage from one policy to another has been too brusque, not taking into account even in its most recent form some of the important requirements of firms. A much more effective policy would be one involving a complex set of measures which create horizontal policies and other organs which facilitate the application of general measures to the specific needs of a sector or branch of production.

We have seen above the characteristics of industrial districts or systems of small firms; we have also discussed some of the general principles which should guide industrial policy. I can now proceed to outline the main aspects of a specific policy. In particular, I will examine two policies, one horizontal and the other specific to the sector. I do not take into consideration either the many measures for professional training in skills or management of the labour market or the fiscal and financial measures in favour of investment or employment, or the initiatives which are urgently needed at a national level to encourage the development of frontier technologies. This is not because I underestimate their importance, but because a division of labour is necessary here.

The technical change underway in the Italian industrial structure requires a more detailed examination of the question: how will the systems of firms be capable of reacting to the introduction of electronic technology? How will these technologies, which involve all sectors of production, be accommodated within this structure of small firms? The reply to this question is strictly tied to what we have said so far; that is, that the capacity to innovate of a system of firms depends absolutely on the collaboration between hundreds of firms and thousands of people in different roles and with different skills. It also depends, therefore, decisively on the level of competence and knowledge of the production process of these thousands of protagonists.

Against this background we must remember that in Emilia skills and knowledge of basic mechanical technology are deep-rooted and widespread among both entrepreneurs and workers. The opportunity of working in both large and small firms has contributed to this diffusion. Furthermore, right from the beginning of this century the existence of many technical institutes has played an important role in the spreading of skills and technical knowledge in the region. The knowledge of mechanics, deeply ingrained in the abilities of the local population, is given high status in the social structure. On the other hand, the new technologies, which are based on electronics, and

264

therefore in a different technological field, are not widely known and the apparatus of production suffers consequently from this lack of skill.

In planning a policy which caters for these needs, we must not forget that a solution based on the import of highly qualified workers is not feasible. The fact that the innovation process is based on the interaction of such large numbers of actors would immediately render it unworkable. This expedient would work well for a large firm, which could, in a relatively short time, equip its research and development department by taking on a limited number of specialists. What is needed is a policy which operates by spreading skills in this field to a large proportion of workers and thence to the tiny cells of the apparatus of production which up till now have worked together to produce innovation and are hindered by the lack of the necessary basic skills. This hold-up caused by a lack of skills, which is already beginning to make itself felt, is a problem of utmost urgency. In other countries, the inability to pass from mechanical skills to electronic skills has made tens of thousands of workers unemployed. The most glaring example of this is the machine-tool industry in the London area.

One way of working towards a solution to this problem of the introduction of new skills into the structure of production could be through the local technical institutes. These could once more be urged to fulfil the role of leader in the diffusion of new skills. This role has been understated in the past but deserves more emphasis. From the beginning of the century to the present these schools have been a central element in the Emilian structure of production. They have been as important in their own way as the technical schools which have had such an influence on the development of German industry. However, notwithstanding their many merits, vocational courses are not sufficient to furnish the basic knowledge necessary to be able to use the new technology creatively. Serious reflection is needed before a strategy can be worked out. To begin with, legislation regarding secondary education in Italy leaves much to be desired. For years there has been talk of reforming both curriculum and structures without even the general outlines and principles having been agreed on. In the meantime, while waiting for the reform to materialize, the curriculum remains the one brought out at the beginning of the 1960s, and it is easy to see that in fields such as computers and electronics which have developed in ways unforeseen twenty-five years ago, it is now totally inadequate. Suffice it to say that official electronics courses include the study of valves as the latest advance in technology, the existence not only of microprocessors but of transistors being completely ignored.

Naturally in most cases the common sense of the teachers has made up for what is lacking. Experimental courses with Ministry of Education approval have been started, changing the content of courses in fact if not in name and adapting them to the needs of modern technology. These initiatives, which are often pursued with great enthusiasm, as in the Aldini Valeriani technical school in Bologna or the Fermi School in Modena, are not sufficient. Not only have the courses to be brought up to date but the number of courses in electronics available to the students for the Emilia region should be increased. This cannot wait for prospective reforms of the whole of the system of secondary education, nor be seen only as part of that reform. The pace of change in the industrial system is rapid, and much more urgent than the forseeable timetable for reforms. The hypothesis to be worked with is that of immediate action which can be co-ordinated with the reform when it is ready.

Even if there is a general consensus that the success of business firms is incompatible with the long wait which a reform implies and there is agreement on the need for immediate action, numerous problems remain to be solved. To increase the number of courses in electronics, the simplest solution would be to convert some of the courses of the last three years of secondary school into electronics courses. Some of the existing courses have lost relevance and can easily be substituted for those which the system of production needs. In practice this solution is largely impracticable because of internal rigidities in the schools themselves. In short, teachers would have to be persuaded to teach new subjects or be made redundant to make way for better qualified ones, the latter being almost impossible given the laws on employment in the Italian education system. Other solutions to the problem must be found, therefore, such as the starting of new courses alongside existing ones both in state schools and in local authority ones, or the creation of new schools outright.

There are, however, long delays in this field such as to warrant an emergency measure over and above the reform of the school system as a whole and not relying on a rearrangement of courses based on persuading and convincing the teachers. The question must be tackled immediately, since it is one of the crucial areas of Emilian economic development and of much greater importance than that of the managerial capacities of entrepreneurs, or of the training of people in marketing or exporting. The market itself is dealing with the latter to some extent. The system of production by itself, however, is not capable of coping with the need to provide people with skills in electronics. The debate on the updating of technical education in the region must assume the same public importance as that on new universities or the role of economic infrastructures.

266

A policy for industrial districts

The second policy measure is much more vertical in character, working on sectors or areas of production. Service centres for industrial districts have been the subject of debate and discussion for some time now, and furthermore are already in operation in several areas in the Emilia region. It seems appropriate here to clarify the analytical background on which they are founded and point out the ideas behind a policy towards them and indicate where their future lies.

The problem put in a nutshell seems to be this: small firms in collaboration with other small firms manage to use and even to produce innovations but are not able, on account of their size, to carry out some of the functions of an entrepreneur which are essential for success. Because of high costs, many aspects of traditional entrepreneurial activity are not possible for small firms. These include gathering funds for complex applied research, getting information about the outcome of the latest research, evaluating with precision and continuity the state of markets, taking advantage of the opportunities which potential markets offer, judging the relative merits of highly sophisticated machinery, controlling access mechanisms and management of trade fairs, organizing the correct reaction to frequent attempts at indirect limitation of competition and overcoming the difficulties tied to the changing standards for products destined for the export market.

These arguments are not sufficient to justify the need for centres built with public funds at general request. It can be argued that these services can, as in other cases, be left to market forces. After all, in the last ten years the structure of private sector services has changed radically. The number of bank branches and the provision of quasi banking services like leasing and factoring has increased; studios for graphic design and advertising have improved in quality and number; the agencies for learning new skills and management consultancies have become more widespread; many specialists in software consultancy have set up, though often under the control of important hardware manufacturers; many laboratories producing models for the fashion industry or designing industrial plants have emerged; the network of transport has expanded. Neither must we forget the role of manufacturers' associations, which goes from the simplest assistance in organizing a payroll and keeping the books to more sophisticated activities like help in obtaining a mortgage, the organization of guarantee associations or buying associations, or the planning of production. However, neither the market nor the producers associations have been able to provide the sorts of services listed in the previous paragraph. The probable reasons for this are twofold: that initial investment is rather high, due to the cost of

267

putting together and co-ordinating the necessary skills for this type of activity, and that the market is restricted because these activities are often linked specifically to an area which has a limited number of firms. Thus, because the market is obviously and understandably insufficient, public policy is necessary. This is not an invasion of the private business by the public authority, but making good the inability of the market to deal with a situation.

This line of analysis has been the inspiration behind those centres which have been formed so far. They include both public and private participants such as ERVET (Regional Economic Planning Board), the Confindustria (the Confederation of Italian Industries), API (Association of Small Firms) and the artisan associations. The centres which already exist rely, quite correctly, on public funds for a limited period of around five years. Entrepreneurs also have to pay for the services they receive, the idea being that the local authority helps to finance the initial investment, including the starting-up expenses, but then the centre becomes progressively self-sufficient.

Not all the centres which have started up so far have had the same objective. Some, such as those in the knitwear, shoe-making, agricultural machinery, and earth-moving equipment industries are centres with general objectives but different tasks depending on the industry they deal with. These, however, aim to operate in respect of all the functions of the firm, from planning and production to marketing. The ceramics centre, on the other hand, which has forged links with the universities of Bologna and Modena, provides only technical services, such as the analysis of the characteristics of kaolin.

Along what lines should a policy for centres of services be developed? First, the decision to involve both producers associations and individual entrepreneurs which has been followed so far should be continued. Centres founded with public funds and without representatives of firms on the governing body would probably be destined to failure. Only entrepreneurs or their associations are able to set up an organization and programme of work which is useful for the firms, and participation in decisions is essential if the firms are to use the services that the centres provide. The failure of the French experience with state-run centres has shown how difficult it is to impose on firms the use of services that they have neither asked for nor helped to set up.

This choice, it must be recognized, makes the formation of centres very laborious and difficult. There are several reasons for this: the entrepreneurs do not always recognize the usefulness of the centres; producers' associations fear that centres could become rivals; there are often problems of precedence between groups; and questions of prestige in the distribution of places on the governing bodies. However, there is no alternative to this system.

A serious limitation of these schemes is that the industries covered by the centres already in operation represent only a small part of the regional economy. Important areas remain without the assistance of service centres. These include the food-processing industry, the tanneries of Parma and Bologna, the wood industry of Parma and Modena, some parts of the mechanical engineering industry such as oil-filled circuits, machine tools for metal and wood, machinery for food packaging and processing, the small chemicals industry, and the tourist industry on the coast. This initial phase has of necessity been one of successive experiments and it would seem reasonable at this stage to substitute a carefully planned policy. This would avoid the danger of reducing the service centres to mere crisis solvers and restricting their future development.

A useful measure would be a census of the local industrial capacities, thus pinpointing the areas in which service centres could be of real use. A map could be drawn of proposed service centres, distinguishing the centres with more general purposes from those with more technical aims. This map, which should be the reference point for future action, could also include more than one centre for the same branch of manufacturing in different areas of the region. It could also show centres linked to each other.

I should also stress the need for legislative measures to provide subsidies to those entrepreneurs who decide independently to form a consortium operating as a service centre. In other words, the work of ERVET on behalf of the service centres, the success of the centres already in operation, and the consequent discussion have stimulated an interest and a demand which must be satisfied. It should also be noted that funds can be made available not only from the region, where money is limited, but also from local authorities and other organizations.

Acknowledgement

An earlier version of this chapter appeared as 'Quale politica industriale per i distretti industriali?' in *Politica ed Economica*, 1984.

Index

Jevons, 130
Journey-to-work flows, 158, 160

Keynes, J.M., 128

Labour costs, 177, 184–5, 208,
  209: in large and small firms,
  83–5, 177, 208
Labour productivity, 85, 112–13
Labour flexibility, 187
Labour market, 143
Labour mobility, 186, 187
Lancashire cotton industry, 158,
  202
Lancashire, 132
Learning by using, 203
Leslie, C., 131
Liguria, 262
Local community, 10–12, 177,
  191–2, 254
Local corporatism, 191
Local economies, 138
Local government, 159, 188–92,
  192
Local labour market areas, 159–60
Localism, 12–15, 175, 178–92
Lombardi, 259
Lombardy, 46, 112, 132, 180
London, 228, 265
Lugo, 225, 228, 232, 234

Manila, 228
Marche, 46, 47, 48, 112, 180,
  184, 229, 230
Mario Valentino, 247, 248
Marshall, A., 20, 21, 22, 128,
  129–31, 136–49, 153, 154, 202
Marshallian industrial district,
  20–1, 132, 136–53, 158–62
Massalombarda, 232
Mature sectors, 262
Mediocredito, 49, 50, 51, 71
Mezzodria, 16–17, 179, 182,
  226–7
Minimum efficient size of firm
  (m.e.s.), 70, 199, 208, 213,
  216, 217

Ministry of Education, 266
Modena, 16, 199, 223, 224, 227,
  232, 259, 260, 266, 269
Modernization of Italian industry,
  35–40
Montanari footwear factory, 232
Montpellier, 239

Naples, 25, 239–58, 260
NEC (north, east, central Italy),
  32, 35–43, 46, 47, 48, 239, 241
New York, 228

Oligopoly, 69
Optimum scale, 208

Padua, 180
Paris, 228
Parma, 269
PCI (Italian communist party), 15,
  19, 23, 180, 182, 184, 188, 189
Peripheral economy, 154
Personalization of demand, 262
Pezzini, M., 25
Piedmont, 46, 112, 184, 262
Ponsacco, 162
Prato, 15, 16, 156–9
Pratten, C.F., 208
Product differentiation, 211, 212
Profits (large and small firms),
  83, 86

Ravenna, 25, 223–5, 227–9, 230,
  231, 232, 233
Reggio Emilia, 199, 223, 232,
  259
Regione, 193, 199
Research and development, 202,
  260
Robertson, D.H., 128
Rosenberg, N., 27, 203, 261
Ruggerini, 259
Ruhr, 132
Russo, M., 8, 22

SACMI, 202
Sassuolo, 232